SECOND PETER & JUDE

SECOND PETER & JUDE

DANIEL L. SEGRAVES

II Peter and Jude

by Daniel L. Segraves

©2000, Word Aflame Press
Hazelwood, MO 63042-2299

ISBN 1-56722-441-5

All Scripture quotations in this book are from the King James Version of the Bible unless otherwise identified. Scriptures noted NKJV are from The New King James Bible, Copyright 1990 Thomas Nelson Inc., Publishers.

All rights reserved. No portion of this publication may be reproduced, stored in an electronic system or transmitted in any form or by any means, electronic, mechanical, photocopy, recording, or otherwise, without the prior permission of Word Aflame Press. Brief quotations may be used in literary reviews.

Printed in United States of America.

Printed by

WORD AFLAME® PRESS
8855 DUNN ROAD
HAZELWOOD, MO 63042-2299

Other Books by Daniel L. Segraves

I Peter: Standing Fast in the Grace of God
Ancient Wisdom for Today's World: Proverbs
Hair Length in the Bible
Hebrews: Better Things, Vol. 1 & 2
Living by Faith: A Verse-by-Verse Study of Romans
James: Faith at Work
Marriage: Back to Bible Basics
Messiah's Name
Themes from a Letter to Rome
You Can Understand the Bible

Order from:
    Pentecostal Publishing House
    8855 Dunn Road
    Hazelwood, MO 63042-2299

Contents

Second Peter: Growing in Grace and Knowledge 11
Introduction to Second Peter 13

  I. Salutation (1:1-2) 31
     A. Author (1:1a)................................... 31
     B. Recipients (1:1b) 35
     C. Greetings (1:2) 40

 II. The Call to Spiritual Growth (1:3-21) 51
     A. The Basis for Growth (1:3-4)..................... 52
     B. The Elements of Growth (1:5-7) 58
     C. The Present Reward of Growth (1:8).............. 65
     D. The Danger of Spiritual Immaturity (1:9)........... 67
     E. The Future Reward of Growth (1:10-11) 71
     F. The Urgency of the Call to Growth (1:12-14)........ 77
     G. The Means of Growth: the Scriptures (1:15-21) 81
       1. Written by Reliable Witnesses: the Apostles
         (1:15-18)..................................... 83
       2. Written by Reliable Witnesses: the Hebrew
         Prophets (1:19-21)........................... 88

III. Beware of False Teachers (2:1-3:7) 93
     A. Characterized by Destructive Heresies (2:1-2)...... 93
     B. Characterized by Covetousness (2:3) 101
     C. Destined for Punishment (2:4-9)................. 102
     D. Characterized by Fleshly Self-will (2:10-14) 116
     E. Characterized by Forsaking the Truth and Going
        in the Way of Balaam (2:15-16) 124

    F. Characterized by Spiritual Emptiness (2:17-18) 133
    G. Characterized by Spiritual Bondage (2:19-22) 137
    H. Characterized by Their Denial of the
       Second Coming (3:1-7) 143

IV. The Certainty of the Second Coming (3:8-14) 155
    A. The Second Coming Will Be Unannounced (3:8-10). 155
    B. Christian Conduct in View of the Second Coming
       (3:11-14) 164

**V. Exhortations in View of the Delay in the
Second Coming (3:15-18)** 173
    A. The Reason for the Delay (3:15-16) 173
    B. Remain Steadfast (3:17) 177
    C. Grow in Grace and Knowledge (3:18) 179

Jude: Beware of False Teachers 183
Introduction to Jude 185

I. Salutation (1-2) 195
    A. Author (1a) 195
    B. Recipients (1b) 198
    C. Greetings (2) 204

II. Purpose for the Letter (3-4) 207
    A. Contend for the Faith (3) 207
    B. Beware of False Teachers (4) 211

III. Warnings from History (5-7) 217
    A. The Destruction of the Israelites (5) 217
    B. The Judgment of Angels (6) 219
    C. The Judgment of Sodom and Gomorrah (7) 225

IV. Characteristics of False Teachers (8-19) 235
    A. They Defile the Flesh (8a) 235
    B. They Reject Authority (8b) 237
    C. They Speak Evil of Dignitaries (8c-10). 238
    D. They Are Greedy and Rebellious (11) 243
    E. They Are Spiritually Empty (12-13). 248
    F. They Face Certain Judgment (14-15). 255
    G. They Are Grumblers and Complainers (16a). 259
    H. They Walk according to Their Own Lusts (16b) 260
    I. They Practice Flattery (16c) 260
    J. They Are Sensual (17-18) 261
    K. They Cause Divisions (19a). 264
    L. They Do Not Have the Spirit (19b) 265

V. Exhortations to Believers (20-23) 267
    A. Build Yourselves Up in Your Most Holy Faith (20a) . 267
    B. Pray in the Holy Spirit (20b) 269
    C. Keep Yourselves in the Love of God (21a). 270
    D. Look for the Mercy of Our Lord to Bring You
       to Eternal Life (21b) 271
    E. Be Merciful to Those Who Doubt (22). 272
    F. Snatch from the Fire Those on the Verge of
       Deception (23a) 274
    G. Show Mercy to the Deceived While Hating
       Deception's Effects (23b) 275

VI. Benediction (24-25) 277
    A. The Believer's Security (24) 277
    B. The Worthiness of God (25) 280

Endnotes 285

SECOND PETER

GROWING IN GRACE AND KNOWLEDGE

Introduction to Second Peter

Two of the shorter books in the New Testament—II Peter and Jude—share a common concern about false teachers infiltrating the church. This theme makes these books especially relevant to the church today, for the errors propagated by those early false teachers are as common now as they were then.

The church has always been the target of those who wish to promote their own theological agendas or aberrant lifestyles.[1] Peter was concerned with false teachers who claimed to be believers but whose heresies denied the Lord (2:1). These teachers were persuasive (2:2). Their motivation was covetousness (2:3). They embraced an immoral lifestyle and were further characterized by rejection of authority, presumption, and self-will. They boldly spoke evil of dignitaries (2:10). They did not know what they were talking about, and they submerged themselves in hedonistic pleasures (2:12-14). Apparently these false teachers were at one time people of genuine faith (2:20-22), but they had forsaken the faith in favor of the fleshly rewards of unrighteousness (2:15). Although they were impressive orators, their words were spiritually empty, appealing primarily to base desires (2:18). These heretics characterized the life of genuine faith as bondage and promised liberty to those who would follow their lead. But the result of following their teaching was slavery to corruptive and addictive behaviors (2:19). Included in their catalog of false doctrine was a scoffing rejection of the second coming of

Christ (3:3-4). The ultimate fate of these teachers was certain destruction (2:1, 12, 17, 20-21).

The Scripture's antidote to the deception of these false teachers, who promoted corrupt theology and perverse behavior, is to develop a life of faith, virtue, knowledge, self-control, perseverance, godliness, brotherly kindness, and love (1:5-7). (See also 1:3; 3:11, 14.) Developing these qualities will assure the believers a life of spiritual fullness, fruitfulness, and stability (1:8, 10), as opposed to the spiritual blindness and amnesia of those who do not grow in these virtues (1:9). Furthermore, believers must constantly be alert against deceptive teaching with its destructive results (3:17). They must grow in grace and in the knowledge of the Lord and Savior Jesus Christ (3:18).

Douglas J. Moo aptly observed that II Peter and Jude "warn us about any tendency to treat sin lightly, to suppose that an immoral lifestyle can be pursued without any penalty."[2] In view of the apparent collapse of morality in the Western world, today's believers should focus more frequently and clearly on the message of these short letters.

We can safely say that the attitudes of the false teachers of whom Peter wrote are typical of the free-wheeling immorality or amorality of our day. It is popularly thought that morality is what one makes it and that each person is his own authority. A bumper sticker that encouraged people to "Question Authority" seemed radical in the sixties, but now this philosophy is a way of life. Not only do people generally believe that they should question authority, but many are quite bold to speak evil of those in authority, even if they do not know what they are talking about.

Introduction to Second Peter

Just like the false teachers in II Peter, many today promote a permissive, hedonistic lifestyle under the illusion that they are rejecting bondage for liberty. In reality, they are rejecting liberty for enslaving, addictive habits, which viciously control their lives.

As people become increasingly enslaved to lust—whether sexual immorality, drug addiction, alcoholism, violence, or greed—believers will stand in starker contrast to them. Those whose faith is in Christ Jesus have "escaped the corruption that is in the world through lust" (1:4).

In I Peter, the apostle was concerned with assuring his readers that they were not alone in their suffering, that they should not be surprised to suffer for their identification with Christ, and that their suffering was only temporary. In conjunction with the theme of suffering, Peter encouraged his readers to remember the certainty of their eternal inheritance and to conduct themselves in such a way as to deflect unwarranted criticism of the church.[3]

II Peter expresses the concerns of a spiritual leader who knew his death was imminent (1:14). The issues that I Peter addresses are matters of great importance, but there is something about an awareness of the nearness of death that sharpens one's focus on the issues of ultimate significance. In his final inspired written communication, Peter wrote to those who shared his faith (1:1-2), encouraging them to develop the virtues that would assure their steadfastness (1:3-15). He traced the origins of the gospel message back to the written Scripture, which is even more authoritative than a visible, audible revelation from God (1:16-21). He viewed the development of Christian virtues as the first priority and reminded his readers of the authority of Scripture, since he knew false teachers would infiltrate the church (2; 3:1-10). In view of the certainty of the Day of the Lord, Peter urged his readers to holy conduct and godliness (3:11-16). In his conclusion he once again warned believers against falling and being led away with error (3:17). The antidote to this danger was (and is) for believers to grow in the grace and knowledge of Jesus Christ (3:18).

The inspired message of II Peter makes the letter especially relevant to the church today, nearly two millennia after Peter wrote it. The threat of destructive heresies (2:1), whether by infiltration from without or by deception from within, is no less serious today than it was in the first century—in fact, it may be greater. The way to avoid being deceived has not changed: it is still to recognize the written Scriptures as having the final authority, to test all teachings by them, and to grow spiritually strong by the development of Christian virtues.

Author, Inspiration, and Place in the Canon

Twenty books of the New Testament were almost universally acknowledged as canonical before the end of the first century. The other seven books—Hebrews, James, Jude, II Peter, II John, III John, and Revelation—experienced some delay in being universally recognized, primarily because of questions about their authorship.[4] Nevertheless, the evidence for the authenticity of these seven disputed books was so strong that each book ultimately gained universal acceptance by the church.

The most significant evidence for the authenticity of II Peter is the letter's internal witness. It claims to be written by Simon Peter (1:1). The author indicated that the

Introduction to Second Peter

Lord Jesus Christ had informed him about his death (1:14)—probably an allusion to John 21:18-19. The author claimed to have been an eyewitness of the transfiguration of Jesus (1:16-18). He mentioned that this was his second letter to write (3:1). He also asserted his standing as an apostle (3:2) and considered Paul his peer (3:15).

With such a consistent and clear testimony of authorship, we must either accept the letter for what it claims to be, or we must reject it. There is simply no room for the assertion that someone falsely claiming to be Peter actually wrote the letter and yet that it is Scripture.

There is ample evidence that the early post-biblical Christian writers accepted II Peter as authentic and inspired. We see this as early as A.D. 96 in I Clement. Moreover, the spurious *Apocalypse of Peter*, written about the middle of the second century, makes use of II Peter, indicating the letter was considered authoritative before that time. Other evidence from the mid-second century includes Aristides and Valentinus (both c. A.D. 130) and II Clement (c. A.D. 150). Evidence from the late second century includes Eusebius's claim that Clement of Alexandria (c. 150-215) wrote a commentary on II Peter in his Bible, the Sahidic version of the New Testament, and Hippolytus (A.D. 180). In the early to mid third century, Origen (c. 185-254) quoted II Peter as Scripture six times.[5] The third-century Bodmer papyrus (P^{72}) also recognized II Peter as canonical.

Some reject the authenticity of the letter on the theory that an authentic letter should have earlier and more extrabiblical endorsement. But we can explain the lack of additional early endorsement by the letter's brevity, the persecution of the church, communication problems in the ancient world, and the possibility that the letter was sent to believers in an area not heavily traveled.[6] Before we could reject the letter because of minimal external endorsement, it would have to be demonstrated that none of these possible reasons for minimal endorsement is indeed its cause. This cannot be demonstrated.

A second reason why some reject II Peter is the alleged differences between the writing style of I and II Peter. But scholars are divided on whether there actually are significant differences,[7] and if there are, they can be explained on another basis than a different author.

One thing is certain: the early church did not accept pseudonymity. If believers had not been convinced that Peter wrote the letter, they would not have accepted it. As Blum has pointed out:

> If epistolary pseudepigraphy was rejected by Christians, then who would have written this letter? Hardly a good man! If it had been a false teacher, what was his motivation? After all, the book does not seem to have any distinctive views that would require presentation under an assumed name.[8]

Pseudonymous works did circulate under Peter's name, including *The Apocalypse of Peter* (c. 135), *The Gospel of Peter* (c. 150-75), *The Acts of Peter* (c. 180-200), *The Teaching of Peter* (c. 200), *The Letter of Peter to James* (c. 200), and *The Preaching of Peter* (c. 80-140). Significantly, early believers did not accept any of these works as authentic. In the final analysis, II Peter earned its place in the canon by virtue of the integrity of its content.

Introduction to Second Peter

Eusebius, the early church historian, acknowledged II Peter as authentic, although he recognized that its status was disputed. By the mid to late fourth century, many prominent leaders, such as Cyril of Jerusalem, Athanasius, Augustine, and Jerome, considered the letter canonical.

In short, all of the internal evidence and the best of the external evidence indicate that the apostle Peter wrote the letter. For further discussion of Peter, see the comments on II Peter 1:1.

From the standpoint of faith, it is not the endorsement of others that authenticates II Peter. Rather, the claims that the letter makes about its own authenticity and the Holy Spirit's witness to the veracity of these claims, both now and over the last two millennia, authenticate the letter.[9]

Date of Composition

According to reliable early tradition, Peter was martyred in about A.D. 65 during Nero's persecution of Christians in Rome.[10] I Peter was written in approximately A.D. 62-64 and certainly no later than July 19, 64.[11] In II Peter, Peter knew his death was near (1:14), he referred to Paul's letters as having already been written (3:15), and he said it was his second letter (3:1). Thus, a reasonable date for II Peter is late A.D. 64 or early A.D. 65.

Place of Origin

The tradition that Peter was martyred in Rome and the fact that he wrote this letter shortly before his martyrdom indicate that he probably wrote II Peter from Rome. This places him at the same location in which he wrote his first letter.[12]

Second Peter

Original Audience

As with I Peter, there are three views concerning the original recipients of this letter. Some think that Peter wrote to a mixed audience consisting of both Jewish and Gentile believers; others suggest that the audience was almost exclusively Gentile; still others are convinced that the original audience was almost exclusively Jewish.

This commentary takes the view that Peter's original audience was almost exclusively Jewish, for some of the same reasons cited in the author's commentary on I Peter.[13]

II Peter 3:1 says, "Beloved, I now write to you this second epistle" (NKJV). If the letter we know as I Peter is his first epistle, both letters have the same audience. In language common to the Jewish Dispersion, Peter addressed his first letter to "the pilgrims of the Dispersion in Pontus, Galatia, Cappadocia, Asia, and Bithynia" (I Peter 1:1, NKJV). If II Peter 3:1 does not refer to the audience mentioned in I Peter 1:1, it seems odd that Peter did not identify his audience more specifically in this letter.

Peter's identification of himself by his Hebrew name "Simon" (from the Hebrew *shema'*, meaning "to hear") in 1:1 seems uniquely appropriate to a letter written to Jewish believers. If his original audience was not Jewish, we are at a loss to explain his use of this name.

Peter's reference to "the present truth" in 1:12 may be a clue that he wrote to a Jewish audience. The present truth would thus refer to the content of the new covenant as distinct from the content of the old covenant. Gentile readers would seem to have no spiritual heritage that would make the concept of "present truth" meaningful.

The negative reference to "fables" in 1:16 would be meaningful to a Jewish audience, who had previously embraced a rich, though spiritually detrimental, lore of Jewish fables. (See I Timothy 1:4; 4:7; II Timothy 4:4; Titus 1:14.)

The fact that Peter had personally ministered to his readers (1:16) suggests—though admittedly it does not require—a Jewish audience. He was specifically an apostle to the Jewish community (Galatians 2:7-8). Peter certainly ministered among Gentiles (e.g., Acts 10), but this piece of information, when placed together with other clues in I Peter, strengthens the case for a Jewish audience.

The clear references to events in the history of Israel are especially appropriate to a Jewish audience. (See 2:1, 4-8, 15-16.) In 2:22, Peter quoted Proverbs 26:11, a proverb most of his Jewish readers would have known since childhood.

Peter's encouragement to his readers to "be mindful of the words which were spoken before by the holy prophets" (3:2) indicates a Jewish audience. Most Gentiles living in the region of Asia Minor during the latter part of the first century would have had minimal knowledge of the pronouncements of the ancient Hebrew prophets. Gentiles Christians, of course, had an interest in the Hebrew Scriptures and sought to learn them, but the Hebrew Scriptures were not yet widely disseminated among Gentiles.

The scoffers to whom Peter referred in 3:3-6 seem to be Jewish because of their reference to the "fathers," the Hebrew patriarchs. What these scoffers had forgotten was the previous state of the world as described in the Hebrew Scriptures.

The apparent reference to Psalm 90:4 in 3:8 indicates a Jewish audience; it seems inappropriate to urge a

Second Peter

Gentile audience not to forget something they would not have known in the first place.

Old Testament themes continue in 3:12-13 with references to the "day of God" and the promise of "new heavens and a new earth." (See Isaiah 65:17.)

Those who think Peter wrote to a Gentile audience suggest the following clues to support their view: (1) Peter wrote "to those who have obtained like precious faith with us" (1:1, NKJV). Since Peter was Jewish, this may suggest a Gentile audience. It need not do so, however. Peter may have used "us" simply in an editorial sense to refer to himself and other Jewish believers who had come to faith in Jesus earlier than those to whom he now wrote. (2) Peter's readers had "escaped the corruption that is in the world through lust" (1:4). Some think it unlikely that Peter would describe a Jewish audience this way. But Jesus often rebuked the religious Jews of the first century for their ignorance and vanity. (See Matthew 15:1-9.) Paul accused the Jews of having a "spirit of stupor," i.e., having ears that could not hear and eyes that could not see (Romans 9:30-32; 11:7-10). (3) Peter referred to the letters of Paul, which were written to the same audience (3:15-16), and Paul wrote to Gentile believers. But Paul intended that at least some of his letters would be circulated to different churches (Colossians 4:16). And his being primarily an apostle to Gentiles would no more prevent him from ministering to Jews than Peter's being primarily an apostle to Jews would prevent him from ministering to Gentiles. New Testament believers understood that all Christian literature was written to them in a broad sense; each letter had a specific original audience, but its usefulness extended to all who believed.

Purpose

II Peter 1:15 reveals this letter's purpose: "Moreover I will be careful to ensure that you always have a reminder of these things after my decease" (NKJV). As Peter anticipated the nearness of his death (1:14), he wished to leave a reminder of the authenticity of the gospel message (1:16-21) and a warning of the impending danger of false teachers (2:1-3) that would survive his passing. II Peter gives direction to all generations of believers that the way to avoid deception is to be assured of the finality of the authority of the written Scriptures (1:19-21) and to develop the virtues that are characteristic of the divine nature (1:3-11). The certainty of the Day of God should be motivation to develop these virtues (3:10-14).

Style and Structure

The letter is written in the style of a last will and testament. This literary device was well known among the Jewish people, having originated with Moses' testament in Deuteronomy. The elements of this style include a reminder of truth (1:12-16; 3:1-2), warnings (1:9-12; 2; 3:17), and exhortations (1:5-7; 3:11, 14).[14] II Timothy is another example of this literary formula.

There are significant parallels between the content of II Peter and of Jude, as shown by the following chart, adapted from Hillyer:[15]

II Peter	Parallel Thought	Jude
2:1	False teachers who deny the Lord	4
2:4	Fallen angels imprisoned in darkness	6
2:6	Burning of Sodom and Gomorrah	7
2:10	Slander of fallen angels	8

II Peter	Parallel Thought	Jude
2:11	Restraint of faithful angels	9
2:12	Slanderers are like brute beasts	10
2:15	Slanderers follow example of Balaam	11
2:17	Slanderers are like storm clouds	2
2:17	Blackness of darkness reserved for slanderers	13
2:18	Slanderers boast, lust, and entice	16
3:3	Scoffers in the last days	18

These parallels have led to speculation about the literary relationship between II Peter and Jude. There are three common schools of thought: (1) II Peter borrowed from Jude. (2) Jude borrowed from II Peter. (3) Both II Peter and Jude borrowed from a common source, now unknown.

In the final analysis, the questions surrounding the relationship of II Peter and Jude have not been resolved. It may seem odd to us that either writer would have borrowed material from the other without acknowledging the source of the material, or that either one would borrow from a third source without acknowledging it. But this is to put the strictures of modern research on an ancient book written during a time when such strictures were not in vogue. An examination of the parallel accounts in Kings and Chronicles and in Matthew, Mark, and Luke will demonstrate that ancient writers borrowed from one another or from common sources without citation.

As Blum has pointed out, regardless of whether II Peter borrowed from Jude, Jude borrowed from II Peter, or both borrowed from a common source, the issues of authenticity, authorship, and inspiration are not necessarily affected.[16] The biblical concept of inspiration certainly allows one author to quote another. For that matter, inspiration allowed Paul's quotes from two Greek poets—Epimenides and Aratus—to be included in Acts 17:28.[17] In addition, it seems that Jude referred to the *Assumption of Moses*, a book no longer extant, when relating the confrontation between the devil and Michael over the body of Moses.[18]

II Peter employs a literary style that is substantially different from the style of I Peter. Green described the literary style in II Peter as "a definite Asiatic style of writing, with a florid, verbose type of diction."[19] This difference does not mean that the same author could not have written both letters. It is common for a writer to vary his or her style when writing for different purposes. There is nothing in II Peter that Peter could not have written.

In spite of the literary differences between I and II Peter, there is also significant similarity between the two letters. Both employ strong Hebraisms (figures of speech used in the Hebrew language) and verbal repetition. Green explained the significance of the vocabulary in both letters:

> Of the words which appear in no other Greek author except later ecclesiastical writers, there are nine in 1 Peter and five in 2 Peter. Twenty-seven words in 1 Peter, twenty-four in 2 Peter are not to be found in any classical author. 1 Peter has thirty-three rare words in common with the LXX [the Septuagint, the ancient Greek translation of the Old Testament], 2 Peter twenty-four. Of the 543 words in 1 Peter, sixty-three are New Testament *hapax legomena* [words that appear only once]; of the 399 words in 2 Peter there are fifty-seven *hapax legomena*.[20]

Recent scholars have used a computer analysis of I and II Peter, which shows that these books are linguistically indistinguishable, to refute those who doubt that Peter authored both books because of differences in literary style and vocabulary.[21]

Summary of Content

The letter begins by identifying the author as Simon Peter, who identified himself as a slave and apostle of Jesus Christ and who wrote to those who shared his faith. He acknowledged that Jesus Christ is both God and Savior and that His righteousness makes faith possible (1:1).

Peter wished his readers grace and peace; he knew these blessings came only through knowing God, who is contextually identified as Jesus (1:2). By His divine power, God has given believers all the resources pertaining to life and godliness that they need; these resources are available to those who know the God who calls them to glory and virtue (1:3). On the basis of the great and precious promises of God, believers partake of the divine nature; they have escaped the corruption of worldly lust (1:4).

Spiritual growth involves the development of specific character qualities. Having begun with faith, believers are to add virtue, knowledge, self-control, perseverance, godliness, brotherly kindness, and love (1:5-7). These qualities assure spiritual maturity and fruitfulness for the believer (1:8). A lack of these qualities indicates spiritual shortsightedness, blindness, and amnesia (1:9). As believers develop these qualities, they make sure their calling and election, remove the possibility of stumbling,

Introduction to Second Peter

and receive assurance of an abundant entrance into the kingdom of God (1:10-11).

Although the letter's original readers were knowledgeable and established in truth, Peter thought it good—in view of his impending death—to remind them of some things (1:12-14). He wanted them to have a reminder that would endure beyond his death (1:15).

He reminded his readers that his witness was not based on fables. Peter had actually seen Jesus transfigured, and he had heard the testimony of the heavenly voice (1:16-18). Even so, Peter recognized the supremacy and finality of written revelation (1:19-21).

Peter's chief concern was with the rise of false teachers from within the believing community (2:1). These teachers would be persuasive, but their motives would be wrong (2:2-3). It was certain that the judgment of God would come upon them, just as it did on rebellious angels, on the sinful population in Noah's day, and on the inhabitants of Sodom and Gomorrah (2:4-6).

The deliverance of Lot from the judgment that came on Sodom indicates that the Lord is just as able to deliver people of faith as He is to judge the unjust (2:7-9). Among those whom God will judge are those whose lives are characterized by lust, rebellion, presumption, self-will, and slander (2:10).

Although even faithful angels do not slander fallen angels, the self-willed rebels described by Peter speak evil when they do not know what they are talking about (2:11-12). The result of their corruption is that they will perish; their reward will be what they have earned (2:12-13). Indications of their corruption include carousing in the daytime, committing adultery, and coveting things (2:13-14).

These corrupt people were apparently once in the right way, but they forsook the truth to follow the example of Balaam (2:15-16). They pretended to be what they were not; their destiny was certain (2:17).

These false teachers had an agenda: they sought to allure those who had escaped from error. In their attempt to allure, they used persuasive but deceptive words, appealing to base desires (2:18). Although they themselves were slaves to corruption, they promised liberty to those who would follow them (2:19).

Another indication that these false teachers once walked in truth is that they had become entangled anew in the pollutions of the world that they had once escaped. Because of this, they were worse off than they were before they first knew the right way (2:20-22).

As in the first letter, Peter reminded his readers of some important things (3:1). He claimed authority for the apostles equal to that of the Hebrew prophets; it was equally important for his readers to remember what the prophets had written and what the apostles had commanded (3:2).

Peter warned his readers that an indication of the last days is those who scoff at the idea of the Second Coming (3:3-4). These scoffers intentionally ignore biblical evidence (3:5-7). To them, the passing of time indicates that biblical prophecies will never be fulfilled, but God does not count time as humans do (3:8). Regardless of how long He waits to fulfill His promises, God will keep His word. The reason judgment has not come earlier is because of God's long-suffering and His desire for all to repent (3:9).

The day will come when all biblical prophecies con-

Introduction to Second Peter

cerning the events of the end will be fulfilled. At that time the present heavens and earth will be replaced. The certainty of this event should motivate believers to live in such a way as to honor God (3:10-14).

Believers should not conclude that because prophecies of the end have not yet been fulfilled they will never be fulfilled. The delay in the Lord's return is due to His long-suffering desire for people to be saved (3:15). Paul had written about this in his letters, too, though unstable people, who had not been taught, misinterpreted Paul's writings, as they do other passages of Scripture, with the result that they bring destruction upon themselves (3:15-16).

Peter forewarned his readers to be alert to the possibility of falling by following the error of the false teachers (3:17). The antidote to falling is to grow in the grace and knowledge of Jesus Christ, to whom the glory belongs now and throughout eternity (3:18).

I
Salutation
(1:1-2)

A. Author (1:1a)

(1a) Simon Peter, a servant and an apostle of Jesus Christ.

Verse 1a. The book begins with the claim that Simon Peter is the author (1:1). Since in his first letter Peter identified himself only by the name Jesus gave him—Peter—some think the identification "Simon Peter" indicates that the work is pseudonymous and that the unknown author appended "Simon" to "Peter" in an attempt to authenticate Peter as the author.

It is unlikely, however, that a pseudonymous author would attempt authentication by identifying himself in a way Peter did not identify himself in his first letter. If Peter had identified himself as "Simon Peter" in his first letter, doubtless anyone attempting to write under his name would have done the same in the second letter. But since Peter did not do that, it would seem strange for anyone using a pseudonym to think that the use of "Simon Peter" would persuade anyone who questioned the authorship of the letter that it was actually written by Peter.

Since early believers did not accept pseudonymity,[22] and since the church did accept the letter as authentic, it

Second Peter

is clear that believers accepted the letter's claim at face value: it was written by the apostle originally known as Simon, whom Jesus named Peter (Mark 3:16).

The name "Simon" is transliterated from the Greek *Symeon*. Symeon is transliterated from the Hebrew *Shime'on*, a form of *shema'*, which means "to hear," in the sense of "to listen" or "to obey." The name "Simon" indicated Peter's Jewishness, and it meant something like "hearing" or "heard."

Jesus gave Simon the name "Cephas" (John 1:42), which is transliterated from the Greek *Kephas*. It comes from the Aramaic kêp̱a', which means "stone" or "rock." "Peter" (Greek, *petros*) has the same meaning. (See Matthew 16:18.)

Among the Jewish people, the meaning of one's name was significant. If a person's name was changed, the meaning of the new name indicated some change of status or destiny or some life transformation. For Jesus to call Simon "Peter" indicated he would be a pillar and foundation stone in the church. (See Galatians 2:9; Ephesians 2:20; Revelation 21:14.)

As in his first letter, Peter identified himself as an apostle of Jesus Christ. An apostle was a messenger, a delegate, or an envoy.[23] As an apostle, Peter represented Jesus Christ. Peter's brother, Andrew, had introduced him to Jesus (John 1:40-42). Jesus called Peter to be a fisher of men (Luke 5:10). (See also Matthew 4:18-22; Mark 1:16-20; Luke 5:1-11.) Peter was listed first among the twelve apostles (Matthew 10:1-4; Mark 3:13-19; Luke 6:13-16). Peter was one of only three apostles permitted to accompany Jesus on special occasions (Mark 5:37; 9:2; 14:33). Once, Andrew was permitted to join this group (Mark 13:3).

Salutation

Peter continued to fulfill a leading role among the apostles after the ascension of Jesus and before the Day of Pentecost, conducting the business that resulted in the replacement of Judas (Acts 1:13-22). After the outpouring of the Holy Spirit, he first proclaimed the gospel to the assembled multitude and answered their question: "Men and brethren, what shall we do?" (Acts 2:14-39).

Peter's leadership among the apostles continued as the church grew and spread beyond Jerusalem. In fact, his was the dominant apostolic influence throughout the first twelve chapters of Acts. In this apostolic role, he proclaimed Jesus to be the Messiah (Acts 3:12-26), he defended the faith before the Sanhedrin (Acts 4:5-12), he protected the purity of the church (Acts 5:1-11), he represented the Jerusalem church (together with John) to the Samaritan believers and was instrumental in ministering the Holy Spirit to them (Acts 8:14-17), he conducted a missionary ministry accompanied by remarkable miracles (Acts 9:32-43), and he introduced the gospel to the Gentiles (Acts 10-11).

Peter was specifically an apostle to the Jewish people, though he occasionally ministered to Gentiles. (See Galatians 2:7-8.)[24]

In this second letter, Peter identified himself not only as an apostle of Jesus Christ but also as a servant of Jesus Christ. The word "servant" is translated from the Greek *doulos*, which means "a slave." This word testifies to Peter's belief in the deity of Jesus, for devout Jews would never confess that they were slaves to any human. The law of Moses instructed the Jewish people to worship the Lord God and to serve Him alone. (See Matthew 4:10; Deuteronomy 6:13; 10:20.) Indeed, the Hebrew word for

Second Peter

worship (*abad*) is closely allied with the idea of serving.

The ancient Jews saw all of life as service and thus worship to God. This included not only involvement in the Temple rituals and reading of the Scriptures, but also work in the fields or any other use of physical energy and skills. Because they viewed themselves as slaves (servants) of Yahweh alone, the Jews refused to acknowledge that they were the servants of anyone else, even when they were politically subjugated. When Jesus said to the Jews, "And you shall know the truth, and the truth shall make you free," they responded with indignation, "We are Abraham's descendants, and have never been in bondage to anyone. How can you say, 'You will be made free'?" (John 8:32-33, NKJV). This is a typical Jewish response; in their mind, they were in bondage only to God, not to any human. The truth, of course, is that throughout their history, Israel had been in bondage to various political oppressors, including Egypt, Assyria, and Babylon. Even at the time Jesus ministered, Israel was a Roman province known as Judaea. But because of the prohibition on serving anyone other than the true God, devout Jews would not admit that they were the servants of any other.

Jewish readers would have understood Peter's claim to be a servant of Jesus Christ as a declaration of the deity of Jesus. A Jew would serve God only; therefore, Jesus is God.

The English word "servant" softens the significance of the Greek *doulos*. The NKJV translates *doulos* as "bondservant." Some translations render it "slave." *Doulos* has to do with complete submission. The English "servant" may imply an employee, but the Greek *doulos* strictly means one who is actually owned or purchased by another. Peter considered himself to actually belong to Jesus Christ; He had purchased Peter, and now Peter's allegiance was to Christ alone.

There may be some significance in which of the New Testament Epistles identify their author as a slave of Jesus and which do not. When we collate all the relevant information, we can reasonably suggest that the New Testament letters which identify the author as a slave of Jesus Christ were written to an audience almost completely or at least significantly Jewish and that the writer intended to demonstrate to Jewish readers the conviction that Jesus is God.[25] Letters written to Gentiles may assert the deity of Christ in other ways, but the Jewish refusal to acknowledge servanthood to another human being would not be so meaningful to Gentiles.

B. Recipients (1:1b)

(1b) To them that have obtained like precious faith with us through the righteousness of God and our Saviour Jesus Christ.

Verse 1b. I Peter is addressed to readers in specific geographic locations. (See I Peter 1:1.) Here, Peter did not specify the location of his readers; he identified them as those who share a common faith. Peter probably did not specify the location of his audience because this was his second letter to the same readers (3:1). There was no need to identify them by location a second time.

"Faith" here is apparently faith in the subjective sense of trust in God. There is no definite article before the word "faith" (Greek, *pistin*). Ordinarily, when "faith" refers to the actual content of what is believed, the definite article precedes it. (See Jude 3.)

Those to whom Peter wrote were people of faith. Like Peter, they trusted in God. More specifically, they trusted in Jesus Christ as their Savior.

The faith held by the readers had been "obtained." This has led some commentators to conclude that "faith" here means, after all, the content or body of doctrinal faith held by believers. But the word translated "obtained" (Greek, *lachousin*) here means that the faith had been appointed or distributed to them; they had received it as a free gift from God. The ability to come to God to receive salvation is a gift of God. (See Acts 11:18; Ephesians 2:8-9.) This includes the ability to believe.

The word translated "like precious" (Greek, *isotimon*) means "of the same kind."[26] The faith of the original readers of this letter was the same kind of faith as held by Peter and the other apostles. It was a faith firmly rooted in the belief that Jesus Christ is both God and Savior and that by His atoning work, He had "bought them" or redeemed them from sin (2:1, 20).

The faith that Peter shared with his readers had been obtained "by the righteousness of our God and Savior Jesus Christ" (NKJV). The word translated "righteousness" (Greek, *dikaiosune*) has a range of meaning; the context determines the specific meaning of the word. In Paul's letters, the word has legal overtones and refers to the way God places believers in right standing with Him on the basis of faith. Some commentators think that in the context of both I and II Peter, we should understand "righteousness" in an ethical sense, meaning fairness or justice.[27] Others think that Peter used the word like Paul to refer to justification by faith.[28]

Salutation

The word "righteousness" has to do with what is right. It is used in reference to uprightness and equity.[29] Here, it does seem best to understand righteousness to refer to God's ethical rightness, equity, or fairness. This is the means by which all believers, whether apostles or the scattered recipients of this letter, obtain faith. God is completely just in that He gives all people, regardless of their ethnic origins, social standing, or gender, the ability to believe on Him. (See John 1:12; 3:16; Acts 11:18; Ephesians 2:8.) Peter first perceived this truth after his visionary encounter with God on a roof in Joppa (Acts 10:34-35).

The phrase translated "of God and our Saviour Jesus Christ" (Greek, *tou theou hemon kai soteros Iesou Christou*) is more precisely translated "of our God and Savior Jesus Christ" (NKJV). The reason is that in the Greek text the definite article "the" (*tou*) appears before the word "God" (*theou*) but not before the word "Savior" (*soteros*). When two nouns (in this case, "God" and "Savior") of the same case and number, as here, are joined by the conjunction *kai* ("and"), and the definite article precedes the first noun but not the second noun, then both nouns refer to the same person or thing.[30] In this instance, Scripture identifies Jesus Christ as both God and Savior.

This is one of a number of places in the Epistles where the New Testament writers clearly identified Jesus as God. Paul wrote, "Christ . . . is over all, the eternally blessed God" (Romans 9:5, NKJV). He also wrote that we should be "looking for the blessed hope and glorious appearing of our great God and Savior Jesus Christ" (Titus 2:13, NKJV). The writer of Hebrews quoted Psalm

45:6-7 to declare that the Son is God (Hebrews 1:8). John wrote that Jesus Christ "is the true God and eternal life" (I John 5:20, NKJV). (See also Colossians 2:9; I Timothy 3:16.)

Moo pointed out that "this is the only place in the New Testament where we read of 'the righteousness of . . . Jesus Christ.' Everywhere else the righteousness is attributed to God. But this reference to Christ is in keeping with the whole tenor of the letter, which consistently puts Christ at the same level as God."[31] (See Romans 1:17; 3:5, 21-22; 10:3; II Corinthians 5:21; James 1:20.) The numerous references to Jesus Christ as "Lord" in this letter underscore Peter's conviction that Jesus Christ is God. (See comments on verse 1a.)

Moo also asserted that "while it would be a gross anachronism to attribute to the apostle at this point a fully worked-out Trinitarian understanding of God, what he says here, along with other similar verses in the New Testament, provides the building blocks for the later elaboration of that central Christian doctrine."[32]

It has become increasingly common for trinitarian theologians to confess that the doctrine of the trinity is not explicit in the New Testament, but to insist that it is implicit. The idea is that it took later generations of Christians to work out the implications of the scriptural claims concerning the nature of God. Thus, Moo and others have declared that the understanding of God as three persons is a "central Christian doctrine," even though it is not explicated in Scripture.

In effect, these writers have admitted that no New Testament writer understood God as three persons. The unintentional implication is that the inspired writers of

Scripture had an inferior view of God compared to later Christians. Moreover, if they lived today, their views of the Godhead would disqualify them from identification as orthodox Christians. Surely this is an untenable suggestion. If Peter and the rest of the writers of the New Testament were genuinely Christian without "a fully worked-out Trinitarian understanding of God," surely today there can be genuine Christians without such an understanding as well, whose understanding of God comes from the same source as that available to first-century believers: the Holy Scriptures.

Insisting that to be a genuine Christian one must understand God in terms of the postbiblical, uninspired creeds adopted at various church councils in the fourth and fifth centuries borders on a belief in authoritative extrabiblical revelation. A typical response to this criticism is that the creeds are authoritative if they accurately reflect the teaching of Scripture, even if they do so in nonbiblical language. But it is precisely here that the problem arises. If the "fully worked-out Trinitarian understanding of God" goes beyond what even an inspired biblical writer would understand, it is doubtful that the postbiblical creeds accurately represent the meaning of those inspired writers.

For Peter, it was enough to declare Jesus Christ to be God. He did not speculate on any distinction of persons in the Godhead. Indeed, Green pointed out that by identifying Jesus as Savior, "Peter is in fact boldly taking the Old Testament name for Yahweh and applying it to Jesus, just as he did in his sermon on the day of Pentecost (Acts ii. 21)."[33]

II Peter refers to Jesus Christ as Savior five times.

Second Peter

(See 1:11; 2:20; 3:2, 18.) This is significant since elsewhere in the New Testament the word "Savior" appears only nineteen times. Eleven of these texts identify Jesus Christ as the Savior.[34] The other eight instances identify God as the Savior.[35]

As Green pointed out, "Saviour is one of the great names of God in the Old Testament."[36] In Isaiah 43:11 Yahweh identified Himself as the only Savior. (See Isaiah 45:21; 49:26; 60:16; Hosea 13:4.) The word "Savior" translates the Hebrew *yasha'*, the basic idea of which is deliverance of some kind. A form of *yasha'* finds its way into the name of the Messiah in the transliteration of the final letters as "sus" (from the Greek *sous*).[37] This gives rise to the meaning of the name "Jesus" as "Yahweh is Salvation." (See Matthew 1:21.)

Peter, a devout Jew, believed the only true God was the God who revealed Himself to the people of Israel as recorded in the Hebrew Scriptures. (See Deuteronomy 6:4.) He also believed this God was the only Savior. Thus, when he identified Jesus Christ as God and Savior, he identified Him as the same God who covenanted with His people Israel, the God who had now made Himself known in the person of Jesus Christ.

C. Greetings (1:2)

(2) Grace and peace be multiplied unto you through the knowledge of God, and of Jesus our Lord.

Verse 2. The initial greeting here is virtually identical with the greeting in I Peter: "Grace unto you, and peace, be multiplied" (I Peter 1:2). Peter's greeting of "grace" was typical in the Greco-Roman world, but—like the writers of other New Testament letters—he also incorporated the common Jewish greeting "peace" (Greek, *eirene*, the equivalent of the Hebrew *shalom*).

Peter's wish for grace (Greek, *charis*) to be multiplied to his readers was not a mere formality. Like Paul, Peter saw the grace of God as far more than simply unmerited favor.[38] In some way, the grace of God is a powerful force by which God motivates and enables people of faith to do what pleases Him. According to Scripture, believers should grow in grace (II Peter 3:18). They should have an ever-increasing capacity for God to motivate and enable them. (See Philippians 2:13.)

The Hebrew idea of peace goes far beyond similar expressions in Western culture. *Shalom* is essentially about holistic well-being. The Western view is fragmentary; it splits people up so that someone can express concern for one's physical well-being with no regard for spiritual well-being. This does not occur in Hebrew thought. *Shalom* embraces both material and spiritual wellness. (See Isaiah 48:22; 57:21; Psalm 34:14; 119:165.) Peter urged his readers to be diligent to "be found of him in peace" (3:14). Contextually, this is a reference to the *eschaton* (last things) and to Peter's hope that at that time God would find his readers to be whole in every way. As II Peter 3:14 further explains, to be "in peace," or "whole," means to be "without spot, and blameless."

In this letter, Peter wished that grace and peace would be multiplied to his readers specifically "through the knowledge of God, and of Jesus our Lord." This is another indication that this letter focuses intentionally

Second Peter

on the person of Jesus, with specific emphasis on His deity.

The word translated "knowledge" (Greek, *epignosis*) goes beyond the usual *gnosis*. By the addition of the preposition *epi*, the meaning of the word is something like "full knowledge."[39] Green pointed out: "A deeper knowledge of the Person of Jesus is the surest safeguard against false doctrine."[40] The word appears again in 1:3, 8; 2:20. In each case, it has to do with knowing Jesus. In 2:21, the related verb *epiginosko* appears, still referring contextually to the knowledge associated with Jesus.

II Peter 1:5-6 and 3:18 use the more common *gnosis*. Since in 3:18 the *gnosis* in view is still knowledge of Jesus, there is strong contextual evidence that we should also understand the *gnosis* of 1:5-6 as knowledge of Jesus. This would make the knowledge that we are to add to virtue a growing knowledge of Jesus, which would fulfill Peter's wish that grace and peace would be multiplied to his readers "in the knowledge of our God and Savior Jesus Christ" (NKJV).

II Peter 1:20 and 3:3 use *ginosko*, meaning "to know," to refer to a knowledge concerning inspiration and a knowledge concerning scoffers who deny the coming of the Lord. Thus, the letter consistently uses various forms of *gnosis* in reference to knowing Jesus, and it uses *ginosko* in reference to other knowledge. Where it elsewhere speaks of some kind of knowledge (1:12, 14; 2:9), it uses the Greek *eido*, which has to do with perception or experience.

The use of *gnosis*, *epignosis*, and *epiginosko* in reference to knowledge of Jesus and the use of other words

Salutation

in reference to other kinds of knowledge suggests that under inspiration Peter used each word purposefully. He was interested in calling his readers to a greater knowledge of Jesus. Since II Peter uses *epignosis*, or a form of it, five times and *gnosis* only three times, and since it once clearly uses *gnosis* to represent knowledge of Jesus, just as it previously used *epignosis*, we should understand it to mean by *gnosis* the same thing it means by *epignosis*. In other words, the use of *epignosis* serves to inform the meaning of *gnosis*. II Peter's use of other words to address knowledge of other kinds underscores this point.

The knowledge Peter was concerned about is "knowledge of God and of Jesus our Lord" (NKJV). The immediate question arising from this phrase is whether it identifies Jesus as God here, as in 1:1. (See comments on verse 1b.) Context has a significant influence on the meaning of words, and for verse 1 to declare that Jesus is "our God and Savior" would ordinarily indicate that verse 2 declares Him to be "our God and . . . Lord."

There is more to consider, however, than context. Specifically, we must consult the Greek text for information on whether the passage continues to identify Jesus as God here.

In verse 1, the phrase translated "of God and our Saviour Jesus Christ" ("of our God and Savior Jesus Christ," NKJV) is *tou theou hemon kai soteros Iesou Christou*. The phrase identifies Jesus as both God and Savior because the definite article, "the" (*tou*), precedes the first noun, "God" (*theou*); but it does not precede the second noun, "Savior" (*soteros*); and the two words are connected by "and" (*kai*).

Second Peter

In verse 2 the phrase "of God and of Jesus" translates *tou theou kai Iesou*. Here, the definite article, "the" (*tou*), precedes the first noun, "God" (*theou*); the definite articles does not precede the second noun, which is the proper name "Jesus" (*Iesou*); and "God" and "Jesus" are connected by "and" (*kai*). To this extent, the grammatical structures of the phrase "of our God and Savior" in verse 1 and the phrase "of God and of Jesus" in verse 2 are identical. The only difference is that in verse 1 the word translated "our" (*hemon*) appears after "God" and before "and." But this does not have any influence on the point we are discussing here.

Much of our understanding of the definite article in Greek has come about during the last two hundred years due to the work of Granville Sharp (1735-1813), an English philanthropist, abolitionist, and linguist. After a thorough study of the definite article in the New Testament, Sharp formulated the following statement, which came to be known as "Granville Sharp's Rule":

> When the copulative [*kai*] [and] connects two nouns of the same case, [viz., nouns (either substantive or adjective, or participles) of personal description respecting office, dignity, affinity, or connection, and attributes, properties, or qualities, good or ill,] if the article [*ho*] [the], or any of its cases, precedes the first of said nouns or participles, and is not repeated before the second noun or participle, the latter always relates to the same person that is expressed or described by the first noun or participle: i.e., it denotes a further description of the first-named person.[41]

Salutation

On the basis of this principle, both the words "God" and "Savior" in verse 1 are descriptive of Jesus Christ.

Most who comment on verse 2, even those who recognize that verse 1 proclaims Jesus to be God, deny that verse 2 so identifies Him. This is because Sharp offered an exception to the above rule:

> There is no exception or instance of the like mode of expression . . . which necessarily requires a construction different from what is here laid down, EXCEPT the nouns be *proper names*, or *in the plural number*; in which cases there are many exceptions; though there are not wanting examples, even of plural nouns, which are expressed exactly agreeable to this rule.[42]

In other words, even if two nouns are joined by *kai* and the first has the definite article but the second does not, the rule may not apply if the nouns are proper names or if they are plural.

We should note, however, that Sharp's exception, as it pertains to proper names, specifically refers to both nouns being proper names. He did not address the situation where only one of the nouns is a proper name. In his exception he also implied that there are some exceptions even to this exception, in which both nouns may be proper names but still refer only to one person, just as is the case with plural nouns.

Based on his understanding of Sharp's exception, Kuehne wrote, "Where . . . one of the nouns is [*Iesous*] (Jesus), the rule cannot be applied with certainty."[43] Although Kuehne understood Sharp's exception to apply

Second Peter

when only one of the nouns is a proper name, he did not understand the exception to mean that when one of the nouns is a proper name the rule can never apply, but only that it did not apply with certainty. Nevertheless, Kuehne rejected the idea that II Peter 1:2 calls Jesus God, on the basis that if one of the nouns is a proper name Sharp's rule does not apply.[44]

Others, however, think that the translation of verse 2 should indicate that Jesus is both Lord and God, just as verse 1 indicates He is both God and Savior. For example, A. T. Robertson wrote, "At first sight the idiom here seems to require one person as in 1:1, though there is a second article (*tou*) before *kuriou*, and *Iesou* is a proper name."[45] Robertson was uncertain whether verse 2 should actually be translated this way, but his uncertainty was due to a textual variant, not the grammar. In other words, if the text does read *tou theou kai Iesou tou kuriou hemon*, Robertson thought that the phrase would require one person, even though *Iesou* ("Jesus") is a proper name and the definite article precedes *kuriou* ("Lord").

It is also interesting to note that one of the newest Bible translations into English, the *New Living Translation*, renders verse 2 as follows: "May God bless you with his special favor and wonderful peace as you come to know Jesus, our God and Lord, better and better."[46] In a footnote, the translators offered an alternate translation: ". . . come to know God and Jesus our Lord," but they clearly believed the former phrase to be more accurate because they included it in the main text.

The textual variant that Robertson alluded to, even if it is not original, may offer a clue as to how verse 2 should be translated. The variant, found in manuscript P (ninth century), some manuscripts of the Latin Vulgate, and some minuscules (later Greek manuscripts written with a form of cursive letters), says "in the knowledge of our Lord."[47] The words "of God and of Jesus" are missing. Green concluded that this shorter reading is original because "it fits the singular *his* of verse 3; and elsewhere in this Epistle it is Jesus alone who is the object of *knowledge* (Greek, *epignosis*)."[48]

Even if we accept the longer reading as original, Green's comments are significant. The singular pronoun "His" in verse 3 normally indicates a singular antecedent. If "God" and "Jesus" in verse 2 refer to two persons, then where is the singular antecedent of "His" in the phrase "as His divine power has given to us all things that pertain to life and godliness" (NKJV)? The last half of verse 3 also contains a singular pronoun, which clearly indicates that verse 2 refers to Jesus as God. It reads, "Through the knowledge of Him who called us by glory and virtue" (NKJV). If verse 3 speaks of the knowledge of "Him," a singular person, then verse 2 also speaks of a singular person when it refers to the knowledge of God.

Green's point that "elsewhere in this Epistle it is Jesus alone who is the object of knowledge" is also significant and true. It would seem strange contextually for one person to be the object of knowledge in 1:3, 8; 2:20 and for two persons to be the object of knowledge in 1:2, especially since 1:2 identifies Jesus—the recognized object of knowledge elsewhere—as God Himself.

We can rarely be certain about the origin of textual variants, but this variant speaks of a singular person in verse 2. For it to develop in the first place, and for it to agree perfectly with the grammar and theme of the rest of the letter, argues persuasively that ancient believers understood the verse to refer to one person only, regardless of which text they followed. In other words, if the longer reading is original, and if ancient believers understood it to refer to two persons, it is very unlikely that a variant which refers to one person could have developed or long endured. Those believers familiar with the older reading would have rejected such a variant early on because it would have so obviously departed from the original meaning of the verse. But if the longer reading is original, and if ancient believers understood it to refer to one person, it is much more likely that a variant that also referred to one person could have developed and endured. Such an error would not have been so glaring and so easily detectable.

Apart from textual and grammatical considerations, we should remember that Peter was a devout Jew, whose theology was defined by the *Shema*: "Hear, O Israel: The LORD our God, the LORD is one!" (Deuteronomy 6:4, NKJV). For Peter and the other apostles, there was only one God, and this God was the Lord. They had no concept of a Godhead consisting of one person who was God and another person who was Lord. Just as Thomas, the devout Jew, had proclaimed of Jesus, "My Lord and My God!" (John 20:28), identifying Jesus as both Lord and God, so Peter believed both words described the same One.

The following evidence indicates that we should understand verse 2 to identify Jesus as God:

1. Verse 1 identifies Jesus as God.
2. Jesus alone is the object of knowledge elsewhere in the letter.
3. Verse 3 uses two singular pronouns to refer back

to a singular antecedent in verse 2.
4. The phrases *tou theou hemon kai soteros* in verse 1 and *tou theou kai Iesou* in verse 2 are identical regarding their definite articles, nouns, and conjunctions.
5. It would have been inconceivable to Peter that God was one person and that the Lord was another.
6. Respectable Greek scholars assert that only one person is in view in verse 2.
7. Granville Sharp's rule does not specifically exclude identity of nouns when only one of them is a proper name. Even if both were proper names, Sharp acknowledged that there may be exceptions to the exception.

In view of the evidence, we can understand verse 2 to mean "grace and peace be multiplied to you in the knowledge of Jesus, our Lord and God."

II
The Call to Spiritual Growth (1:3-21)

This section of II Peter teaches that spiritual growth is the antidote to the deception of false teachers. (See 2:1-3.)

The basis for spiritual growth is that God has given to believers everything they need for life and godliness. These resources come through the knowledge of God (verse 3). God has promised these resources to all believers, and they enable us to share in God's nature and to escape the corruption of sin (verse 4).

The eight elements of spiritual growth are faith, virtue, knowledge, self-control, perseverance, godliness, brotherly kindness, and love (verses 5-7). None of these is sufficient in isolation from the other elements; we must develop them in conjunction with each other.

The reward for spiritual growth is the promise of spiritual fruitfulness (verse 8).

If believers do not mature, they lack spiritual vision and forget the transforming effect of the Atonement in their lives (verse 9).

Another benefit of spiritual growth is avoidance of stumbling and the promise of a victorious entry into the eternal kingdom (verses 10-11).

Peter urgently exhorted his readers to grow spiritually because he knew his death was near (verses 12-14). Since he could write only so much to them at this point in his

Second Peter

life, he focused on the most important issues.

The Scriptures are the means of spiritual growth. God inspired reliable witnesses to write them: the Hebrew prophets and the New Testament apostles (verses 15-21).

A. The Basis for Growth (1:3-4)

(3) According as his divine power hath given unto us all things that pertain unto life and godliness, through the knowledge of him that hath called us to glory and virtue: (4) whereby are given unto us exceeding great and precious promises: that by these ye might be partakers of the divine nature, having escaped the corruption that is in the world through lust.

Verse 3. The singular pronouns "his" and "him" refer back to Jesus, whom verses 1-2 identify as God, Savior, and Lord. The term "divine power" is a Hebrew periphrasis (indirect expression) for God.[49] (See Luke 1:35.) "His divine power" means that God Himself has given us all things pertaining to life and godliness.

The phrase "life and godliness" is a hendiadys meaning "a godly life."[50] A hendiadys is a "literary figure whereby one idea is expressed by two (or occasionally three) nouns linked by a simple 'and.' The first noun is treated as the main substantive, with the second (and third) taken adjectivally."[51]

Like the writings of Paul and John in other places,[52] II Peter uses a series of words that were laden with significance in the Hellenistic world. Though it occasionally uses the language of Greek philosophy, it does not use the words to mean what they meant to Hellenists. Instead, it infuses the words with new meaning that is uniquely Christian.

These words include *arete*, "virtue;" *theias koinonoi phuseos*, "partakers of the divine nature;" *eusebia*, "godliness;" and *phthora*, "corruption." Hellenists used *arete* to refer to virtue as a pagan ethic.[53] They used *eusebia*, which literally means "good worship,"[54] to refer to piety as a pagan ethic.[55] *Theios* referred to the "divine," but again from the perspective of Greek thought.

Green pointed out how II Peter uses these words:

> Peter is simply taking the language of the opposition, disinfecting it, and using it back on them, charged with Christian meaning. . . . The writer is putting his Christian doctrine into Greek dress for the purposes of communication, without in the least committing himself to the pagan associations of the terms. Indeed . . . he makes a frontal assault on Stoic and Platonic presuppositions who taught, respectively, that by *phusis* (nature) or *nomos* (law) a man became partaker of the divine. No, says our author; it is by grace, by the gospel promises, that this comes about. Furthermore, the aorist *apophugontes* ["having escaped"] reminds us that we are not moving in the realms of Platonism but Christianity. We are made partakers of the divine nature not *in escaping* from the natural world of time and sense, but *after escaping* the "world" in the sense of mankind in rebellion against God.[56]

According to some systems of Greek philosophy, humanity could eventually escape the corruption of the world—which to them meant the material world—by the practice of certain virtues. One supposedly became a partaker of the divine nature through the practice of these virtues.[57] This is not the message of II Peter. According to II Peter, believers have already escaped the corruption that is in the world at the beginning of their Christian life; this escape is the starting point, not the goal. And they participate in the divine nature not by the practice of certain virtues but on the basis of the "exceedingly great and precious promises" of God.

Underscoring the Jewishness of the original recipients of this letter, Keener pointed out:

> That Peter's immediate cultural context is Diaspora Judaism rather than Greek paganism may be indicated by how he defines physical "corruption" or "decay": its source is lust (v. 4; cf. 2:14; 3:3). Immortality was available, as the Greeks wished, but it was made available only through purification from sin (1:9); and the Greek concept of immortality is qualified by the biblical hope in the kingdom and hence future resurrection (cf. 1:11).[58]

Keener pointed out that the false teachers that this letter refutes "are simply Diaspora Jews almost completely overtaken by Greek thought."[59]

It is evident that Greek thought still permeates Western culture—even Western Christianity—into the third millennium. In response to the perceived decay of morality in our society, many have issued calls to return to the perceived virtue of former days. A careful study of our history may reveal that the perception of a past virtuous age is more illusion than fact. But the idea that the practice of certain virtues can solve social ills is a reflection of Greek philosophy. It is a kind of "pull yourself up by your own bootstraps" philosophy, which assumes that we can become better people by acting better. This is not the message of II Peter. The epistle does not tout a self-improvement program by which we can improve our lot in life. Rather, the starting point is faith, not virtue (verse 5). Where there is no faith, there is no genuine basis for character development.

Certainly all of us would like to live in a society where everybody practiced "old-fashioned virtues." But this view not only provides a self-deceptive vision of the past through the rosy-tinted glasses of nostalgia; it also fails to reckon with the fallenness of all humanity and our utter inability to measure up to God's standard of righteousness by our own efforts. (See Romans 3:23.) What every generation needs is not a renewed call to virtue, but a fresh proclamation of the gospel with its life-changing power. As the hearts of people change, their social structures will change, but not until then.

Everything we need for godly living comes through the knowledge of Jesus Christ, who has "called us by glory and virtue" (NKJV). He has called us by His own glory and virtue. The reading of the Textus Receptus, reflected in the KJV and translated "to glory and virtue," is an ancient reading. It can be translated "by glory and virtue," as in the NKJV. The critical Greek text follows another ancient reading, which means "to his own glory and virtue."[60] The primary difference is that the Textus Receptus has *dia*, which means "through" or "by," where the critical text has *idia*, which means "to his own."

The Septuagint version of Isaiah 42:8, 12 attributes both glory and virtue to Yahweh. Since Jesus is God, II Peter attributes glory and virtue to Him. It is the glory and virtue of Jesus that attract people to Him. "Virtue" here is not the virtue of Greek paganism but the Hebrew concept of "virtue in action, concrete deeds of excellence."[61] As it relates to Jesus, "virtue" expresses "the manifestation of divine power, i.e., miracle."[62]

The Hebrew concept of glory virtually equated the glory of God with God Himself. The New Testament frequently describes Jesus as the very glory of God. (See II Corinthians 4:6; Hebrews 1:3; James 2:1.) To the Hebrews, the glory of God was the invisible God visibly present.[63] In Christ Jesus, the incarnation of God, the glory of God is permanently revealed.[64]

The "call" is the universal call to believe on the Messiah. As the glory of God present on this earth, and through the miraculous demonstration of His virtue, Jesus calls all people to believe on Him. (See John 1:7; 3:14-18; 5:39-40; 12:32; II Peter 3:9.)

Verse 4. The word "whereby" refers back to the glory and virtue of Jesus Christ. On the basis of His glory and virtue, believers receive "exceedingly great and precious promises" (NKJV). This phrase does not just mean that the promises have been made but that they have actually been fulfilled. It certainly refers to the promises Jesus Himself made during His time on earth, including the promise of the Holy Spirit. (See Acts 1:8.) But there is no need to limit these promises to those made after the Incarnation; the exceedingly great and precious promises include those made by the Hebrew prophets and fulfilled in the life and ministry of Jesus. (See Acts 13:32-33.) The

The Call to Spiritual Growth

fulfillment of these promises makes believers "partakers of the divine nature."

II Peter does not mean here that believers in some way become divine. Believers are not gods. They are not subsumed into God. Rather, "believers come to share in some essential qualities that are characteristic of God himself."[65] Elsewhere, it is clear that believers are to be conformed to the image of Christ. (See Romans 8:29.) The Greek word translated "partakers" (*koinonia*) has to do with fellowship or sharing. Believers have fellowship with or share in the characteristics of God's nature in conjunction with escaping "the corruption that is in the world through lust" (NKJV). This is not something that believers strive to do; it is something that they have done. The word translated "having escaped" (*apophugontes*) is in the aorist tense, indicating this is something that happened in the past. The escape occurs when believers become recipients of the great and precious promises, including the promise of regeneration by the new birth. (See I Peter 1:3, 22-23; 2:2; John 3:3-5.)

Another way to say that we are partakers of the divine nature, in Pauline terminology, is to say that we are "in Christ" or that we have "put on Christ."[66] By means of our union with Christ, His righteousness is imputed or reckoned to us. (See II Corinthians 5:21.) To be identified with Him in His righteousness is to share in His divine nature.

II Peter does not identify corruption with the material universe, as did the Hellenists. It identifies corruption with lust, or evil desires. The "world" here is not the physical planet, but the society of people in rebellion against God. Again, this was in opposition to Greek thought.

According to Scripture, believers escape the corrupting influence of sin by receiving the great and precious promise of the new birth. This is the same thing as saying they are "partakers of the divine nature."

B. The Elements of Growth (1:5-7)

(5) And beside this, giving all diligence, add to your faith virtue; and to virtue knowledge; (6) and to knowledge temperance; and to temperance patience; and to patience godliness; (7) and to godliness brotherly kindness; and to brotherly kindness charity.

It was common among Stoic philosophers to make lists of virtues to promote moral advancement.[67] But when New Testament writers used such lists, it was not to promote Greek thought. They used lists to enhance communication with readers who were already familiar with this literary device, but the inspired writers brought new meaning to such lists.[68] As Green has pointed out, "The great difference between Stoic and Christian ethics is that the latter are not the unaided product of human effort, but the fruit of our being partakers of the divine nature."[69]

Hillyer has pointed out that a more literal translation of verses 5-7 would read as follows: "In . . . your faith richly provide goodness; in . . . your goodness, knowledge; in . . . your knowledge, self-control," and so forth.[70] This is because each phrase begins with the preposition *en*, which means "in." The words suggest an "organic union, a cluster of fruits on the living branch of faith."[71] These various character traits do not exist in isolation from each other; each is integrated with all the others to

The Call to Spiritual Growth

provide a full-orbed spiritual maturity.

Verse 5. The translation "and beside this" (KJV) seems to undertranslate the Greek *kai auto touto de*, which is more precisely translated "but also for this very reason" (NKJV). The call for us to grow spiritually is not something in addition to the new birth but something we should do because of the new birth. Since believers partake of the divine nature in regeneration, they should give "all diligence" to develop the character qualities that were evident in the life of Christ.

II Peter also uses the word translated "diligence" (Greek, *spouden*) in 1:10, 15, and 3:14. For believers to give "all diligence" indicates that nothing should be lacking in their effort to grow spiritually. The miracle of God's grace in regeneration has made spiritual growth possible for believers, but it is, nevertheless, up to them to diligently apply the resources God has given them to reach toward spiritual maturity. Philippians 2:12 describes this process as "work[ing] out your own salvation with fear and trembling" (NKJV). This does not mean we are to earn our salvation; it means that, having been saved, we are to conscientiously live out all the implications of our salvation.

Scripture everywhere declares that salvation is a free gift from God, not a reward God gives those who earn or deserve it by their efforts. But, as Blum has pointed out, "the new birth does not rule out human activity."[72] Blum quoted Berkhof, who defined sanctification as "a work of God in which believers co-operate."[73] Hillyer put it, "God does his part; we must cooperate and do ours."[74]

II Peter 1:1 declares that faith is a gift of God. Here, Scripture calls believers to add to their faith. This is something believers must do as the grace of God enables

Second Peter

them. (See Philippians 2:13.) God extends the gift of faith (Ephesians 2:8-9), but the development of virtue, knowledge, self-control, perseverance, godliness, brotherly kindness, and love is the responsibility of the believer. It would, of course, be impossible to develop these characteristics apart from the enabling and influence of the Holy Spirit, but believers develop these Christian graces only as they, empowered by the Holy Spirit, apply themselves to the process of maturity.

As the KJV translates *eipchoregeo*, spiritual growth is a matter of "adding." The rich symbolism behind this word takes its significance beyond the mere idea of addition, however:

> In the great days of ancient Athens, the plays of dramatists like Aeschylus, Sophocles, and Euripides required large and costly choruses. But when such a play was put on, some wealthy, public-spirited Athenian defrayed the vast outlay on the chorus—and consequently was known as the *choregos*. The noble productions were extravagantly expensive, but *choregoi* vied with each other in their generosity. . . .
>
> Believers, Peter is saying, must be lavish in the time and effort they put into developing their Christian lives—not being satisfied with getting by on the minimum, but striving like the *choregos* of old to achieve the finest and most attractive production.[75]

Because the *choregos* joined with the state and the poet in producing the plays, the word came to mean "generous and costly co-operation."[76] This classical meaning is in view here because chapter 1 later uses the same word

The Call to Spiritual Growth

to describe the abundant entrance of believers into the everlasting kingdom (verse 11). Believers are to spare no effort in developing the character qualities described here; they are to be lavish in the development of virtue, knowledge, and so forth. It is impossible for believers to expend too much effort on spiritual growth. In doing this, the believer is cooperating with God.

With their God-given gift of faith as the starting point, believers must add virtue. The same word translated "virtue" here (*arete*) has already appeared in verse 3, where it refers to the virtue of Jesus Christ, the manifestation of His divine power.[77] *Arete* was a common word in Greek literature, used to describe the full achievement of intended purpose. For example, the virtue or excellence of a knife is to cut. The excellence of a horse is to run.[78] The excellence of soil is to be fertile.[79] The virtue of Jesus Christ is seen in the demonstration of His deity.

What is the believer's virtue? The believer's ultimate virtue comes in the achievement of his highest purpose: conformity to the image of Jesus Christ. (See Romans 8:29; Ephesians 4:24; Colossians 3:10.) This involves the full range of character qualities seen in Christ, as summarized in Luke 2:52 to include physical, social, mental, and spiritual development.

The believer is to be generous in the development of knowledge. In some contexts, *gnosis* ("knowledge") may be distinct from *epignosis* ("full knowledge"). II Peter uses both words, however, to mean the specific knowledge of Jesus Christ. (See comments on verses 2-3.) A certain sign of spiritual growth is fuller and more intimate knowledge of the person of Jesus Christ. This is not just knowledge about Jesus; it is to know Jesus. This kind of knowledge comes only by intimate and regular communion with Him in prayer and through careful study of the Scriptures, which reveal Him to us.

The next area for spiritual growth is temperance, or self-control. As the word (*egkrateia*) is used in Greek literature, it means mastering one's desires and passions, specifically one's sensual appetites.[80] This is a particular concern in II Peter, for the false teachers who would infiltrate the church would have "eyes full of adultery and that cannot cease from sin" (2:14). The same word appears in the list of the fruit of the Spirit in Galatians 5:23. Self-control to the Greek moralists was simply the exercise of one's power of choice to control the passions instead of being controlled by them.[81] This is not the Christian perspective. (See Romans 7:15-24.) For Christians, "self-control" is really "Christ-control," as believers yield their members as instruments of righteousness to the indwelling Spirit (Romans 6:12-13).

In the process of spiritual growth, believers are to develop patience. The word translated "patience" (*hupomone*) has to do with endurance during the trials of life. The Greek word literally means "to bear up under." The New Testament frequently uses it in the context of bearing up under suffering. (See II Corinthians 1:6; 6:4; Colossians 1:11; II Thessalonians 1:4; James 1:3; 5:11; Revelation 1:9.) This kind of patience is enhanced by a grasp of the broad message of Scripture (Romans 15:4), which reveals how God has worked in the lives of those who have trusted Him in the midst of painful circumstances. When a believer has done the will of God, all that remains is to be patient until God works His will (Hebrews 10:36).

Godliness (*eusebia*) is necessary to spiritual development. Greek philosophers used this word, which literally means "good worship," to mean piety. The word's meaning in Scripture goes beyond this. In a Christian sense, godliness has to do with reverence as "a very practical awareness of God in every aspect of life."[82] The New Testament uses the word several times.[83] Its first mention is from Peter's lips, when he denied that it was by his *eusebia* (translated "holiness") that the lame man was healed (Acts 3:12).

Verse 7. Another indication of mature character is growth in brotherly kindness. The word translated "brotherly kindness" is *philadelphia*, which also appears in I Peter 1:22. (See Romans 12:10; I Thessalonians 4:9; Hebrews 13:1.) *Philadelphia* actually means more than kindness; kindness could be a mere outward show of good manners, which, though significant, does not necessarily signal a real change of heart. *Philadelphia*, a compound word formed from *phileo* ("love") and *adelphos* ("brother"), literally means "brotherly love."

In secular Greek literature, the word referred to love for blood brothers.[84] In biblical thought, *philadelphia* means the love believers have for each other. To love the brethren is an indication of the genuineness of regeneration. (See I John 3:14-18; 4:7-8, 11-12, 20-21.) According to Jesus, the command to love one's neighbor (Leviticus 19:18) is second only to the *Shema*, the command to love God. (See Matthew 22:37-40; Deuteronomy 6:4.) Jesus illustrated the kind of love in view here with the parable of the good Samaritan. (See Luke 10:25-37.) The biblical idea of love is never limited to a feeling, however emotionally one may be attached to another. Biblical love is connected to concrete actions.

Second Peter

This point is especially clear when we study the Greek word *agape*, which Scripture presents as the ultimate expression of spiritual growth. The KJV translates *agape* as "charity" in this case, as in twenty-seven other places in the New Testament. It translates *agape* as "love" eighty-six times and as "dear" once. I Corinthians 13:4-8 gives the classic definition of *agape*, associating it with specific behavior rather than with feelings.

Bible interpreters commonly attempt to make a sharp distinction between *phileo* and *agape*. As Moo pointed out:

> Much has been written on the different Greek words that the New Testament uses for "love." Many of these writings make the mistake of thinking that the different Greek words are invariable in meaning and always distinct from one another. One often hears, for example, that *eros* refers to sexual love, *philia* to family love, and *agape* to distinctively Christian love. . . . Unfortunately, matters are more complicated than this. The Greek words for love do not have an invariable meaning and, in fact, overlap quite a bit. Nor is the word *agape* an exclusively Christian word.[85]

The meaning of a word is influenced by the context in which it is used. Here, by using *philadelphia* in close proximity to *agape*, II Peter indicates that brotherly love is one expression of *agape*. In other words, *philadelphia* is not necessarily something other than *agape*.

If we think of the characteristics in II Peter 1:5-7 as existing in isolation from each other, it is difficult to identify *philadelphia* as *agape*. Moreover, the passage states we are to add each quality to the previous quality, indicating a distinction. But the Greek text has the preposition *en* ("in") before each quality, suggesting that we should develop each quality within the other qualities. A literal translation of verses 5-7 would read something like this:

> (5) But also for this very reason, giving all diligence, in your faith lavish virtue, in virtue knowledge, (6) in knowledge self-control, in self-control perseverance, in perseverance godliness, (7) in godliness brotherly kindness, and in brotherly kindness love.

Rather than representing these character qualities by individual pearls on a string, we can better represent them by nested boxes, each within the other. As each box is opened, another is revealed.

Scripture sees faith, hope, and love as the three abiding virtues (I Corinthians 13:13). I Peter refers to faith five times, to hope four times, and to love five times. Although II Peter does not focus on hope—the virtue of hope has a high profile in I Peter, but II Peter is more concerned with making sure the readers avoided the seduction of false teachers—it is significant that the list of characteristics pertaining to spiritual growth begins with faith and ends with love. II Peter is in perfect harmony with the rest of Scripture on Christianity's defining traits.

C. The Present Reward of Growth (1:8)

(8) For if these things be in you, and abound, they make you that ye shall neither be barren nor unfruitful in the knowledge of our Lord Jesus Christ.

Second Peter

Verse 8. "If these things be in you" could imply a question as to whether some of readers possess these characteristics. Actually, there is no subjunctive (conditional) mood in the sentence. The word "if" does not appear in the Greek text. The first portion of the verse (*tauta gar humin huparchonta kai pleonazonta*) translates literally as "for these things being in you and abounding." *Huparchonta* ("being") and *pleonazonta* ("abounding") are present active participles indicating the state of affairs as they presently are. The verb translated "make" (*kathistesin*) by the KJV is in the present tense, active voice, indicative mood, indicating that the readers are presently, at the time of the writing, neither barren nor unfruitful.

All the qualities in the preceding list are resident within the divine nature that believers receive when they are born again. They are there, in abundance, within the believer. They guarantee the believer's effectiveness and productivity. But they can have their effect only when the believer cooperates with the Holy Spirit to develop them in a lavish way.

The word translated "barren" (*argous*) is elsewhere translated "idle" (Matthew 12:36; 20:3, 6; I Timothy 5:13) and "slow" (Titus 1:12). Biblical faith is never associated with spiritual inactivity. A believer may be at rest, but he is not to be idle or spiritually aimless.

The word translated "unfruitful" (*akarpos*) literally means "no fruit." It also occurs in Matthew 13:22; Mark 4:19; I Corinthians 14:14; Ephesians 5:11; Titus 3:14; Jude 12. To be fruitless is a consequence of being idle. To be fruitful is a consequence of being actively occupied in kingdom work.

The Call to Spiritual Growth

Here, as in verses 2, 6, 2:20, and 3:18, believers are to develop in their knowledge of the Lord Jesus Christ. Certainly they know Him—they have, after all, been made partakers of the divine nature—but it is inherent in the Christian life that one should increase in personal, intimate knowledge of Jesus. Paul wrote, toward the end of his life, "That I may know Him and the power of His resurrection, and the fellowship of His sufferings, being conformed to His death" (Philippians 3:10, NKJV). Those who develop an ever more intimate knowledge of our Lord Jesus Christ will have little trouble detecting false teaching and false teachers. A clear vision of the biblical Jesus makes all others seem shallow and counterfeit by comparison.

D. The Danger of Spiritual Immaturity (1:9)

(9) But he that lacketh these things is blind, and cannot see afar off, and hath forgotten that he was purged from his old sins.

Verse 9. The person who lacks the qualities listed in verses 5-7 is "blind, and cannot see afar off." It may at first seem strange for blindness to precede shortsightedness, but this is the order of words in the Greek text. The word translated "cannot see afar off" is a form of *muopazo* (from which comes the English "myopia"), and it means "nearsighted." One possible translation of the phrase is "he is so near-sighted that he is blind."[86] Although we could understand this phrase to mean that such a person is blind to heavenly things and can see only earthly things, the grammar of the verse suggests another

Second Peter

meaning. We can read *muopazon* as a causal participle, in which case the meaning would be that the person is blind because of willfully shutting his eyes.[87]

This meaning is indicated by the next phrase, which describes this person as having forgotten that he was purged from his old sins. The words translated "hath forgotten" (*lethen labon*) can mean only that this person has deliberately forgotten.[88] The general idea of this verse, then, is that those who do not progress in the qualities inherent in the divine nature are deliberate in their spiritual blindness and in their forgetfulness of the transforming power of the Atonement. (See II Corinthians 4:4; I John 2:11; Revelation 3:17.)

Bible commentators commonly explain the phrase "hath forgotten that he was purged from his old sins" to mean forgetfulness of the events surrounding water baptism. Green wrote:

> Peter may have in mind here the public confession and vows taken by converts at their baptism (cf. Acts ii.38, xxii. 16). Their *old sins* would then be those committed before they became Christians, the cleansing of which would be an essential corollary of being made a partaker of the divine nature. The man who makes no effort . . . to grow in grace is going back on his baptismal contract.[89]

According to Hillyer:

> The convert, by failing to make the effort to grow in grace . . . has in effect willfully turned his or her back on the stand for Christ made at baptism. That

was when past sins, that is, sins committed in the old life before conversion, were confessed. In the sacrament the believer was cleansed, forgiven, and so enabled to make a fresh start (1 Pet. 3:21; Rom. 6:1-14).[90]

Caffin commented, "St. Peter is apparently thinking of the one baptism for the remission of sin."[91] Caffin then referenced Acts 2:38 and 22:16. Blum wrote, "Perhaps Peter had in mind those who turn away from their commitment at baptism."[92] Although not certain the reference is to baptism, Moo observed, "This is possible, since the New Testament presents baptism as related to the forgiveness of sins and as a standard part of coming to Christ."[93]

In view of Peter's declaration on the Day of Pentecost, "Repent, and be baptized every one of you in the name of Jesus Christ for the remission of sins" (Acts 2:38), it seems reasonable that being cleansed from "old" sins (i.e., sins committed prior to coming to Christ) refers to water baptism. Peter also commanded the Gentile believers at Cornelius's home "to be baptized in the name of the Lord" (Acts 10:48). Furthermore, I Peter says that the salvation of Noah's family through the flood is "an antitype which now saves us—baptism (not the removal of the filth of the flesh, but the answer of a good conscience toward God), through the resurrection of Jesus Christ" (I Peter 3:21, NKJV).[94]

If baptism is in view here, this phrase underscores the connection between baptism and forgiveness of sin. This is not to suggest the doctrine of baptismal regeneration (being born again by baptism itself). Baptism is of no value at all apart from active faith. (See Mark 16:16.) But for those who have placed their faith in Christ Jesus for salvation and have confessed their sins and turned from them in repentance, water baptism stands connected with these events in effecting the remission or forgiveness of sins.[95] From the biblical evidence, any attempt to disconnect baptism from the cleansing effect of Christ's atoning work is as invalid as any attempt to disconnect repentance or faith from the salvation experience.[96]

The radical transformation that occurs at the new birth involves several events, including the conscious decision to trust Jesus Christ alone for salvation, confession of sin and of the intent to forsake sin as a way of life, water baptism, and Spirit baptism. Attempts to isolate and disconnect these events do not spring from biblical evidence, but from the need to conform biblical evidence to theological speculations of postbiblical generations.[97] Rather than isolating each of these events as a defining moment, the New Testament uses them almost interchangeably to describe some aspect of regeneration. It does so because each event in the salvation experience in some way stands for the whole. From the holistic perspective of Jewish thought, we cannot view the various aspects of one's regeneration in isolation from the other aspects. Whether the focus is on faith, repentance, water baptism, or Spirit baptism, the total picture is regeneration in its completeness.

If II Peter refers here to something other than water baptism, it seems strange that it makes specific reference to "old" (*palai*) sins. The New Testament recognizes that the blood of Jesus Christ continually cleanses believers from sin as they maintain their faith in Him (e.g., I John

1:7-8), but II Peter here speaks of specific sins—old, or former, sins—that had been cleansed at a specific point in time. Contextually, these sins were cleansed when the readers were made partakers of the divine nature, i.e., at regeneration.

In short, it was not just cleansing from sin that some had forgotten, it was their cleansing from specific sins, those sins they had committed in their old lives prior to coming to Christ. By failing to progress in the implications of their regeneration by developing the qualities of verses 5-7, these people gave evidence that they had willfully and intentionally turned away from the light of the gospel to spiritual blindness. In other words, they had forgotten the transformation that occurred at their new birth.

Clearly, then, there is no alternative for the believer but to apply himself to the issues of spiritual growth. Failure to do this indicates spiritual regression. There can be no static spirituality. The only alternative to spiritual progress is to stumble (verse 10).

E. The Future Reward of Growth (1:10-11)

(10) Wherefore the rather, brethren, give diligence to make your calling and election sure: for if ye do these things, ye shall never fall: (11) for so an entrance shall be ministered unto you abundantly into the everlasting kingdom of our Lord and Saviour Jesus Christ.

Verse 10. The word translated "calling" (*klesin*) appears eleven times in the New Testament.[98] In each case the KJV translates the word as "calling," with one exception where it uses "vocation." *Klesin* is from *kaleo*, which means "to call."

The word translated "election" (*ekloge*) occurs seven times in the New Testament.[99] It means "to select" or "to choose."

Theological debate revolves around the meaning of "calling" and "election." Those who adhere to some form of Calvinism assert that before He created human beings God elected some to be saved. Strict Calvinists who hold to the view of "double election" believe that at the time He elected some to be saved God also elected others to be lost. The harshness of this view has led many Calvinists to moderate their position to "single election," the idea that God elected some to be saved and passed over everyone else. The end result is, of course, the same.

For example, Green declared that Peter's words here go "to the heart of the paradox of election and free will."[100] Furthermore, Green asserted that "*election* precedes *calling* (cf. Rom. viii. 30)."[101] Green's comments reflect the tendency that we all have to impose preconceived theological views on Scripture. As far as the meanings of the words are concerned, II Peter simply indicates that the readers had been called and chosen. Specifically, God had called them to salvation and had chosen them to be saved.

II Peter places the calling before the election, and the same order appears in Revelation 17:14, where those who are with the Lamb are "called, and chosen, and faithful." Contrary to Green's assertion, Romans 8:30 does not indicate that election precedes calling. This passage says, "Moreover whom He predestined, these He also called"

(NKJV). There is something that precedes predestination, however: "For whom He foreknew, He also predestined to be conformed to the image of His Son" (Romans 8:29, NKJV). The salvation process, which ultimately leads to glorification (Romans 8:30), begins with the foreknowledge of God, not with predestination. God knows all things. (See Psalm 139:1-6; Isaiah 46:10; 48:5; 57:15; Jeremiah 1:5; 23:24; Romans 11:2; I Peter 1:2.) Since He knows all things, past, present, and future, He knows who will come to Him. But this is quite a different thing than saying that God has predestined certain individuals to be saved and others to be lost. God's foreknowledge of the choices people will make is not at all the same as God making their decisions for them. Although God knows who will be saved or lost, He still leaves the choice up to the individual, and it is a free choice. (See John 3:16; Revelation 22:17; Acts 17:30; II Peter 3:9.)

Those whom God foreknows will come to Him; they are "predestined to be conformed to the image of His Son" (Romans 8:29, NKJV). This is the calling according to His purpose as in Romans 8:28. Green's view is that the calling of Romans 8:30 is the same as the calling of II Peter 1:10. But context determines meaning, and the context of Romans 8:30 indicates that the calling there is not the initial calling to salvation but the call to be conformed to the image of Christ. The call to salvation is universal; God calls all to repent of their sins and come to Christ. But He extends the call of Romans 8:30 only to those who have previously responded to the universal call to salvation.

Rather than explaining away the order of words in this verse (and in Revelation 17:14), it would be better to

Second Peter

recognize that the order in II Peter is divinely inspired. God calls all to salvation; those who respond to that call are chosen by God to be saved.

This verse challenges another aspect of Calvinism—the view that those whom God has chosen to be saved cannot lose their salvation. (See 2:1, 19-22.) II Peter urges us to diligently make our calling and election "sure" (*bebaian*). The implication is that such diligence is necessary for the assurance of salvation. In doing "these things"—the things of verses 5-7—the believer receives assurance that he will "never fall."

The word translated "fall" (*ptaisete*, from *ptaio*) appears four times in the New Testament. (See Romans 11:11; James 2:10; 3:2.) Those who think that the elect cannot under any circumstance lose their salvation focus on the possible meaning "to make a mistake, go astray, sin."[102] That is, they view this "fall" as something short of the loss of salvation. This meaning appears in James 2:10; 3:2. James 3:2 states that "we all stumble [*ptaiomen*, from *ptaio*] in many things" (NKJV). But if all believers, including James, regularly stumble, how could II Peter assure us that the possibility of never stumbling is within our grasp? Though sinning or "coming to grief"[103] is a possible meaning of *ptaio*, given the right context, that is not its meaning here. Here, the context defines the word to mean "loss of salvation."[104] As Moo has pointed out:

> The "stumbling" here is of a final nature, denoting a fall that prevents one from getting to heaven. . . . The "stumbling" here is the opposite of "receiving a rich welcome into the eternal kingdom of our Lord

and Savior Jesus Christ" (v. 11) and seems to be equivalent to the "falling" that Jude contrasts with being presented faultless before the Lord in the last day (Jude 24).[105]

Believers who diligently apply themselves to spiritual growth, as II Peter 1:5-7 describes, have assurance that they will be fruitful in their knowledge of the Lord (verse 8) and that they will never lose their salvation.

Verse 11. Believers who diligently apply themselves to spiritual growth and to the development of Christ-like character, as verses 5-7 describe, have the promise that God will supply them an abundant entrance into the everlasting kingdom of Jesus Christ, our Lord and Savior. This is in direct opposition to the loss of salvation that verses 9-10 describe. This potential loss is a consequence of failing to grow spiritually.

For the second time, the word *epichoregeo* appears. Verse 5 translates it as "add," but the word carries the cultural meaning "to lavish." (See comments on verse 5.) Here, the word is translated as "ministered" ("supplied," NKJV). Together with the word "abundantly," the idea is that those who are diligent in growing spiritually will be rewarded with a lavish, extravagant reception into the eternal kingdom. As someone wryly pointed out, the biggest surprise many Christians will have when they get to heaven will be to discover that God is happy to have them there!

The phrase "everlasting kingdom" occurs only here in the New Testament. It may be that Peter identified the kingdom as "eternal" in view of his imminent death; when we face eternity, the temporary and transitory nature of life on earth stands in stark contrast to life in the eternal realm.

Second Peter

There is no intent to distinguish here between the "kingdom of our Lord and Savior Jesus Christ" and the more common "kingdom of heaven" or "kingdom of God."[106] The kingdom belongs to the Son of Man (Matthew 13:41; 16:28) and the Son of God (Luke 1:33). Jesus identified the kingdom as His own (John 18:36). (See Luke 1:32; 23:42; II Timothy 4:1, 18; Hebrews 1:8.) Since the kingdom belongs to Him, Jesus shares it with those who follow Him. (See Luke 22:28-30.) The kingdom swallows up all human authority (Revelation 11:15), and the "saints of the Most High" participate in ruling over it (Daniel 7:27).

Although there is some sense in which believers are already in the kingdom (Colossians 1:13), there is also a sense in which their entrance into the kingdom is still future (Acts 14:22). Theologians refer to this as the "already, but not yet" phenomenon of New Testament eschatology (doctrine of the last things). Essentially, a kingdom is where a king exercises his rule and authority.[107] It is the king's domain.

An overview of the use of the word "kingdom" throughout Scripture indicates a broad range of meanings for "kingdom of God" and related terms. God intended ancient Israel to be a kingdom of priests (Exodus 19:6). In a literal and political sense, the "kingdom of the LORD" existed where David and his descendants ruled. (See II Samuel 7:16; II Chronicles 13:8.) In a final earthly sense, the kingdom of God will be manifested in the rule of Jesus Christ, David's greatest Son, over the earth during the Millennium.[108]

Both John the Baptist and Jesus came preaching the nearness of the kingdom of God. (See Matthew 3:1-2;

4:17.) God took His kingdom from Israel and gave it to the church because Israel's spiritual leaders rejected their true King, Jesus (Matthew 21:43; I Peter 2:9; Romans 14:17). As it exists in the church, the kingdom is in a mystery form that the Hebrew Scriptures did not reveal. (See Matthew 13:1-52, especially verses 11 and 35; Ephesians 3:3-6.)

Although the kingdom is currently in mystery form, we may be sure that God will literally fulfill every kingdom promise He made to ancient Israel. Although Jesus' disciples still misunderstood the mystery form of the kingdom when they asked Him, "Lord, will You at this time restore the kingdom to Israel?" (Acts 1:6, NKJV), He did not deny that He would restore the kingdom. Instead, He answered, "It is not for you to know times or seasons which the Father has put in His own authority" (Acts 1:7, NKJV).

The declaration that the kingdom belongs to Jesus Christ identifies Jesus as God Himself. (See comments on verse 1.) II Peter is the only book in the New Testament to identify Jesus as both "Lord and Savior" in one descriptive term. Indeed, it uses the phrase four times. (See 2:20; 3:2, 18.) The structure of the phrase "Lord and Savior" is identical to "God and Savior" in verse 1. The parallelism between the phrases is obvious; they have equivalent meaning.

F. The Urgency of the Call to Growth (1:12-14)

(12) Wherefore I will not be negligent to put you always in remembrance of these things, though ye know them, and be established in the present truth.

(13) Yea, I think it meet, as long as I am in this tabernacle, to stir you up by putting you in remembrance; (14) knowing that shortly I must put off this my tabernacle, even as our Lord Jesus Christ hath shewed me.

Verse 12. Peter resolved not to be negligent to remind his readers of these things because of the danger of their falling and thus failing to enter the kingdom of the Lord and Savior Jesus Christ. He would be diligent to remind them to make their calling and election sure, so they could have an abundant entrance into the kingdom of Christ. He was confident they already knew what he wrote to them, but he also knew the value of being reminded of truth. (See verse 13.)

It was common for New Testament writers to remind their readers of truths they already knew. Paul and Jude both joined Peter in this practice (Romans 15:15; Philippians 3:1; II Timothy 2:14; Titus 3:1; Jude 5). In a larger sense, Peter intended both of his letters to be a reminder (3:1).

Peter's readers knew and were established in "the present truth." This phrase indicates a fixed body of truth.[109] (See Jude 3.) It must be a reference to the new covenant, a distinct body of truth incorporating the "exceedingly great and precious promises" of verse 4. There is no warrant here to infer that truth is constantly changing and that truths are now being revealed which were not known during the first century. We find the truth of verse 12 in the words of the Hebrew prophets and the commandments of the apostles. (See 3:2.)

The word "established" is from *sterizo*, a form of

which also appears in I Peter 5:10, where it means to make something firm.[110] Here the use is much the same. The readers know and are firmly established in new covenant truth. If indeed they are, they will know that the natural faith response to the radical transformation at the heart of the new covenant—the new birth—is to progress from spiritual infancy to maturity by the development of Christ-like character.

Verse 13. Peter believed it was right, so long as he was alive, to continue to remind his readers of the things in his letter. This reminder would "stir them up." The word "stir up" (*diegeiro*) has to do with awakening or arousing from sleep; it is used metaphorically of arousing the mind. II Peter 3:1 uses the word again.

We can never take for granted that because a person knows some specific aspect of truth, regardless of the nature of the truth, he will act on it. Those who embrace and act on truth are those whose minds are "stirred up." They are mentally alert not only to the academic nature of truth but also to its importance in daily life and for eternity.

The word "tabernacle" ("tent," NKJV, repeated in verse 14) is metaphorical here. It comes from *skenoma*, a tent. Scripture uses it in reference to the Tabernacle as the dwelling place for God. Here Peter used it to refer to his physical body as the dwelling place for his nonphysical self. Paul used the same metaphor in II Corinthians 5:1-10.

It would be a mistake to think that Peter and Paul embraced "Greek dualism, with its perishable body and immortal soul."[111] Those who are strongly influenced by Greek dualism tend to read into the Scriptures the idea of a perishable body, which is inherently evil (since it is material), and an immortal soul, which will exist forever

Second Peter

in some kind of disembodied state. This is not the teaching of Scripture.[112] The Hebrew perspective, which is the biblical perspective, views humans holistically. There is no attempt to fragment humans into virtually unrelated parts. There is certainly no denial that humans are both material and immaterial, but Scripture views both aspects of the human condition as integrated. The body is not evil in itself but is virtually a neutral entity, which can be acted upon by the sin principle or by the Holy Spirit. (See Romans 6:12-13.)

Biblical anthropology (doctrine of humanity) sees humans as "living souls" (Genesis 2:7), or "living beings" (NKJV). The body is just as much a part of a person as the immaterial part. The body is not destined to be discarded, but to be resurrected. After death, persons do not merely become disembodied souls. In the resurrection, they are the same persons they were before, with the same bodies they had before, although their bodies are uniquely equipped by means of the resurrection for life in the realm of the Spirit. They will have "glorious bodies" (Philippians 3:21), but they are bodies nevertheless. (See I Corinthians 15:35-58.)

The body is the "outward man," which is perishing, even as the "inward man" is being renewed daily (II Corinthians 4:16). But even though the body will—in this sense—be "dissolved," Paul did not yearn for a disembodied state (II Corinthians 5:1-4). He wanted to move from the status of mortality to immortality.

Verse 14. Peter knew the time for his death was at hand. Some have speculated that Jesus may have further revealed to Peter the nearness of his death, and this could be the case. But as far as scriptural evidence is con-

The Call to Spiritual Growth

cerned, John recorded Jesus' words to Peter foretelling Peter's martyrdom at an advanced age. (See John 21:18-19.) Now that Peter had reached this age, he knew the fulfillment of Jesus' words could not be long in coming.

G. The Means of Growth: the Scriptures (1:15-21)

(15) Moreover I will endeavour that ye may be able after my decease to have these things always in remembrance. (16) For we have not followed cunningly devised fables, when we made known unto you the power and coming of our Lord Jesus Christ, but were eyewitnesses of his majesty. (17) For he received from God the Father honour and glory, when there came such a voice to him from the excellent glory, This is my beloved Son, in whom I am well pleased. (18) And this voice which came from heaven we heard, when we were with him in the holy mount. (19) We have also a more sure word of prophecy; whereunto ye do well that ye take heed, as unto a light that shineth in a dark place, until the day dawn, and the day star arise in your hearts: (20) knowing this first, that no prophecy of the scripture is of any private interpretation. (21) For the prophecy came not in old time by the will of man: but holy men of God spake as they were moved by the Holy Ghost.

Now that II Peter has emphasized the importance of spiritual growth, it turns our attention to the means of spiritual growth, namely, the trustworthy testimony of the apostles and the holy men of God who had previously

Second Peter

spoken by the Holy Spirit. The testimony of previous holy men was recorded in the Hebrew Scriptures, and the written testimony of the apostles was equally reliable (3:2).

Apparently the false teachers that had infiltrated the ranks of the believers (2:1-3, 12-22; 3:3-5) questioned Peter's authority and perhaps the authority of the other apostles (1:16, 18; 3:2). It seems that they specifically denied the reality of the future coming of the Lord (1:16; 3:3-4, 8-10, 13). If so, these false teachers could have been promoting the same or a similar error as that of Hymenaeus and Philetus, who denied any future resurrection (II Timothy 2:17-18). Some of the Corinthians embraced the same error (I Corinthians 15:12).

The denial of a bodily resurrection was common among Greek thinkers of Peter's day.[113] As it infiltrated the church, this teaching "was probably an early form of Gnosticism that emphasized a spiritual resurrection over against the Christian belief in a future bodily resurrection."[114] False teachers attempted to harmonize their view with Scripture by appealing to the believer's identification with Christ in His death and resurrection at baptism (Colossians 2:12; Romans 6:3-5) and by claiming that the second coming of Christ was fulfilled when the Spirit came upon the waiting believers at Pentecost.[115]

A more recent counterpart of such a teaching is the "never die" doctrine taught in some circles of Pentecostalism in the early twentieth century. As is ordinarily the case with false teaching, this one made a misguided appeal to specific passages of Scripture. (See John 8:51; 11:26.) A similar, apparently more recent error, is the idea that at the new birth believers receive a kind of "heavenly flesh" that is incorruptible.

Although false teachings of this sort may give lip service to the second coming of Jesus and to the bodily resurrection of believers, they deny the significance of these events by the claim that the transformation Scripture associates with the Second Coming has already occurred.

The biblical teaching is that the physical body—even of believers—is perishing (II Corinthians 4:16), that everyone has an appointment with death (Hebrews 9:27), that the transformation of the body will occur at the resurrection (I Corinthians 15:51-54), and that the resurrection awaits the future coming of the Lord Jesus (I Corinthians 15:20-23).

1. Written by Reliable Witnesses: the Apostles (1:15-18)

Verse 15. Peter wanted to be sure that his readers had a reminder of his teaching even after his death. Some think that Peter referred to his influence on Mark as Mark wrote his gospel.[116] Others think that Peter referred to the letter he was writing at the moment.[117] Then there is the view that the reference is not to any specific writings, but that Peter simply intended to continue his ministry up until the time of his death, with the idea that his ministry would continue to strengthen the church after his departure.[118]

Peter referred to his coming death as his "decease." "Decease" translates a form of the Greek *exodus*, which appears elsewhere in the New Testament only in the account of the Transfiguration, where it speaks of Jesus' coming death (Luke 9:31), and in Hebrews 11:22, where it speaks of the exodus of the Israelites from Egypt. It may be significant that Peter used this unusual word (in the New Testament) in such close proximity to his discussion of the Transfiguration (verses 16-18). The death of Jesus was by crucifixion, and Peter would die a martyr's death. (See John 21:18-19.) Legend has it that Peter was also crucified, but upside down at his own request because he did not think himself worthy to die in precisely the same manner as Jesus.

Verse 16. It seems that false teachers criticized the teaching of Peter and other apostles concerning the coming of the Lord Jesus Christ as being based on clever fables. Peter assured his readers this was not so: He and James and John spoke with the authority of eyewitnesses of the Transfiguration, which was a precursor of the Second Coming. (See Matthew 17:1-9; Mark 9:2-10; Luke 9:28-36.)

The word translated "fables" (*mythos*), from which comes the English "myth," appears five times in the New Testament. Twice it has to do with Jewish fables (I Timothy 1:4; Titus 1:14). Once it has to do with "old wives' fables" (I Timothy 4:7).

Peter and other apostles had made known to first-century believers the "power and coming" of the Lord Jesus Christ. The word for "coming" (*parousia*) appears twenty-four times in the New Testament. In all but seven cases, it refers to the second coming of Jesus.[119] In six cases it refers to the coming of various individuals to a specific place or to the presence of a person at a place.[120] In one case it refers to the coming of the man of sin (II Thessalonians 2:9).

The use of *parousia*—whether it refers to Jesus, to human beings, or to the man of sin—indicates a literal

The Call to Spiritual Growth

presence. We cannot spiritualize the term to mean that Christ already has come or will come in the future in some figurative way. His coming will take place as literally as His departure. (See Acts 1:10-11.) Thus, we cannot say that the second coming of the Lord Jesus Christ occurred when the Holy Spirit came upon the waiting disciples on the Day of Pentecost or that it occurs when the Holy Spirit comes upon believers today. As glorious as these events are, they do not fulfill the literal bodily presence required by the meaning of *parousia* or by the words of the angels in Acts 1. When Peter, James, and John saw the transfigured Jesus, it was a "sneak preview" of the Second Coming. Although Jesus was transfigured, He was still present bodily.

Although "power" and "coming" could refer to separate things—the power (*dynamis*) of Jesus and the specific event of His second coming—it is more likely that the words form an hendiadys. They refer to Christ's "powerful coming" or to His "coming in power."[121] (See Matthew 24:30.)

The word translated "majesty" (*megaleiotes*) appears only twice more in the New Testament. (See Luke 9:43, where it is translated "mighty power," and Acts 19:27, in reference to the goddess Diana.) It has to do with the perception of divine majesty, whether real or imagined. As used here, the word indicates that at the transfiguration the apostles saw a visible expression of Christ's divine nature.

Verse 17. Peter, James, and John not only witnessed the transfiguration of Jesus, but they also heard the voice of God the Father authenticating Jesus as His "beloved Son." (See verse 18; Matthew 17:5-6; Mark 9:7; Luke 9:35.)

Second Peter

The words "excellent glory" are "a typically Hebraic periphrasis for God, comparable with the 'divine power' and 'divine nature' of i. 3, 4. . . ."[122] Thus, in this verse, "excellent glory" is synonymous with "God the Father." The Transfiguration focused on the coming glorification of Jesus as the Son of Man. (See Matthew 16:28; 17:9, 12; Mark 8:38; 9:9, 12; Luke 9:26, 44.)

On three occasions a voice from heaven spoke to or about Jesus—at His baptism (Matthew 3:13-17; Mark 1:9-11; Luke 3:21-22), at the Transfiguration, and at the conclusion of His prayer that the Father would glorify His name (John 12:28). Trinitarians commonly use these episodes to teach that the Father and Son are distinct persons. They reason that if God the Father speaks out of heaven to or about the Son who is upon the earth, they must be distinct persons. This view is complicated, however, by unanswerable questions as to what this would mean regarding the relationship between the Father and the Son. If the Father and the Son together compose one God,[123] in what meaningful way can they be two persons? If such were the case, at the very least the word "persons" would have to be redefined to preserve biblical monotheism.[124] Scripture will not permit any form of polytheism or tritheism.

"The voice of God . . . is . . . used in Scripture as a metaphor referring to his person. . . . This lies behind the later (Aramaic) Jewish practice of referring to God enigmatically as 'the Voice' or 'the Word.'"[125] (See Psalm 29:3-8.) Jesus is, of course, "the Word made flesh." (See John 1:1, 14.)

Rather than seeing the "voice of God" episodes in the life of Jesus as evidence for distinct persons, we should

The Call to Spiritual Growth

look for their meaning contextually. In the context of the Transfiguration, the voice was divine endorsement of the "Son of Man" as the very one who would come in glory. (See Matthew 16:27-28.) The "Son of Man" motif is significant; it is an intentional focus on the genuine and full humanity of the Messiah. When the focus is on His divine nature, He is identified as the "Son of God."

The Transfiguration declared the permanence of the Messiah's humanity (i.e., it is the Son of Man who will come in glory) and the integrity of His person (i.e., it was the Son of Man Himself who was transfigured, indicating that this human being was also divine).

Every biblical reference to the Father speaking to the Son or the Son speaking to the Father contextually defines the Son in terms of His humanity. (See, e.g., Isaiah 42:1 and the prayers of Jesus.) There is no biblical example of the Father speaking to the Son as God or of the Son as God speaking to the Father.[126] That Jesus was at once both God and man complicates any discussion of the relationship between the Father and the Son, rendering any explanation somewhat unsatisfactory, but we must approach the problem from the biblical and Hebrew perspective of monotheism, not from the perspective of Greek philosophy.

The Messiah (i.e., "Christ") received from God the Father "honor and glory." This may again be an "hendiadys to denote the majesty of Christ's appearance. But the terms may have specific individual significance, 'honor' referring to exalted status and 'glory' to Christ's splendid appearance."[127]

Verse 18. Peter, James, and John heard the voice from heaven that spoke during the Transfiguration. Thus two of their senses were involved in this revelation: seeing and hearing. No doubt Peter mentioned that they heard the voice to underscore the legitimacy of their testimony. Even though a person sees something, he may not understand what he sees. Or if a person merely hears something, he may misunderstand what he hears.[128] But when a person both sees and hears, the reliability of his testimony is heightened.

To say that the mountain upon which the Transfiguration occurred was "holy" simply means that it was set apart for God's use. (See Exodus 3:5; 15:13; Joshua 5:15; Psalm 2:6.)

2. Written by Reliable Witnesses: the Hebrew Prophets (1:19-21)

Verse 19. Interpreters differ on the meaning of the Greek phrase translated as "we have also a more sure word of prophecy." It could be translated in such a way as to indicate that the testimony of the apostles authenticated the Hebrew prophets. The NKJV follows this possibility with the translation "we have the prophetic word confirmed." On the other hand, the phrase could mean, as the KJV indicates, that the words of the Hebrew prophets authenticated the testimony of the apostles.[129]

It seems best to understand the phrase to mean that the written Scripture is the final and ultimate authority, superior even to visions or audible revelations. This meaning arises from the immediate contextual emphasis on the written Scripture as the product of the influence of the Holy Spirit on holy men (verse 21). I Peter 3:2 also suggests this meaning by placing emphasis first on the words of the holy prophets and secondly on the commandment of the apostles. In other words, the commandment of the apostles is authoritative because it follows the pattern established by the holy prophets; the holy prophets are not authoritative only because the apostles agree with them. The holy prophets were authoritative before the apostles came on the scene.

In addition, if the idea is that the apostles' experience at the Transfiguration validates the prophecies of holy men, it seems strange that Peter needed to assert the authenticity of those prophecies by discussing their origin in the moving of the Holy Spirit (verse 21). The validation of the apostles would have been enough; there would have been no need to explain that holy men did not speak by their own will but by the influence of the Holy Spirit.

In addition, the general tenor of the New Testament demonstrates the apostles' belief that the written Scriptures were the final authority. In order to demonstrate the truth of the gospel message, they constantly appealed to the Hebrew Scriptures. We see this in the sermons in Acts, Romans 15, I Peter 2, and the books of Hebrews and Revelation.

II Peter informs its readers that they should take heed to the "more sure word of prophecy," an apparent reference to the Hebrew Scriptures, or at least to the Messianic prophecies contained in the Hebrew Scriptures. Then, in a poetic turn, it compares the Hebrew Scriptures to a light shining in darkness. It continues the poetic description by depicting the coming of the Lord as the dawning of the day and the rising of the day star in the hearts of believers.

Second Peter

The Bible uses a variety of images to describe its characteristics. Here, it is a "light shining in darkness." In Psalm 119:105, it is a lamp illuminating one's path.[130] The idea is that, apart from the truth of Scripture, the world is a place of darkness. Only the inspired Scriptures provide illumination in a world where sin has darkened human understanding.

The dawning of the day and the rising of the day star are references to the second coming of Jesus. "The day" refers to eschatological events, as in "the day of God" (3:12) or "the day of the Lord" (I Thessalonians 5:2). (See Romans 13:12; II Thessalonians 2:2.) Jesus is the light of the world (John 1:9; 8:12; 9:5; 12:35-36, 46; Matthew 4:14-16). Jesus identified Himself as the "bright and morning star" (Revelation 22:16). (See also Revelation 2:28; Numbers 24:17; Malachi 4:2; Luke 1:78-79.) The morning star is Venus, which often appears just before dawn, but "it merges in the human imagination with the sun itself."[131]

That the day star arises "in your hearts" is not a denial of the literal return of our Lord. It is simply a poetic description of "the subjective results of Christ's actual coming. When he comes, an illuminating transformation will take place in believers."[132]

Until the coming of the Lord, believers must heed the Scriptures in order to avoid being deceived by false teachers. These teachers may, like those about whom II Peter is concerned, deny the Second Coming in some way, or they may introduce other aberrant doctrine. Regardless, the Bible is the final authority. Moreover, any visionary experience or charismatic pronouncement must bow to and conform to Scripture.

The Call to Spiritual Growth

Verse 20. Verses 20 and 21 affirm the doctrine of the inspiration of Scripture. (See II Timothy 3:16.) The statement "no prophecy of the Scripture is of any private interpretation" has been understood in a variety of ways. Here are three suggested meanings: (1) Scripture is not of private origin, i.e., it did not originate with those who wrote it. (2) No passage of Scripture can be interpreted in isolation from the rest of Scripture. (3) Private individuals cannot authoritatively interpret Scripture; in other words, the church alone has this prerogative.

In the context, the first of these views seems most likely. Contextually, the discussion is not about interpreting revelation but about the origin of revelation. If verse 20 is about the interpretation of Scripture, the verse is disconnected from verse 21. Although it is true that we cannot interpret any specific portion of Scripture in isolation from its immediate and larger contexts, that does not seem to be the issue here. Finally, there is no hint in Scripture that individuals are prohibited from reading and interpreting Scripture; indeed, individuals are encouraged to read and interpret the Bible for themselves. (See Acts 17:11; II Timothy 2:15.) Biblical interpretation is not restricted to any ecclesiastical hierarchy.

"Knowing this first" means "recognize this truth to be of utmost importance."[133] This phrase underscores the interpretation of verse 19 that the written Scripture is the ultimate authority, even over visionary revelations. Believers must never allow Scripture to slip from its place as the final determinant of faith and practice.

Verse 21 reiterates that prophecy, which verse 20 defines as the prophecy in Scripture, did not originate with the will of any human being. This is precisely why it

Second Peter

is authoritative. If the Scripture originated with human will, it could be inspiring literature, but it would in the end still be mere human opinion. But Scripture is authoritative because "holy men of God spoke as they were moved by the Holy Spirit" (NKJV).

The men involved in writing Scripture were holy in the same sense that the mountain of the Transfiguration was holy: God set them apart for special use. They struggled with the same temptations and sins as do all human beings (e.g., David and Solomon), but when it came to the writing of Scripture, they were "moved by the Holy Spirit."

A form of the word translated "moved" (*phero*) appears in Acts 27:15, 17 to describe how the wind in a ship's sails will move ("drive" in the KJV) the ship across the water. Though this is helpful in understanding how the Holy Spirit "moved" men (i.e., the "movement" did not originate with them; they merely "put up their sails"), it may be more helpful to notice that another form of the same word appears in II Peter 1:17-18, where it is translated "came." Though the voice from heaven was authoritative, it was no more authoritative than the written Scriptures, for they originated from the same source as the heavenly voice. Since they predated the heavenly voice, they even take priority over it as the "more sure word of prophecy" (verse 19).

So II Peter makes the point that the testimony of Peter and the other apostles is trustworthy because they were personal recipients of revelation that is in complete harmony with the prophecies of the holy men who were moved by the Holy Spirit to write Scripture. Anyone who teaches contrary to the testimony of Peter and the other apostles is simply a false teacher. (See 2:1; 3:3-5.)

III

Beware of False Teachers
(2:1-3:7)

II Peter 1 characterizes Peter and the other apostles as reliable witnesses and true teachers (1:16-18), and it proclaims the inspiration and thus the trustworthiness of the Hebrew prophets (1:19-21). II Peter 2 gives attention to false teachers infiltrating the community of believers. These false teachers were the current counterpart of the false prophets who infiltrated the ancient community of Israel.

Verses 1-3 speak of these false teachers in the future tense, while verses 10-22 speak of them in the present tense. Several explanations have been given for this. The most plausible is that II Peter alludes to earlier prophecies that warned of the coming of false teaching, warnings that were being fulfilled at the time of its writing.[134]

A. Characterized by Destructive Heresies
(2:1-2)

(1) But there were false prophets also among the people, even as there shall be false teachers among you, who privily shall bring in damnable heresies, even denying the Lord that bought them, and bring upon themselves swift destruction. (2) And many shall follow their pernicious ways; by reason of whom the way of truth shall be evil spoken of.

Second Peter

Verse 1. The word "also" refers back to the true prophets of 1:20-21. In addition to true prophets who were moved by the Holy Spirit and whose teaching thus did not originate with them, there were false prophets among the people. By definition, the Holy Spirit did not move on these false prophets; that is, their teaching did originate with them.

"The people" (*laos*) is a common way for Scripture to refer to the nation of Israel. The false prophets had insinuated themselves "among the people." False teaching is always more dangerous when it is propagated by those who claim to stand in solidarity with their intended victims. Paul warned the Ephesian elders that they would face this problem. (See Acts 20:29-31.) The presence of false prophets among the ancient Israelites was not unusual. (See Deuteronomy 13:1-11; 18:20-22; Isaiah 9:15; 28:7; Jeremiah 23:14; 14:14; Ezekiel 13:3.) Unfortunately, it is all too common in the Christian community as well—as Jesus warned. (See Matthew 7:15; 24:11, 24; Mark 13:22; Luke 6:26; I John 4:1.)

Those who promoted false belief among the ancient Israelites were false prophets. Those who promote false belief among Christians are also false teachers. Perhaps those who introduced "destructive heresies" did not, in this case, claim divine authority for new revelation but claimed to interpret more accurately the revelation already given in Scripture. This may have made their deceptive teaching even more enticing; if they had claimed to be prophets giving new authoritative revelation, believers may have more readily rejected their prophecies when they did not square with Scripture. But since they claimed to be teaching the Scriptures—which

Beware of False Teachers

Christians already believed to be authoritative—it may have been more difficult for some to detect their errors.

These false teachers will "secretly bring in destructive heresies" (NKJV). This is the only time the word translated "secretly bring in" (*pareisaxousin*) appears in the New Testament. It suggests that these false teachers are crafty or surreptitious in introducing false teaching. They do not blatantly deny cardinal truths. They give lip service to Scripture, pretending to be committed to it as the final authority. They pretend to be people of faith, who honor the true God. They have an agenda, however, that exploits the people of God. (See verse 3.)

Later Christian writers used the word transliterated "heresies" (*haireseis*) to identify people who embraced teachings that varied from what they considered orthodox and historic.[135] But in the first century, the word had a broader range of meaning. *Hairesis* means "choice," and it describes various religious sects or their beliefs. (See Acts 5:17; 15:5; 24:5, 14; 26:5; 28:22.) Paul used it for divisive teaching in the early church. (See I Corinthians 11:19; Galatians 5:2.) The church was to reject those who refused to abandon divisive teaching after receiving two admonitions (Titus 3:10). This apparently means they were not to have any place of leadership or influence in the church.

The heresies that false teachers introduced are "destructive" (*apoleias*, translated "damnable" by the KJV). They are "destructive opinions."[136] Specifically, these heresies are Christological in nature; they in some way pervert the biblical teaching concerning the Messiah. These opinions result in "denying the Lord that bought them."

Second Peter

A consideration of the larger context indicates that the destructive heresies of the false teachers have to do with libertinism. By "denying the Lord that bought them," they do not allow Jesus to be the Lord of their lives. Although He had "bought them," these false teachers deny His rights of ownership over them. (See I Corinthians 6:20; 7:23; I Peter 1:18-19; Revelation 5:9; 14:3-4.) *(Agorasanta,* translated "bought," has to do with redemption and indicates that those so redeemed are now the property of the one who redeemed them.[137]) They embrace moral impurity, despise authority, speak evil of things they do not understand, carouse, and are covetous (verses 10, 12-14). They promise liberty to those who follow them (verse 19), an apparent reference to liberty from moral restraint. A similar libertine teaching invaded the church at Corinth. (See I Corinthians 6:13-20.)

The word translated "Lord" (*despoten*) has to do with absolute ownership and control.[138] The point here is that those who have been "bought," or redeemed, by the Lord owe Him exclusive allegiance. But the lifestyle that the false teachers embrace and promote denies the Lord His redemptive rights. In other words, the lives of those who have been redeemed should be characterized by submission to authority, moral purity, abstinence from evil speaking, moderation, and the absence of covetousness.

These false teachers bring on themselves "swift destruction." Although this could mean that their destruction is imminent, it may also mean that their destruction, whenever it occurs, is certain.[139] They may think things will always continue along as they are and that they will never face God in judgment, but they are mistaken. (See 3:3-5.)

Beware of False Teachers

Similarly, Jude wrote, "For certain men have crept in unnoticed, who long ago were marked out for this condemnation, ungodly men, who turn the grace of our God into lewdness and deny the only Lord God and our Lord Jesus Christ" (Jude 4, NKJV). Apparently this type of false teaching was not an isolated problem in the first century.

Another reference to false teaching occurs in I Timothy 4:1-5, although in that case, the emphasis was ascetic rather than libertine. Moreover, the New Testament teaches that the day will come when people will seek out teachers who will tell them what they want to hear (II Timothy 4:1-4).

Ideas have consequences, and nowhere is this truer than with theology. The Scriptures assert a standard of truth, which is internally consistent. Deviation at any point can corrupt the entire body of belief. Although some things may not be as significant as others (e.g., one's view of the identity of the "sons of God" of Genesis 6), it is essential that believers make an honest, prayerful, and diligent attempt to understand Scripture correctly (II Timothy 2:15). What may seem a minor deviation on any point relating to the nature of God, the person of Christ, or salvation can have devastating consequences when followed to its logical conclusion.

It is essential to define words in a way that is faithful to the biblical testimony. We must allow words to mean what the Bible defines them to mean. For example, those who embrace Arianism (e.g., Jehovah's Witnesses) confess that Jesus is Lord, but they define this to mean that He is something less than Yahweh Himself. Mormons identify themselves as Christians, but they declare that the biblical witness to the Father, Son, and Holy Spirit

Second Peter

means that there are three gods. It is not enough to use the right words; we must give the words their correct biblical meaning.

There is no room in this verse for the Calvinistic view of limited atonement. John Calvin taught that Christ died for—and thus redeemed—only those God had predestined to be saved. Those not included in the unconditional election are not included in the Atonement. But this verse asserts that the false teachers deny the Lord "who bought [redeemed] them." They have been redeemed, but they have rebelled against the One who redeemed them. Clearly, they are lost. Their "latter end is worse for them than the beginning" (verse 20, NKJV). It would have been better for them never to have known the way of righteousness (verse 21).

The doctrine of these false teachers seems eerily similar to that of the opponents of "Lordship salvation," over which great debate occurred in evangelicalism during the 1980s. Some evangelical scholars taught that it is possible to accept Jesus as Savior without accepting Him as Lord. In other words, people can be saved without allowing Jesus to be the Lord of their lives. These teachers desired to affirm the biblical teaching of salvation by grace through faith, not of works (Ephesians 2:8-9).

But Jesus is one integrated person who is at once both Savior and Lord. It is necessary not only to believe on Him as one's Savior but also to surrender to Him as Lord. It is interesting that four times II Peter identifies Jesus as Lord and Savior, in the process of correcting the false teaching that one does not need to allow Jesus to be the Lord of one's life. (See 1:11; 2:20; 3:2, 18.)

Verse 2. II Peter predicts that the heresies of false

teachers would be popular. "Many will follow their destructive ways" (NKJV). It is regretful that large numbers of believers would turn from biblically faithful teaching to embrace false teaching. But people may embrace false teaching for a variety of reasons. They may be insufficiently grounded in the broad scope of fundamental biblical truths. They may be locked into spiritual immaturity. (See Hebrews 5:11-14; I Corinthians 3:1-2.) They may have a personal agenda. (See II Timothy 4:1-4.) Or they may be honest, sincere people who are simply deceived by plausible but deceptive words (verse 3).

The Greek text upon which the KJV is based repeats *apoleiais* in this verse. It is translated "damnable" in verse 1 and "pernicious" here. *Apoleiais*, from *apollumi*, has to do with being ruined or destroyed.[140] The NKJV follows this text and translates the word as "destructive." *Apoleiais* appears in II Peter in the Received Text in 2:1 ("damnable"), 2 ("pernicious"), 3 ("damnation"), 3:7 ("perdition"), 16 ("destruction"). If we follow this text, verse 2 reiterates the destructive nature of the teaching that would be secretly introduced.

There is, however, a significant textual variant at this point. Where the Received Text has *apoleiais* in verse 2, the critical text has *aselgei*, "a strong word for reckless and hardened immorality."[141] Whether or not *aselgei* is the original reading in verse 2, it does appear in the Received Text of 2:7 (translated "filthy" by the KJV) and in 2:18 (translated "wantonness" by the KJV). It also appears in I Peter 4:3 (translated "lasciviousness" by the KJV). If *aselgei* is original in verse 2, it further identifies the false teaching not just as destructive (which verse 1 has already pointed out) but also as specifically involving

Second Peter

sexual immorality. Sexual immorality is obviously in view in 2:7, 10, 14, 18.

The description of the Christian life as the "way of truth," a Hebraism meaning the "true way," is a metaphor from the Hebrew Scriptures. (See Psalm 119:30; Genesis 18:19.) In other words, people of faith conform to a specific standard of conduct and ethical behavior.[142] This is their way of life. Throughout the Book of Acts, the Christian life is "the way." (See Acts 9:2; 19:9, 23; 24:14, 22.) This phrase underscores that Christianity is characterized by a distinctive lifestyle. It is impossible to follow the "true way" and to live in a way that is indistinguishable from the surrounding society of unbelievers. In the context of II Peter, one aspect of the "true way" is a life of moral purity in opposition to the sexual libertinism of the prevailing culture.

The false teachers in view here obviously still claim to be genuine believers, or there would be no occasion for the "way of truth" to be blasphemed. They have not disassociated themselves from the community of faith. Where this is the case, the only solution is for people of genuine faith to disassociate themselves from those who pervert the true way. (See I Corinthians 5.)

In I Peter, we see the same concern for believers to live in such a way as to silence critics of the church. (See I Peter 2:12, 15; 3:15-16; 4:14-16.) To blaspheme is to speak evil. It is not uncommon for Scripture to warn of the danger of believers living in such a way that unbelievers would speak evil of them or of God. (See II Samuel 12:14; Isaiah 52:5; Romans 2:23-24[143]; I Timothy 6:1; Titus 2:5.) Blasphemy will characterize the last days (II Timothy 3:1-2), but there should be no basis for any evil thing spoken against Christians. Indeed, the thing that should be most winsome about Christians is their way of life, a way characterized by the fruit of the Spirit (Galatians 5:22-23), a way that is obviously superior to life apart from Christ.

B. Characterized by Covetousness (2:3)

(3) And through covetousness shall they with feigned words make merchandise of you: whose judgment now of a long time lingereth not, and their damnation slumbereth not.

Verse 3. The motivation of the false teachers who will rise up among the community of believers is covetousness. They have a heart "exercised with covetous practices" (verse 14, [i.e., they are "experts in greed."[144]]). They have "forsaken the right way and gone astray, following the way of Balaam the son of Beor, who loved the wages of unrighteousness" (verse 15, NKJV). Because Balaam allowed greed to blind him completely to what was right, verse 16 describes him as mad, or insane. (See also Numbers 22; Jude 11.)

Here we clearly see that "the love of money is a root of all kinds of evil, for which some have strayed from the faith in their greediness" (I Timothy 6:10, NKJV; see I Timothy 6:3-11.) Covetousness is at the root of many sins, often including the sin of teaching falsehood. Church history and current events are replete with examples of those who taught what they knew to be wrong for the financial reward. But those who teach the truth are never motivated by greed. (See I Thessalonians 2:5.)

Second Peter

The word translated "feigned" ("deceptive," NKJV) is *plastois*, from which comes the English "plastic." The word has to do with something that is fabricated, made up. These false teachers simply create their teachings out of thin air; they have no basis in biblical authority. It may be that they pay lip service to Scripture—they may even quote it or read from it in an attempt to establish legitimacy for their teaching—but they twist the Scriptures to give them a meaning that the Holy Spirit never intended. (See 3:16.)

The word translated "merchandise" is from *emporeuomai*, which is transliterated into English as "emporium." This word underscores the covetousness of the false teachers. The word speaks of trading with the intention of making a profit. In this case, the false teachers use those they deceive to make a profit for themselves. In the words of the KJV, the people they deceive are their merchandise.

It is certain that false teachers will answer to God for their error: "For a long time their judgment has not been idle, and their destruction does not slumber" (NKJV). The idea is that although these false teachers may seem to be getting away with their deception, judgment is hanging over them; the destruction that awaits them is not asleep.[145] After God has suffered long with them to give them an opportunity to repent, they will certainly perish. (See 3:9.)

C. Destined for Punishment (2:4-9)

(4) For if God spared not the angels that sinned, but cast them down to hell, and delivered them into

chains of darkness, to be reserved unto judgment; (5) and spared not the old world, but saved Noah the eighth person, a preacher of righteousness, bringing in the flood upon the world of the ungodly; (6) and turning the cities of Sodom and Gomorrha into ashes condemned them with an overthrow, making them an ensample unto those that after should live ungodly; (7) and delivered just Lot, vexed with the filthy conversation of the wicked: (8) (for that righteous man dwelling among them, in seeing and hearing, vexed his righteous soul from day to day with their unlawful deeds;) (9) the Lord knoweth how to deliver the godly out of temptations, and to reserve the unjust unto the day of judgment to be punished.

History proves conclusively that those who rebel against God always pay the appropriate penalty. The earliest example of this truth is the angels who sinned (verse 4). Human examples include the wicked people of Noah's day (verse 5) and the inhabitants of Sodom and Gomorrah (verse 6). But when God judges the wicked, He does not confuse the righteous with them: He spared Noah and Lot (verses 5-8). The point is that God will judge false teachers, but He will deliver those who resist their deceptions (verse 9).

Verse 4. God's punishment of the angels who sinned illustrates the certainty of the judgment of God upon those who sin. God punished those angels by casting them down to hell (*tartarus*).[146] There they are "reserved unto judgment" in "chains of darkness."

That these angels are reserved unto judgment indicates that *tartarus* is not their final fate. It is temporary, as they await their ultimate destiny. The destiny of Satan, the most significant angelic defector, is eternal torment in the lake of fire (Revelation 20:10), and we may be sure all lesser fallen angels share the same fate. (See Matthew 25:41, 46.) Believers will in some way participate in judging these fallen angels. (See I Corinthians 6:3; Revelation 20:4-6.)

The use of *tartarus* rather than *hades* or *gehenna* (the more common words translated "hell") is significant. II Peter borrows *tartarus* from Greek mythology, where it represents "the subterranean abyss to which disobedient gods and rebellious human beings were consigned."[147] That is, in Greek mythology Tartarus was a literal, physical cavern of some kind beneath the surface of the earth. Thus, II Peter borrows a word from the cultural milieu of the first century and invests it with new meaning to represent the penalty now exacted upon rebellious angels. It is not the only New Testament book to invest new meaning into pagan words or concepts.[148]

The use of *tartarus* does not mean a literal, physical hole beneath the earth where fallen angels are held captive. Instead, these angels are in "chains of darkness." This is metaphorical language, referring not to literal, physical chains but to the spiritual darkness now captivating fallen angels. Having rejected the light in which they previously dwelt, they now stumble in darkness.[149]

The use of "chains" to describe the "darkness" that binds fallen angels seems "to suggest that God has restricted the scope of the (evil) angels' activity as a result of their sin."[150] We see a parallel in Revelation 20:1-3, where an angel binds Satan with "a great chain," casting him into a "bottomless pit" for one thousand years, thus

Beware of False Teachers

placing a specific limitation on his activity that prevents him from deceiving the nations until the thousand years are completed. When this restriction is removed, Satan goes out to deceive the nations (Revelation 20:7-8).[151]

Angels are spirit beings (Hebrews 1:7) whom God created to exist in the spiritual realm of light, truth, and revelation. (See I John 1:5-7; John 1:4-5, 7-9.) As a consequence of their sin, He has banned them from the realm of existence for which He created them. They now exist in a realm of darkness, falsehood, and lies. (See John 8:44.) Since they rebelled against God, it was necessary for Him to prepare an alternate destiny for them—punishment in everlasting fire. (See Matthew 25:41, 46.)

The reference to the angels who sinned has given rise to a great deal of speculation as to the time and nature of their sin. It is appropriate to survey these speculations, but we should keep in mind that II Peter itself does not identify the nature or time of this sin. Nor does Jude in its parallel reference (Jude 6). In the final analysis, any attempt to determine with absolute certainty the time or nature of this sin is speculation.

One view is that II Peter speaks of the angels who joined Satan in his initial rebellion against God.[152] (See Isaiah 14:12-15; Ezekiel 28:11-19; Revelation 12:3-4.) Another view is that II Peter describes the events of Genesis 6:1-2, with the assumption that the "sons of God" were angels who somehow married "daughters of men."[153]

An objection to the first view (angels who rebelled with Satan) is that "if Satan and the sinning angels were confined until the day of their judgment, Satan and his demons would not be free today to roam the world enticing men to sin."[154] This objection fails, however, because

II Peter does not state that these angels are physically or geographically confined. The "hell" to which they have been cast down is *tartarus*, not *hades* or *gehenna*.[155] II Peter does not suggest that spirits can be confined to the geographical, physical location of a hole beneath the surface of the earth. These fallen angels are not bound in physical chains but in "chains of darkness," or "chains" characterized by darkness, a reference to spiritual darkness.

The second view (angels marrying women) is based largely on the assumption that the *Book of Enoch* (or *I Enoch*) influenced II Peter at this point.[156] The *Book of Enoch* is a first-century-B.C. pseudepigraphical work (book rejected as part of Scripture), and it has a highly developed angelology and eschatology.[157]

There is no direct evidence that the *Book of Enoch* influenced Peter; this view is drawn largely from an apparent quotation by Jude from the *Book of Enoch*[158] and from the supposed influence of Jude on II Peter. But even Jude's reference to a prophecy in the *Book of Enoch* does not indicate that Jude endorsed all of the content of this pseudepigraphical work. Just as Paul quoted the Greek poets Cleanthes and Aratus, Menander, and Epimenides without endorsing anything else they wrote (Acts 17:28; I Corinthians 15:33; Titus 1:12), Jude could have quoted a reliable account of Enoch's prophecy found in the *Book of Enoch* without endorsing anything else in the book. Jude did not confer on the *Book of Enoch* the status of Scripture, nor did Paul upon the pagan poets he quoted. And the possibility exists that Jude quoted a prophecy of Enoch that was common knowledge among the Jewish people, having been preserved by oral tradition.[159]

Regardless of the occasion upon which these angels sinned, the point is that God did not spare them from the penalty of their sin, and neither will He spare false teachers from the consequence of their attempt to seduce the people of God with heresies. (See 2:1, 9.)

Verse 5. II Peter's next example to demonstrate the certainty of judgment upon the false teachers is the destruction of the ungodly in the flood of Noah's day. (See Genesis 6:5-22; 7.) I Peter mentions this event as well, presenting the salvation of Noah's family as a type of the salvation of New Testament believers through baptism.[160] (See I Peter 3:20-21.)

Here, the "world" (*kosmos*) refers to the people who perished in the flood. The Scripture describes them as "ungodly" (*asebon*), which means they had absolutely no time for God.[161] Genesis more specifically describes them as violent (Genesis 6:11, 13). With the exception of Noah and his family, the people of that day were characterized by great wickedness; they were obsessed with evil (Genesis 6:5, 8-10; 7:1).

Of the three examples of the certainty of God's judgment upon false teachers (verses 4-8), this is the first to mention the certainty of deliverance for the godly. Even though Noah and the other seven people who were delivered (Noah's wife, their three sons, and their wives) represented a miniscule minority of the population of the world, God did not overlook them in the almost universal wickedness of the day.

This example provides hope for the church. It may seem that false teachers enjoy great success—the sheer numbers of their followers may overwhelm those who are faithful (verse 2)—but God will not confuse the faithful

Second Peter

with the faithless. As we see also in the example of Lot (verses 6-8), God will do whatever is necessary to spare those who trust Him from His judgment upon those who do not trust Him. (See I Thessalonians 5:9; Revelation 3:10.)

There is no reference in the Old Testament or elsewhere in the New Testament to Noah as a "preacher of righteousness." The description, or similar ones, appears in ancient literature.[162] No doubt Jewish oral tradition—demonstrated to be true in this case by its inclusion in the New Testament—preserved the account of Noah preaching righteousness. We should not think of his preaching as equivalent to modern preaching in Christian pulpits. The word translated "preacher" (*keryka*) means Noah was a "herald" of righteousness. Regardless of how he interacted with the godless society of his day, Noah's life was a brilliant beacon of right living in the midst of oppressive spiritual darkness.

Verse 6. The next example of the certainty of the judgment of God upon those who sin is the destruction of Sodom and Gomorrah. (See Genesis 18:16-33; 19.) The Lord told Abraham, "The outcry against Sodom and Gomorrah is great, and . . . their sin is very grave" (Genesis 18:20, NKJV). Many of the men of Sodom participated in the sin of homosexuality (Genesis 19:4-8), but it was apparently a consequence of deeper root sins: pride, fullness of food, abundance of idleness, and a lack of concern for the poor and needy. (See Ezekiel 16:49; compare with I John 2:15-17.)

The destruction of Sodom and Gomorrah was a uniquely appropriate example, for the false teachers of II Peter promoted moral impurity, rebellion, carousing in

Beware of False Teachers

the daytime (indicating idleness), and hedonism (10, 13-14, 18-19; 3:3). The destruction of Sodom and Gomorrah is "an example to those who afterward would live ungodly" (NKJV). If God held Sodom and Gomorrah accountable for their sins, He will certainly hold others accountable who follow their example. In fact, since the judgment of God upon sin is directly related to the revelation one has received, the judgment of God upon some will be even more severe than upon Sodom and Gomorrah. (See Matthew 10:15; 11:23-24; Luke 12:47-48; Romans 2:11-16.) No doubt the false teachers of II Peter will receive more severe judgment, for they were recipients of great revelation. They heard the gospel and knew the Lord, but they denied Him. (See 2:1, 15, 20-22; 3:5.)

The same word translated "ungodly" in verse 5 appears in verse 6; it describes those who have no time for God. All who think they have no time for God should soberly consider the fate of Sodom and Gomorrah. In any society, it seems difficult to imagine that life as it is known could come to an end in the judgment of God. But this has happened again and again in the history of the human race, although the examples of God's intervention may not always be as dramatic as the Flood or the destruction of Sodom and Gomorrah. Wisdom reminds every generation that buildings can crumble, standards of living can deteriorate, governments can be overthrown, and the very fabric of society itself can be ripped apart. Indeed, the veneer of civilization is quite thin. This truth is revealed all over again with every natural disaster or political upheaval that results in rioting, looting, and general mayhem.

God turned the cities of Sodom and Gomorrah into

ashes. The meaning of *tephrosas* is that they were "covered with ashes." This is the only time in the New Testament that this word appears, but it occurs in Dio Cassius's description of Pompeii after Mount Vesuvius erupted in A.D. 79.[163]

That Sodom and Gomorrah was "condemned . . . with an overthrow" (*katastrophe katekrinen*) means that they were condemned to extinction.[164] Some scholars speculate that the "ruins of Sodom and Gomorrah are probably hidden beneath the waters of the shallow southern end of the Dead Sea."[165] Strabo described the Dead Sea area as "a land of ashes." Hillyer concluded:

> The means used by God to destroy Sodom and Gomorrah was the rain of brimstone and fire, probably brought about by the igniting during an earthquake of the concentrated chemical deposits in the region (salt, potash, magnesium, calcium chloride, bromide) that give the Dead Sea its extraordinary buoyancy but fatally affect fish.[166]

Verses 7-8. Just as God saved Noah from the destruction that came upon the ungodly world of his day, so He saved Lot from the destruction of Sodom and Gomorrah. Abraham was right: God will not destroy the righteous with the wicked (Genesis 18:23). These examples bring hope to the church. Regardless of how wicked the world around us—even the professing church world—seems to be, and regardless of how closely connected we may seem to be with that world (as Noah was associated with the world of his day and Lot was with Sodom and Gomorrah), God will deliver the godly even as He reserves the unjust for judgment (verse 9). The certainty of judgment for the ungodly is as sure as the certainty of deliverance for the godly.

It may seem strange to speak of Lot as "just" or "righteous." The KJV translates both words from *dikaios*. We tend to think of Lot as worldly, weak, and compromising, and so the Book of Genesis generally depicts him. (See Genesis 13:10-13; 19:1.) But the entire basis of Abraham's bargain with God was that Lot was a righteous man living among wicked people. (See Genesis 18:23-33.) When Lot refused to turn his angelic visitors over to the men of Sodom, the Sodomites said of him, "This one came in to stay here, and he keeps acting as a judge" (Genesis 19:9, NKJV). They obviously sensed Lot's continuing disapproval of their behavior.

Regardless of his mistakes, it is clear that Lot never lost his faith in God. He received the angels, honoring them and insisting that they stay in his home (Genesis 19:1-3). He refused to turn them over to the depraved men of Sodom, and he identified the desires of those men as wicked (Genesis 19:4-7). Lot believed the testimony of the angels about the coming destruction of the city and tried to convince his sons-in-law to flee with their families (Genesis 19:12-14). He accepted the Lord's merciful deliverance (Genesis 19:15-17).

Lot made many wrong choices in life and suffered the consequences—including the loss of his wife, daughters, and sons-in-law—but he never embraced the godlessness of those around him. Instead, he was "oppressed by the filthy conduct of the wicked," which "tormented his righteous soul from day to day by seeing and hearing their lawless deeds" (NKJV). In this sense Lot may have been better than some professing Christians today who are no

Second Peter

longer troubled by rampant godlessness and immorality. To the extent that we accept as normal, or even as a legitimate alternative lifestyle, the behavior that Scripture identifies as an abomination to God, we have become conformed to this present world (Romans 12:2).

The word translated "vexed" in the KJV ("oppressed," NKJV) is *kataponein*, and it appears elsewhere in the New Testament only in Acts 7:24 to describe the oppression of an Israelite by an Egyptian whom Moses killed. In some way, Lot was troubled by the behavior of the wicked as the Israelite had been by his Egyptian oppressor.

The word translated "filthy" (*aselgeia*) indicates unbridled lust and excess. These people were wicked (*athesmos*), a word which describes one who breaks through lawful restraint to gratify his lust. The word occurs in the New Testament only here and in 3:17.[167]

What may seem most incredible about the story of Sodom and Gomorrah is that, as wicked as the people were, God was willing to spare them if only He could have found ten righteous people in these cities (Genesis 18:32). If it may seem to us that God should bring judgment on certain segments of our society, we should keep in mind that God in His mercy is open to reasons to delay judgment. One reason He considers valid is the presence of the godly among the wicked. The reason God is open to delaying judgment is to give sinners time to repent (3:8-9). This may explain why the judgment of God has not already come upon our world today. (See II Thessalonians 2:7.)

Verse 9. Now we come to the conclusion of the sentence that began in verse 4. God did not spare sinning angels or those who had no time for Him in the days of Noah and Lot, but He delivered Noah and Lot from the

Beware of False Teachers

destruction around them. These divine actions demonstrate a general principle: the Lord knows how to deliver the godly while at the same time reserving the unjust for judgment. II Peter presents this truth to comfort faithful believers: Those who remain faithful will be delivered from the destructive consequences of false teaching, but those who teach "destructive heresies" (verse 1, NKJV) will face the judgment of God.

Here, as elsewhere in the New Testament, the word "know" means "to be able."[168] In the English language, we see this meaning in a statement like "He knows how to play the piano," which means "He is able to play the piano." God does not just have a theoretical knowledge of how to deliver the godly; He is able to do it and does do it. The manner by which He delivered Noah and Lot demonstrates God's limitless ability. If the destruction is limited to one specific area, God can remove the godly, as He removed Lot. If it is worldwide, He can still deliver the godly, as He did with Noah.

Those who are promised deliverance are the "godly" (*eusebeis*). Those who experienced destruction in the flood and in Sodom and Gomorrah were the "ungodly" (*asebon*, verse 5; *asebein*, verse 6). These are related words that come from *sebomai*, which means "to revere, to worship." Those who will be punished have no time for God; those who will be delivered have time for God. II Peter uses *asebon* again in 3:7, where it declares that the present heavens and earth "are reserved for fire until the day of judgment and perdition of ungodly men" (NKJV).

Although the KJV and NKJV translate *peirasmou* as plural in the word "temptations," the word is actually singular, meaning "temptation, trial, test." It appears in the singular form in the Received Text upon which the KJV and NKJV are based, in the third edition of the United Bible Societies text, and in the twenty-sixth edition of the Nestle-Aland text. The only text that has the plural form of the word is that of Tischendorf (1865-72). If plural, the word is probably a reference to temptations or trials in general; if singular, it probably means a specific trial defined by the context.

Green commented that the singular "test" is "somewhat analogous to the 'bring us not to the test' of the Lord's Prayer, the final test of apostasy from God. It was from this test that Noah and Lot emerged victorious; they stood alone among mockers and unbelievers."[169] On the two other occasions where Peter's writings use a form of *peirasmos*, they clearly mean trials that prove the genuineness of faith rather than simple temptations to sin. (See I Peter 1:6-7; 4:12.)

The immediate context here and the use of *peirasmos* elsewhere for a trial of faith indicate that in this verse the same kind of trial is in view. The doctrines of the false teachers might be seductive and convincing, but they will not deceive the godly. Thus the godly will escape the judgment that will come upon the false teachers and those who embrace their doctrines.

It would be a terrible mistake to think there are no consequences of false teaching. If the truth makes one free, error brings one into bondage (John 8:32). This is true regardless of the nature of the false teaching. Whether it promises liberty (see verse 19) or introduces unnecessary requirements with the claim that they will make one more pleasing to God (see Galatians 5:1;

Beware of False Teachers

Colossians 2:8, 16, 18-23; Acts 15:28), false teaching brings people into bondage. All teaching that twists Scripture to make false promises to people does the same, even if the intention of the teacher is good and the promises are alluring. This includes any teaching that promises Christians complete freedom from pain and suffering and guarantees them health and wealth if only they have enough faith.[170] Though God does often graciously grant His children health and plenty, these are not universal promises. God is working out issues in our lives far more significant than material prosperity and freedom from pain; He is more concerned about eternal values and the development of the character of Christ within us. (See Romans 8:28-29.)

Not only does God know how to deliver the godly; He also knows how to "reserve the unjust unto the day of judgment to be punished." The Greek text at this point will permit either the translation of the KJV or that of the NKJV (with similar translations in other modern English versions): "to reserve the unjust under punishment for the day of judgment." If we follow the translation of the KJV, the point is that God will ensure that in the end the unjust will be judged and punished. If we follow the alternate translation, it means that the unjust are somehow being punished even as they await their final judgment.

The word translated "punished" (KJV) is a present passive participle (*kolazomenous*), indicating the ongoing nature of the punishment. If we follow the translation of the KJV, the punishment that will result from the future judgment will be ongoing. In the case of the alternate translation, the unjust are now experiencing some kind of ongoing punishment. This parallels the idea in verse 4, where the angels who sinned are presently in chains of darkness, "reserved unto judgment." For human beings, we see this kind of ongoing punishment while awaiting final judgment in the story of the rich man and Lazarus (Luke 16:19-31.)

We must leave open the question of whether this punishment is present or future. Since the word is in the present tense, it certainly could be present. But it is not uncommon for the New Testament to use the present tense to represent some future event; the future passive participle is rare in Koine Greek. For instance, II Peter 3:11 uses a present participle to represent the future dissolving of all things.[171]

Regardless of when this punishment occurs, those who are punished are the false teachers of 2:1. The epistle continues to describe their character and teachings in 2:10-22 and 3:1-7.

D. Characterized by Fleshly Self-will (2:10-14)

(10) But chiefly them that walk after the flesh in the lust of uncleanness, and despise government. Presumptuous are they, selfwilled, they are not afraid to speak evil of dignities. (11) Whereas angels, which are greater in power and might, bring not railing accusation against them before the Lord. (12) But these, as natural brute beasts, made to be taken and destroyed, speak evil of the things that they understand not; and shall utterly perish in their own corruption; (13) and shall receive the reward of unrighteousness, as they that count it pleasure to riot in the day time. Spots they are and blemishes, sporting

themselves with their own deceivings while they feast with you; (14) having eyes full of adultery, and that cannot cease from sin; beguiling unstable souls: an heart they have exercised with covetous practices; cursed children.

The false teachers infiltrating the early church were obsessed with sexual immorality and rejected any kind of authority. They expressed bold obstinacy by fearlessly speaking evil of "dignitaries" (NKJV). There were brazen enough to do what even angels would not do. In a sense, they behaved like animals. They did not have to understand something to speak evil of it. Although they joined with believers in the love feasts (fellowship meals) of the first-century church, their motive was not love but self-indulgence. They refused to engage in constructive work but "carouse[d] in the daytime" (NKJV). They were ceaseless sinners; they were consumed with adultery and were experts in covetousness. They enticed the unstable to follow their destructive ways. As children who were cursed because of their behavior, they were destined to receive the reward of unrighteousness.

Verse 10. The false teachers of chapters 2 and 3 are special examples of God's ability to "reserve the unjust unto the day of judgment to be punished" (verse 9). The point of the references to sinning angels (verse 4), to the ungodly in the days of Noah (verse 5), and to the ungodly in Sodom and Gomorrah (verses 6-8) was to demonstrate that these false teachers would not escape the judgment of God.

A warning like this underscores the importance of correctly interpreting Scripture. Twisting Scripture to say something it does not mean is destructive (3:16). In the end it is the same as adding to or taking away from Scripture. (See Deuteronomy 4:2; Proverbs 30:5-6; Revelation 22:18-19.) Whether a false teacher twists, adds to, or takes away from Scripture, he declares that God has said something He did not say or that He has not said something He did say.

In warning against false doctrine Paul wrote, "Remind them of these things, charging them before the Lord not to strive about words to no profit, to the ruin of the hearers. Be diligent to present yourself approved to God, a worker who does not need to be ashamed, rightly dividing the word of truth. But shun profane and idle babblings, for they will increase to more ungodliness. And their message will spread like cancer" (II Timothy 2:14-17, NKJV). The words in this text indicate the seriousness of false teaching: "no profit," "ruin," "ashamed," "babblings," "ungodliness," "cancer."

It is essential for those who teach to be meticulous in their work, for teachers "shall receive a stricter judgment" (James 3:1, NKJV). In the context of teaching, "if anyone does not stumble in word, he is a perfect man" (James 3:2, NKJV).

The false teachers of II Peter walked "after the flesh in the lust of uncleanness." The word "flesh" can mean a wide variety of things in the New Testament.[172] In this context, it clearly means the "sin principle." The false teachers walked according to the principle of sin that is inherent in human existence due to Adam's influence. (See Romans 5:12, 19.) They yielded themselves without reservation to the lust (*epithymia*, "craving") of sin.

The phrase "them that walk after the flesh in the lust

Beware of False Teachers

of uncleanness" suggests sodomy.[173] "Lust of uncleanness" could be either a genitive of quality, meaning "unclean lust," or an objective genitive, meaning something like "in their craving for the unclean." Moo suggested the literal translation "going after flesh in a passionate longing for defilement."[174] Further, "the reference is to sexual sin, probably including, in light of Peter's reference to Sodom and Gomorrah in verse 6, homosexuality."[175]

It may seem strange that false teachers who promoted and engaged in homosexual behavior would have any interest in religious pretense. But during a bleak period in Israel's history, sodomites were provided dwellings in or next to the Temple in order to engage in perverted sexual relations with those who came to worship a wooden image that had been set up in the Temple. Josiah purged the Temple of these sodomites and the image (II Kings 23:7). Since II Peter introduces the discussion of false teachers by comparing them with false prophets in ancient Israel (2:1), it should not be surprising that false teachers in the New Testament would introduce the same kinds of abominations as did false prophets in the Old Testament.

The false teachers in II Peter were presumptuous and self-willed. The word translated "presumptuous" (*tolmetes*), which occurs only here in the New Testament, indicates they were daring. They had no fear of the consequences of their evil deeds. The word translated "self-willed" (*authades*) appears also in Titus 1:7, which says this trait must not characterize a bishop. The word indicates that these false teachers were concerned only about pleasing themselves. They were arrogant.

An indication of the arrogance of the false teachers is that they were "not afraid to speak evil of dignitaries"

(NKJV). Who were these dignitaries (*doxas*, "glories")? There are various possibilities. The reference could be to angels (verse 11), as Jude 8-9 may suggest. Perhaps the false teachers mocked the idea of angels—somewhat in the spirit of the Sadducees (Acts 23:8)—or spoke evil of angels. Verse 12 may suggest this. Another possibility is that these false teachers spoke evil of church leaders, such as the apostles. They did apparently accuse the apostles of following "cunningly devised fables" (1:16). Perhaps, as they promoted their perverse religion, they mocked those who taught truth. They did scoff at the teaching concerning the Second Coming (3:3-4). Some interpreters think that the reference is to these false teachers speaking evil of the Lord. This may be indicated in verse 1 by their denial of "the Lord that bought them." Finally, the verse may not refer to any specific authority but may simply characterize the false teachers as generally rebellious.[176]

Regardless of the specific nature of their rebellion, these false teachers indulged in a sin comparable to witchcraft (I Samuel 15:23). Like witchcraft, theirs was a false religion.

Verse 11 compares the false teachers' evil speaking unfavorably to the behavior of angels who, even though "greater in power and might, do not bring a reviling accusation against them before the Lord" (NKJV). The point is that the false teachers do something even angels will not do.

The Greek text here is ambiguous on two points: (1) Who are the angels greater than, with regard to their power and might? (2) Whom do the angels not bring a reviling accusation against?

The text could mean that the angels are greater in power and might than the false teachers or the dignitaries of whom the false teachers speak evil. Those against whom the angels do not bring a reviling accusation could be the false teachers or the dignitaries. In the final analysis, we may not be able to resolve these questions.[177] Regardless, a general principle emerges from this verse: the false teachers speak evil of those who are superior to them; angels will not speak evil even of those who are inferior to them. We see an example of this in the parallel reference in Jude 8-9. The archangel Michael, in his dispute with the devil about Moses' body, "dared not bring against him a reviling accusation, but said, 'The Lord rebuke you!'" (Jude 9). If a faithful angel refused to revile an angel who was unfaithful, it revealed the error of false teachers who reviled those who were faithful.

It is a sign of defection from faithfulness to God to speak evil of others. Although faithful angels will not speak evil even of those inferior to them, Satan has become the accuser of brethren. (See Revelation 12:10; Zechariah 3:1-3.) Those who speak evil of others are following Satan's example.

It is significant that angels do not bring reviling accusations against others "before the Lord." Green pointed out:

> Unlike the false teachers who are careless of the lordship of Christ and are free with their insults, the angels so revere their Lord as they live all their lives in His presence, that no insulting language is allowed to pass their lips, even though it would be richly deserved.[178]

Scripture consistently warns against the sin of evil speaking. (See Proverbs 26:28; Ephesians 4:31; James

Second Peter

3:9-10; 4:11.) When we are aware that God is constantly evaluating not only our actions but also our words, we will be more careful in our speech.

Verse 12. The behavior of the false teachers in speaking evil even of things about which they had no understanding was like that of "brute beasts made to be caught and destroyed" (NKJV). Their destiny was to "utterly perish in their own corruption." Like animals, these false teachers displayed no understanding. (See Psalm 32:9.) Just as animals act out of instinct rather than understanding, so these false teachers acted out of instinct, but their instinct was that of fallen, rebellious people.

The things not understood by the false teachers are probably things pertaining to the role of angels in the divine economy. (See Jude 8-10.) And in view of their wanton sexual immorality, these false teachers simply did not comprehend the reasons for or the value of moral purity. In their animalistic behavior, there was no evidence that they connected sexual restraint with virtue. They are first-century examples of those who believe in and practice sexual "freedom," and II Peter says they will find that the penalty of this "freedom" is corruption so complete that it will lead to their destruction.

Verses 13-14. The destruction that will come upon the false teachers is "the wages of unrighteousness" (NKJV). (See Romans 6:23.) There are consequences to actions. The specific unrighteous actions of these false teachers included taking pleasure in carousing in the daytime, being consumed with adultery, being habitual sinners, enticing unstable people to sin, and practicing covetousness until they were experts in it.

The condemnation of carousing in the daytime does

Beware of False Teachers

not legitimize carousing at night! Carousing ("riot," KJV) is wrong whenever it occurs. Rather, it shows that even the degenerate Roman society disapproved of daylight debauchery.[179] Among drinkers, it was acceptable to be intoxicated at night. (See I Thessalonians 5:7.) On the Day of Pentecost, Peter responded to the accusation that the disciples were drunk with the defense that this could not be so, since it was only nine o'clock in the morning (Acts 2:13, 15). Even in modern society, those who drink in the evening hours usually frown on those who begin drinking early in the day. But these false teachers saw no need for restraint at any time.

It was common for the church in the first century to practice "love feasts" in conjunction with communion. The purpose of these feasts, which were full meals modeled after the Passover,[180] was to celebrate the fellowship of the body of Christ. They began to deteriorate, however, as wicked people infiltrated them, like the false teachers in view here, and abused them, like the carnal Christians in Corinth. (See I Corinthians 11:20-22, 27-34; Jude 12.) By the time of Hippolytus, Christians conducted their love feasts during daylight hours to avoid the rumors spread by unbelievers.[181] Common rumors included the accusation that Christians practiced incest (because believers considered themselves to be brothers and sisters) and cannibalism (because in the Lord's Supper they partook of the "body" and "blood" of the Lord). Eventually, the love feasts were discontinued altogether. The abuse of the love feasts by people like the Corinthians with their drunkenness and the false teachers with their immorality no doubt lent credence to the rumors spread by the critics of Christianity.

Second Peter

These false teachers were "spots and blemishes" on the Christian community. (See Jude 12.) Their character was precisely the opposite of the character of Christ, who was "without blemish and without spot" (I Peter 1:19).

To say that these false teachers had "eyes full of adultery" means that they saw every member of the opposite sex as a candidate for an illicit affair. They had so completely given themselves over to sin that it had become a way of life for them; they could not cease from sin. They enticed those who were unstable to follow them in their deceptions.

The same word translated "unstable" here (*asteriktous*) appears again in 3:16, which warns of those who twist the Scriptures to their own destruction as a result of being unstable. Here, to be unstable means not to be firmly and deeply rooted in the essentials of the Christian faith. Those who were stable would have immediately rejected the advances of these false teachers.

The phrase translated "trained in covetous practices" (NKJV) indicates that by practice ("trained" comes from the Greek word transliterated "gymnasium") they had become experts in coveting. They had developed a keen desire for things not belonging to them and to which they had no right.

Because of their ongoing commitment to false teaching and rebellious practices, God had cursed these false teachers. They were laboring under His condemnation for sin.

E. Characterized by Forsaking the Truth and Going in the Way of Balaam (2:15-16)

(15) Which have forsaken the right way, and are gone astray, following the way of Balaam the son of

Bosor, who loved the wages of unrighteousness; (16) but was rebuked for his iniquity: the dumb ass speaking with man's voice forbad the madness of the prophet.

Verse 15. The false teachers had "forsaken the right way" and had "gone astray." It was common in the ancient world to characterize a philosophy or religion as a "way." The idea is that one's belief system determines the path one follows in life.[182] We might say today that one's worldview determines one's lifestyle.

Both the Old Testament and the New Testament characterize the life of obedience to God as a "way." (See Deuteronomy 11:26-28; I Samuel 12:23; Ezra 8:21; Acts 9:2; 13:10; 19:9, 23; 22:4; 24:14, 22.) A life of rebellion against God is also known as a "way." (See Psalm 1:1, 6; Proverbs 2:12-15; II Peter 2:15; Jude 11.) There is no idea in Scripture that we can sever our belief system from our behavior. Neither Christianity nor rebellion against God can be mere intellectual exercises; belief produces behavior.

In a recent debate between two physicists, one a believer in Christ and the other an atheist, on the presence and possible significance of design in the universe, the atheist denied any moral law. "It is wrong to torture children," he said, "because I say so." He seemed to believe that because he thought it was wrong to torture children, and because other humans thought so too, that was the determining factor. But what about societies where the torture (or even the slaughter) of children is acceptable or even desirable—to say nothing of other atrocities? It is impossible to hold consistently to a biblical worldview and to practice godlessness; it is also

Second Peter

impossible to reject the existence of God and to hold consistently to a biblical lifestyle.

The false teachers had traded the "right way" for the "way of Balaam." They had once been in the right way, which means they had followed the path of obedience to God. But in their rebellion they had "gone astray." This verse, together with verses 19-22, indicates that these false teachers had not always been false teachers. They had "known the way of righteousness" (verse 21) but had turned from it. In biblical thought, to "know" means to know experientially, not just theoretically. We cannot harmonize these verses with the Calvinistic view of unconditional election and the perseverance of the saints. It is possible for a person to know the truth but to exercise his will in rebellion against God to the point of losing his salvation.

These false teachers had forsaken the right way for a specific error: the way of Balaam. Balaam's way was the way of greed: he "loved the wages of unrighteousness." Although Balaam professed allegiance to God, he refused to take God's first answer as His final answer (Numbers 22:12). When King Balak increased the number and honor of the princes he sent to Balaam and promised to honor Balaam greatly, Balaam claimed that his allegiance to God was greater than his interest in gold and silver (Numbers 22:15-18). But Balaam's willingness to seek further direction from God revealed his hope that he could, after all, go with the princes of Balak to curse Israel.

To refuse to take God's first answer as His final answer is to reveal a genuine lack of trust in God. It demonstrates the belief that our own way is better than

Beware of False Teachers

God's way and that with enough persistence we may persuade God to change His mind and to come around to our way of thinking.

The false teachers' covetousness mirrored Balaam's greed. (See verse 14.) Other "wages of unrighteousness" that they loved were adultery and the empty promise of liberty (verses 14, 19).

Here we find an interesting example of the way the context of Scripture helps define words and phrases. Verse 13 uses the phrase "reward of unrighteousness" (KJV) or "wages of unrighteousness" (NKJV), from *misthon adikias*, to describe the penalty these false teachers would receive, which verse 12 describes as destruction and perishing. This was not what these false teachers hoped for. But verse 15 uses precisely the same phrase to describe the wages these false teachers hoped to receive. Such a difference in meaning for the same phrase in such closely related texts demonstrates the dangers inherent in "proof-texting." God did not intend for us to read the Bible as a string of isolated verses; we are to read it contextually and holistically.

The Greek text upon which the KJV is based reads that Balaam was the son of "Bosor." The Hebrew Scriptures consistently identify Balaam as the son of "Beor." (See Numbers 22:5; 24:3, 15; 31:8; Deuteronomy 23:4; Joshua 13:22; 24:9; Micah 6:5.) "Beor" is also the reading in the fourth-century Greek text B, in ancient Syriac, Coptic, and Armenian versions, and in the Septuagint.

If "Bosor" is the original reading in II Peter, it may be an intentional play on words. The consonants in "Bosor" are the same as in the Hebrew word for "flesh" (*basar*).

Second Peter

Perhaps II Peter indicates that Balaam was in the strictest sense the son of "flesh," or the sin principle. If so, like Balaam, the false teachers walked "according to the flesh" (verse 10). The Hebrew name "Beor" (*be'or*) comes from the Hebrew *ba'ar*, which means "to burn, consume, kindle, or be kindled." It is possible that the pronunciation "Bosor" may have been characteristic of those from Galilee, whose dialect distinguished them from Judeans. (See Matthew 26:73.)

That Balaam was greedy and that he counseled Balak to use the women of Moab to entice the men of Israel to sin made him a uniquely appropriate model for the false teachers. (See Numbers 25:1-3; 31:15-17.) They too were greedy and sought to seduce others by the promise of liberty to engage in sexual immorality with impunity.

Verse 16. The account of Balaam's talking donkey appears in Numbers 22:21-33. God's anger was aroused because Balaam was on his way at the request of Balak, the king of the Moabites. This may seem strange in view of God's second response to Balaam: "If the men come to call you, rise and go with them; but only the word which I speak to you—that you shall do" (Numbers 22:20, NKJV). But God's first response had been, "You shall not go with them; you shall not curse the people, for they are blessed" (Numbers 22:12, NKJV). Balaam refused to take God's first answer as His final answer; this indicates a lack of trust in God and His wisdom.

It may be that God, for His own purposes, will grant desires that are in opposition to His will to those who do not fully trust Him. He may allow those who think they know better than He does to experience the consequences of their stubbornness. Thus, just because God

Beware of False Teachers

permits something does not mean it has His approval. No one can confidently say, "This must be acceptable to God because He hasn't stopped me!" Although God certainly can put obstacles in our paths, as He did with Balaam, He may allow us to persist in our stubbornness in order to demonstrate to us the folly of our ways.

We see an example of this principle in ancient Israel's testing of God in the desert. "And He gave them their request, but sent leanness into their soul" (Psalm 106:15, NKJV). This verse refers to Numbers 11, which records Israel's complaint about the manna that God miraculously provided. Instead of gratefully accepting His provision, the Israelites wept and said, "Who will give us meat to eat? We remember the fish which we ate freely in Egypt, the cucumbers, the melons, the leeks, the onions, and the garlic; but now our whole being is dried up; there is nothing at all except this manna before our eyes!" (Numbers 11:4-6, NKJV). As a consequence, "the anger of the LORD was greatly aroused; Moses also was displeased" (Numbers 11:10, NKJV). After Moses complained to the Lord about this situation, the Lord told him to tell the people, "Consecrate yourselves for tomorrow, and you shall eat meat; for you have wept in the hearing of the LORD, saying, 'Who will give us meat to eat? For it was well with us in Egypt.' Therefore the LORD will give you meat, and you shall eat. You shall eat, not one day, nor two days, nor five days, nor ten days, nor twenty days, but for a whole month, until it comes out of your nostrils and becomes loathsome to you, because you have despised the LORD who is among you, and have wept before Him, saying, 'Why did we ever come up out of Egypt?'" (Numbers 11:18-20, NKJV).

Second Peter

The way God provided the enormous amount of meat needed to supply this much for 600,000 men, to say nothing of women and children, was by means of "a wind [that] went out from the LORD, and it brought quail from the sea and left them fluttering near the camp, about a day's journey on this side and about a day's journey on the other side, all around the camp, and about two cubits above the surface of the ground. And the people stayed up all that day, all night, and all the next day, and gathered the quail . . . and they spread them out for themselves all around the camp" (Numbers 11:21, 31-32, NKJV).

But although the Lord had responded to their crying and provided the meat, "while the meat was still between their teeth, before it was chewed, the wrath of the LORD was aroused against the people, and the LORD struck the people with a very great plague" (Numbers 11:33, NKJV).

The phrase translated "but sent leanness into their soul" in Psalm 106:15 could be translated "but sent a wasting disease among them."[183] Whether the reference is to some sort of diminished spiritual capacity or to the plague itself, the point is that, because of human stubbornness, God sometimes grants something that is not His will. The reason is to allow people to experience the temporal consequences of rebellion against God in order to awaken them to eternal values.

As Balaam made his way with Balak's princes, riding his donkey, "the Angel of the LORD took His stand in the way as an adversary against him" (Numbers 22:22, NKJV). The irony of this story is that Balaam's donkey was more sensitive to spiritual things than Balaam: "Now the donkey saw the Angel of the LORD standing in the way with His drawn sword in His hand, and the donkey turned

Beware of False Teachers

aside out of the way and went into the field. So Balaam struck the donkey to turn her back onto the road" (Numbers 22:23, NKJV).

This was enough to illustrate Balaam's folly, but the story has hardly begun: "Then the Angel of the LORD stood in a narrow path between the vineyards, with a wall on this side and a wall on that side. And when the donkey saw the Angel of the LORD, she pushed herself against the wall and crushed Balaam's foot against the wall; so he struck her again" (Numbers 22:24-25, NKJV).

As we learn later in the story, the donkey was actually protecting Balaam from death (Numbers 22:33). The donkey's final attempt so provoked Balaam that he struck her with his staff: "Then the Angel of the LORD went further, and stood in a narrow place where there was no way to turn either to the right hand or to the left. And when the donkey saw the Angel of the LORD, she lay down under Balaam; so Balaam's anger was aroused, and he struck the donkey with his staff" (Numbers 22:26-27, NKJV).

Here what has already been a fascinating story turns even more dramatic: "Then the LORD opened the mouth of the donkey, and she said to Balaam, 'What have I done to you, that you have struck me these three times?'" (Numbers 22:28, NKJV). A talking (and counting!) donkey is amazing enough, but the part of the story that most clearly demonstrates Balaam's complete lack of spiritual sensitivity is that he carried on a conversation with the donkey, apparently without stopping to consider that such a marvel as a talking donkey could be only a miracle of God! Balaam answered the donkey, "Because you have abused me. I wish there were a sword in my hand, for now I would kill you!" (Numbers 22:29, NKJV).

Second Peter

This story illustrates just how stubborn a rebel against God can be. Balaam completely ignored the phenomenon of an ordinarily obedient donkey three times behaving in an unusual way, and he apparently did not even notice anything unusual about the donkey's ability to talk! He was so intent on his own way that the donkey's behavior caused him to fly into a rage. Balaam stands here in the company of people of all ages who have thought they could deal with God's warnings by eradicating them.

But the donkey was not finished with Balaam: "Am I not your donkey on which you have ridden, ever since I became yours, to this day? Was I ever disposed to do this to you?" (Numbers 22:30, NKJV). The donkey's unusual behavior should have caused Balaam to realize that not everything was as it should be. But instead of getting the point, Balaam again answered the donkey, "No" (Numbers 22:30).

At this point "the LORD opened Balaam's eyes, and he saw the Angel of the LORD standing in the way with His drawn sword in His hand; and he bowed his head and fell flat on his face" (Numbers 22:31, NKJV). Now the Angel spoke to Balaam: "Why have you struck your donkey these three times? Behold, I have come out to stand against you, because your way is perverse before Me. The donkey saw Me and turned aside from Me these three times. If she had not turned aside from Me, surely I would also have killed you by now, and let her live" (Numbers 22:32-33, NKJV).

Even at this point, Balaam's repentance seems half-hearted: "I have sinned, for I did not know You stood in the way against me. Now therefore, if it displeases You, I will turn back" (Numbers 22:34, NKJV). How could there have been any question in Balaam's mind that his actions dis-

Beware of False Teachers

pleased the Lord? But this is the nature of those who "forsake the right way." They develop a kind of spiritual insanity. As Peter wrote, "A dumb donkey speaking with a man's voice restrained the madness of the prophet" (NKJV).

In short, II Peter uses Balaam's story as an appropriate illustration of the folly of the false teachers. Like Balaam, they were so mad with their error that they could not hear the voice of God in those who sought to reprove them. They had rejected the Word of God just as Balaam had rejected God's first answer and were now "willfully" forgetful (3:5).

The talking donkey was certainly an unusual miracle, but it did not tax God's ability. A miracle is simply God doing something differently than He ordinarily does. Beasts lack understanding (see comments on verse 12); they act by instinct, not by the powers of a rational mind. But God can override what is natural and orchestrate what we would call supernatural events. This is the exception to the rule, however.

F. Characterized by Spiritual Emptiness (2:17-18)

(17) These are wells without water, clouds that are carried with a tempest; to whom the mist of darkness is reserved for ever. (18) For when they speak great swelling words of vanity, they allure through the lusts of the flesh, through much wantonness, those that were clean escaped from them who live in error.

Verse 17 describes false teachers as dry wells and empty clouds. Refreshing well water and rain clouds are

Second Peter

obvious metaphors for the spiritual life imparted by the words of true teachers. (See Jeremiah 2:13; John 6:63; Philippians 2:16.) False teachers claim to possess life-giving words, but those who follow them find the claim to be empty. (See verse 18.) Verse 19 describes the content of their false teaching: it promises liberty. This is apparently the promise of liberty from the moral restraints inherent in the Christian lifestyle. (See verses 10, 12-15.) But instead of liberty, this falsehood results in slavery to corruption. In the final analysis, sin cannot be mastered; it masters those who indulge in it. The words of false teachers, rather than producing spiritual life, spread like a cancer. (See II Timothy 2:16-17, NKJV.)

The description of these false teachers as "clouds that are carried with a tempest" suggests their instability and the lack of substance of their teaching.[184] They may come on the scene with great fanfare, with the ostensible promise of great spiritual insight, but they are blown about with every wind of doctrine (Ephesians 4:14). They tend to have some "new" thing, but their teaching quickly becomes stale.

False teachers are destined to an eternity in the "blackness of darkness" (NKJV). (See Jude 13.) Scripture uses various images to depict the final fate of those who rebel against God. It is sometimes described as "outer darkness" (Matthew 8:12; 22:13). This "outer darkness" is synonymous with the "lake of fire" (Matthew 25:30, 41).

A rich mythical lore has developed concerning the nature of hell. It is popular to think of hell as a kind of "devil's heaven," where Satan rules supreme, aided by his imps. In this fiction, Satan takes gleeful delight in torturing his hapless victims. This is contrary to the biblical reality. Instead:

> Hell is not the headquarters of evil, not the palace of Satan. . . . Hell is the destination toward which moral agents, human beings or angels, take a step each time they choose evil over good. . . . Hell is not a torture chamber to which some sadistic deity consigns well-meaning, if perhaps misguided, people. Hell is the logical and inexorable outcome of the careers of freely willing sinners, to which a regretful God allows them to go. . . . Hell is where God gives up—literally gives up creatures to their chosen end.[185]

C. S. Lewis wrote:

> In the long run the answer to all those who object to the doctrine of hell is itself a question: "What are you asking God to do?" To wipe out their past sins and, at all costs, to give them a fresh start, smoothing every difficulty and offering every miraculous help? But He has done so, on Calvary. To forgive them? They will not be forgiven [i.e., they will not accept forgiveness]. To leave them alone? Alas, I am afraid that is what He does.[186]

The word translated "reserved" (*terein*) appears also in I Peter 1:4. An unfading, incorruptible, undefiled inheritance is reserved in heaven for people of faith, but blackness of darkness is reserved for false teachers and those who follow them.

Verse 18. Since these false teachers are "wells without water," the "great swelling words" they speak are empty. The word translated "great swelling" (*hyperonka*) means "of excessive bulk" or "swollen beyond natural size."[187] False teachers do not lack for words. They may be fluent orators, but there is no lasting value to their message. They appeal specifically to the baser instincts of human beings: the lusts of the flesh, lewdness (NKJV).

It seems that at least part of the error of these false teachers was the idea that there is no meaningful connection between the material and immaterial components of human nature. In their view, nothing done with the physical body had any effect on one's spiritual well-being. This was the error of the ancient Valentinians, who "were adept at presenting the young believers with high-sounding talk which acted as a cover for the basest of obscenity."[188] But the biblical view of human nature is holistic. Man is a unity; what he does with his body affects his whole personality, just as what he does with his spiritual nature affects his whole personality.[189]

The false teachers attempted to allure "the ones who have actually escaped from those who live in error" (NKJV). Like wolves preying on sheep, these teachers of error targeted individual believers. Some scholars suggest that the word translated "error" (*plane*) refers to paganism, thus identifying the recipients of this letter as Gentiles. Although *plane* can refer to paganism, it is doubtful that the evidence supports this claim. The New Testament uses this word to describe any kind of error. The chief priests and Pharisees used this word in their request to Pilate to set a guard about the tomb of Jesus (Matthew 27:62-64). They viewed the disciples of Jesus as being in deception. James, in a letter to Jewish believers, used the word to describe the error that a brother could fall into (James 5:19-20). Since James used the word to an audience that was clearly Jewish (James 1:1), it is doubtful that the presence of the word here demands a Gentile audience for II Peter.

Instead of "the ones who have actually escaped" (NKJV), some Greek manuscripts have here "the ones who are barely escaping." The question is whether the reading should be *ontos apophugontas* ("actually escaped") or *oligos apopheugontas* ("only just escaping"). If it is the latter, the false teachers specifically targeted new believers, described in verse 14 as "unstable souls."

G. Characterized by Spiritual Bondage (2:19-22)

(19) While they promise them liberty, they themselves are the servants of corruption: for of whom a man is overcome, of the same is he brought in bondage. (20) For if after they have escaped the pollutions of the world through the knowledge of the Lord and Saviour Jesus Christ, they are again entangled therein, and overcome, the latter end is worse with them than the beginning. (21) For it had been better for them not to have known the way of righteousness, than, after they have known it, to turn from the holy commandment delivered unto them. (22) But it is happened unto them according to the true proverb, The dog is turned to his own vomit again; and the sow that was washed to her wallowing in the mire.

Verse 19. The false teachers of II Peter 2:1 sought to seduce their prey with promises of liberty. The liberty

Second Peter

they promised was apparently freedom from moral restraint. There is a grammatical connection between the "liberty" promised and the "corruption" to which the false teachers themselves were slaves.[190] In other words, the false teachers had become slaves of their "liberties."

The New Testament endorses the value of self-restraint, even in morally neutral areas. For example, Paul wrote, "All things are lawful unto me, but all things are not expedient: all things are lawful for me, but I will not be brought under the power of any" (I Corinthians 6:12). There are more important questions than whether something is "lawful" or permissible. Here are the more important questions: (1) is this helpful (expedient), and (2) is this addictive?

The Christian life is not about practicing every liberty we may feel. It is about ordering our lives in a disciplined way, freely choosing to limit our freedoms to contribute to spiritual growth and to broaden our ministry to others.

There is, of course, no genuine liberty to engage in corrupting practices. The word translated "corruption" (*phthoras*) appears twice previously in the letter, once in 1:4 and again in 2:12. In 1:4, the corruption occurs through lust. In 2:14, the corruption seems to be connected to the "lust of uncleanness," to the rejection of authority, to presumption, and to self-will (2:10). Further evidence of the corruption of these false teachers is that they "count it pleasure to carouse in the daytime" (2:13, NKJV), they have "eyes full of adultery" (i.e., they see every woman as a potential sexual conquest), they "cannot cease from sin," they entice "unstable souls," they are experts in covetousness, they are accursed (2:14), they have "forsaken the right way" (2:15), and they "allure through the

Beware of False Teachers

lusts of the flesh, through lewdness" (2:18, NKJV).

If believers exercise restraint even in morally neutral areas, following Paul's example, it diminishes the possibility that they will ever be seduced into thinking it is permissible to take immoral liberties in areas of absolute certainty. Specifically, when something has the potential of being addictive, the wisest decision is to abstain from it. Or when something does not contribute in any way to wholesomeness of character, mind, emotions, body, or spirit—even if it may be morally neutral—the wisest decision is to abstain from it. This seems to be Paul's idea in his assertion that he will abstain from things that are not helpful and that he will not be brought "under the power" of anything (i.e., he will not become enslaved by or addicted to anything).

This does not mean that believers must walk through life on proverbial eggshells, living in constant fear of making the wrong decision. God does give "us richly all things to enjoy" (I Timothy 6:17, NKJV). In many areas of life, there is no one decision that is right for everyone. We must take into account that we are individuals; each of us is shaped by a variety of factors, including biological, sociological, and psychological influences. Thus, something that may be potentially addictive for one person may not be for another.[191] Moreover, something that may be genuinely helpful for one person—whether spiritually, mentally, emotionally, physically, or in building character—may not be for another. Hard and fast rules are difficult to draw up in areas where Scripture is silent.

It is certain, however, that those who live a life of thoughtful self-restraint will not readily succumb to the lie that they should have liberty to engage in obviously

Second Peter

destructive and addictive behaviors. And some behaviors are obviously self-destructive and addictive. As Scripture points out, the corruption engaged in by these false teachers was enslaving. Any practice that overcomes a person brings him into bondage, or enslaves him. By its very nature, sin is addictive and enslaving. As Moo put it, "The indulgence of the flesh leads inexorably to enslavement to the flesh."[192]

There is always the temptation to abuse genuine Christian liberty, using it as an excuse for self-indulgence. (See Romans 6:14-16; Galatians 5:13; I Peter 2:16.) But to do this is to deceive oneself; it is self-destructive.

The statement "for of whom a man is overcome, of the same is he brought in bondage" is a proverb that "originated from the practice of enslaving enemies captured in wartime."[193] Because of the personal pronoun ("whom"), some think it is a reference here to being enslaved by a person. But "a proverb tends to shift its referents depending on the situation to which it is applied."[194] Contextually, it seems clear that the reference here is to the enslaving power of sin, not to people.

Verses 20-21. A straightforward reading of these verses indicates that the false teachers had once been genuine believers. The language here is the language of conversion. They had "escaped the pollutions of the world through the knowledge of the Lord and Saviour Jesus Christ." To say that they are "again entangled therein" indicates that they had once not been entangled. Elsewhere II Peter connects the knowledge of God to salvation. (See 1:2-3, 8; 3:18.) They had "known the way of righteousness" but had "turn[ed] from the holy commandment."

It is apparent from these words that it is possible to

lose one's salvation. (See also Romans 11:21-22[195]; I Corinthians 10:1-12; Hebrews 3:12-19; 6:4-6; 10:26-29, 38[196]; James 5:19-20[197]; Jude 4-6.) When this happens, the final destiny of the person who loses his salvation is worse than it would have been had he never been saved. Peter heard Jesus tell a story about a man whose "last state . . . is worse than the first" (Matthew 12:43-45). That story no doubt influenced his words here.[198]

The statement that these false teachers had previously "escaped the pollutions of the world" is quite similar to the previous statement that the readers had "escaped the corruption that is in the world" (1:4). In that context, those who escaped the world's corruption are "partakers of the divine nature," they are genuine believers who have received "all things that pertain to life and godliness, through the knowledge of Him" (1:3). They are genuine, saved believers.

It would be very strange for II Peter to use virtually identical language twice in such close proximity to mean radically different things. If those mentioned earlier in this brief letter who "escaped the corruption that is in the world" were actually saved, so were those who "escaped the pollutions of the world."

The word translated "escaped" in verse 20 (*apophugontes*) is a form of the same word translated "escaped" in verse 18 (*apophugontas*). If the people who were being allured had "actually escaped" (NKJV) or were even "just escaping" (NIV, indicating they were new believers) from those who live in error, their escape was real.[199] If the escape in verse 18 was real, so was the escape in verse 20.

The good news in verse 20 is that those who know the Lord and Savior Jesus Christ have escaped the pollutions

Second Peter

of the world. The word translated "pollutions" (*miasmata*) appears only here in the New Testament, but it is from *miaino*, which appears in John 18:28, Titus 1:15, Hebrews 12:15, and Jude 8, with the idea of defilement. To know Jesus Christ as Lord and Savior is to escape from all that defiles.

Having turned "from the holy commandment," these false teachers were "again entangled . . . and overcome." Though they had once escaped the defilements of the world, they were now entangled in them again. They had been "overcome." The word translated "overcome" (*hettao*) appears also in verse 19 to describe those who have been overcome and brought into bondage by corruption.

Here is a sad picture. These false teachers had, like everyone else, been slaves to sin. Then they had found freedom from sin by knowing Jesus. But because they turned away from Him, they returned to their former slavery to sin. But they had not merely reverted back to their previous state. Instead, "the latter end is worse with them than the beginning." As verse 21 points out, it would have "been better for them not to have known the way of righteousness, than, after they have known it, to turn from the holy commandment delivered unto them." II Peter is in agreement here with the general tenor of Scripture on this subject: people will be judged according to what they know. (See Matthew 10:14-15; 11:20-24; Luke 12:47-48.) This does not mean anyone will be saved by ignorance, for no one lives up fully to what he does know, however limited his level of revelation may be. (See Romans 1-3.) But it does mean that when God pronounces His final judgment on each person, no one will be able to accuse Him of injustice. He will hold each person accountable precisely for the opportunities given to him. (See Romans 2:12; 3:4.)

Verse 22. To graphically illustrate this point, II Peter offers two proverbs, one biblical and one secular. The first—"A dog returns to his own vomit"—comes from Proverbs 26:11. The other—"[A] sow, having washed [returns] to her wallowing in the mire"—may be drawn from a seventh- or sixth-century B.C. book, *Ahiqar*.[200]

These two proverbs are very appropriate if the original audience of this letter was Jewish. The Jewish community considered pigs unclean, based on their inclusion in the list of unclean animals in the law of Moses. They also despised dogs. (See Matthew 7:6; Philippians 3:2; Revelation 22:15.)

The implication of these proverbs is that those who know Jesus Christ and who turn away from Him have put themselves in the category of those who are unclean. Their rejection of Christ and their promotion of corruption are as disgusting as it is for a dog to eat its own vomit and for a sow, once washed, to wallow in filth. The word translated "mire" (*borboros*) appears only here in the New Testament. Its range of meaning includes "slime, dung, filth."

II Peter expresses no sympathy for false teachers who had once known "the way of righteousness" (verse 21).[201] Typically, such teachers are not content to wallow in filth themselves; they must convince others to turn from Christ and join them.

H. Characterized by Their Denial of the Second Coming (3:1-7)

(1) This second epistle, beloved, I now write unto you; in both which I stir up your pure minds by way

of remembrance: (2) that ye may be mindful of the words which were spoken before by the holy prophets, and of the commandment of us the apostles of the Lord and Saviour: (3) knowing this first, that there shall come in the last days scoffers, walking after their own lusts, (4) and saying, Where is the promise of his coming? for since the fathers fell asleep, all things continue as they were from the beginning of the creation. (5) For this they willingly are ignorant of, that by the word of God the heavens were of old, and the earth standing out of the water and in the water: (6) whereby the world that then was, being overflowed with water, perished: (7) but the heavens and the earth, which are now, by the same word are kept in store, reserved unto fire against the day of judgment and perdition of ungodly men.

At this point, the letter turns its focus from false teachers (chapter 2) back to the recipients of the letter (chapter 1). The letter is addressed "to those who have obtained like precious faith with us" (1:1); it identifies the recipients as "brethren" (1:10). Beginning in 3:1, it identifies the recipients as "beloved." This continues in 3:8, 14, and 17.

By the literary device of virtually identical phrases, II Peter, in the beginning of chapter 3, signals to its readers that it is returning to the general context and focus of chapter 1. II Peter 1:13 says, "Yes, I think it is right, as long as I am in this tent, to stir you up by reminding you" (NKJV). The phrase "to stir you up by reminding you" is from *diegeirein humas en hupomnesei*. II Peter 3:1 says, "I stir up your pure minds by way of reminder"

(NKJV). The words, "I stir up your . . . by way of reminder" are from *diegeiro humon en hupomnesei*. The parallel is obvious. II Peter 1:20 says, "Knowing this first, that no prophecy of Scripture is of any private interpretation" (NKJV). The phrase "knowing this first" is from *touto proton ginoskontes*. II Peter 3:3 says, "Knowing this first: that scoffers will come in the last days, walking according to their own lusts." The Greek words translated "knowing this first" are identical with 1:20. Chapter 1 emphasizes the danger of forgetfulness (1:9, 12, 13, 15). Chapter 3 does the same thing (3:1, 5, 8). II Peter 1:16-21 addresses the certainty of the coming of the Lord. The epistle returns to that theme in 3:3-16.[202]

This section of II Peter still deals with false teachers. Because of willful forgetfulness, they deny the certainty of the coming of the Lord (3:3-5).

Verses 1-2. The recipients of this letter are identified as "beloved" here and in verses 8, 14, and 17. After the vivid portrayal and harsh condemnation of the false teachers in the previous chapter, it seems that Peter wished to assure his readers of his tender love for them. He was convinced that they—in contrast to the false teachers—had "pure minds."

The reference to the current letter as "this second epistle" quite naturally leads us to suppose that the first epistle was the letter of I Peter. Some scholars reject this idea, thinking that the purpose of I Peter was not to "stir up" their "pure minds by way of reminder" (NKJV). Some also point out that if a forger wished to convince his readers that his work was authentic, this is precisely the kind of formula he would use.[203] But the reference to a previous epistle is not so specific that it positively prohibits it

Second Peter

from being I Peter. And neither should we be surprised to find Peter himself referring to this letter as a "second epistle." Perhaps a forger would use this technique to validate his work, but nothing prohibits a genuine author from making references to other works he has written. And although it may certainly be that Peter wrote letters other than those that appear in the canon, as Paul possibly did,[204] nothing here requires that the "first epistle" to which he alluded here was something other than the canonical I Peter.[205]

Peter's purpose in this and the previous letter was to "stir up your pure minds by way of reminder" (NKJV). (See 1:13.) As noted in the introduction to this section, we can trace the theme of the importance of remembrance throughout chapter 1 and this chapter. Peter intended to "stir up" the minds of his readers by reminding them of things they already knew.

The spiritual power of memory does not come simply by recalling some historical event or other information. It is, instead, "the dynamic process of applying the truths [remembered] to the new situations and problems that the believer confronts."[206] Scores of references in the Old Testament urge God's people to remember past events in such a way as to influence their decisions and behavior in the present.[207] II Peter represents this kind of remembering as the antidote to the deception of false teachers. As the readers actively recall the words of the Old Testament prophets and of the apostles and apply them to their lives, they will avoid falling prey to deceivers.

The first readers of this epistle had "pure minds." Depending on a textual variant, II Peter either uses a phrase identical to or very much like Plato's phrase for "wholesome thinking" (*eilikrine dianoia*).[208] If so, Peter, like Paul, appropriated current proverbs or sayings to express a Christian truth, in this case that "their minds were uncontaminated by the lust and heresy all around them."[209]

II Peter admonishes its readers to remember "the words which were spoken by the holy prophets" (the Old Testament) and "the commandment" of "the apostles of the Lord and Saviour." The contextual indication is that they should remember what the holy prophets had spoken concerning the coming of the Lord Jesus Christ. (See 1:16, 19-21; 3:4-9, 13.) But what is the "commandment" of the apostles that they are to remember?

In every other use of the word translated "commandment" (*entole*), the reference is to "some kind of demand or requirement."[210] This seems to be how II Peter 2:21 uses the word. Based on the typical use of *entole*, Moo asserted that "commandment" here means "the basic demand that believers conform to the image of Christ, becoming holy even as the God who called them is holy."[211] Perhaps that is the meaning here. The consistent meaning of *entole* elsewhere and the close proximity of this use with 2:21 are significant matters and would ordinarily be determining factors without question. How is it, then, that many commentators see the word "command" as referring to what the apostles had said concerning the return of Christ?[212]

Sometimes in Scripture, a word that ordinarily has a specific range of meaning takes on quite a different meaning in a new context.[213] Words are defined by their contexts. In this case, the immediate context of "commandment" is the words that the holy prophets had spoken concerning the coming of the Lord. Further, in what seems to be a parallel to 3:2, "we" in 1:16 refers to what the apostles had said concerning the coming of the Lord, a message confirmed by the Old Testament prophets (1:19-21). The reference to the words of the holy prophets and the apostles leads immediately into a discussion of the coming of the Lord (verses 3-14). Verses 15-16 specifically refer to Paul, an apostle, who had written in his epistles "of these things," apparently the coming of the Lord.

The most accurate understanding may be as follows: In the context, "commandment" does refer to what the apostles had said concerning the coming of the Lord, but the word is particularly appropriate because they generally connected the promise of the coming of the Lord with a command to be prepared for His coming. That is certainly the case here. (See verses 14, 17-18.)

To join together the words of the holy prophets and the commandment of the apostles in this fashion is an unspoken claim to equality of authority between the Hebrew prophets and the New Testament apostles. Peter would never have done this if he did not consider the words of the apostles to be equally authoritative as the words of the prophets.

Verses 3-4. One of the indications of the "last days" is the appearance of scoffers who mock the idea of the second coming of Christ. (See comments on 1:16; 2:19.) Other indications, found elsewhere, include the departure of some from the faith as they heed deceiving spirits and demonic teaching (I Timothy 4:1); the departure of some who have embraced "antichrist" teaching (I John 2:18-23; 4:1-3)—the "antichrist" teaching denied the reality of the

Beware of False Teachers

Incarnation; and the appearance of false Messiahs (Matthew 24:4-5).

The future reference here ("scoffers will come") does not mean that these scoffers had not already arrived at the time Peter wrote. In 2:1, the reference to false teachers is also future tense, but it is clear through the rest of chapter 2 that they were already present. We see that the scoffers were already at work by the present-tense statement in verse 5 that "they willfully forget." II Peter apparently uses the future tense because it "is indirectly quoting the prediction of Jesus himself."[214] (See Matthew 7:15; 24:4, 5, 11, 24; Mark 13:22.)

For the New Testament church, the "last days" began on the Day of Pentecost. (See Acts 2:17.) Like II Peter, other New Testament writings refer to the "last days" in a way that makes clear they had already arrived. (See II Timothy 3:1-9; Hebrews 1:2; James 5:3.) John was certain that the "last hour" had come (I John 2:18).

Since almost two thousand years have passed since the beginning of the "last days," some may think that the first-century believers were wrong. They were not. In the Bible, the "last days" is a period of time following the "time past." The first coming of Jesus Christ, the premier event, long anticipated by prophets in the "time past," inaugurated the "last days," because there is no event in the future that will eclipse the significance of the appearance of the Messiah. Even His second coming is dependent upon His first coming. In a sense, the first coming of the Messiah is the hinge of time: everything before it is "time past"; everything after it is "latter." (See Hebrews 1:1; I Peter 2:10.) Nothing will supersede the new covenant that was established in conjunction with the first coming of the Messiah. (See

Matthew 26:28.) It is the "last" covenant, or the covenant for the "last days."

These scoffers follow their own lusts. The word translated "lusts" here also appears in 1:4 and 2:10, 18. The word refers to strong, evil desires. They do not wish to believe in the coming of Jesus Christ, because if the promises of that event are true, they must answer to Him for their self-indulgent lifestyle.

These scoffers, on the basis of their mistaken notion that God had never intervened in His creation, rejected the coming of Christ. In this sense, their view seems similar to the Deism that flourished in England in the seventeenth and eighteenth centuries and in the United States in the late eighteenth century. Deists confessed belief in God as Creator, but they held that He created the universe with natural laws that would perpetuate the order of the created realm apart from any further involvement by Him.

The "fathers" in view here are the patriarchs of Israel—Abraham, Isaac, and Jacob—or other ancient ancestors of the Jewish people. (See Acts 3:13, 22; 7:2, 11-12, 15, 19, 32, 38-39, 44-45, 51-52; Romans 9:5; 11:28; 15:8.)

Verse 5. The false teachers who claimed that "all things continue as they were from the beginning of creation" (verse 4, NKJV) had, by an exercise of their will, forgotten the dramatic episodes of God's direct intervention in His creation. Specifically, they forgot the destruction of the flood of Noah's day (verse 6). This intervention was the direct result of nearly the entire human population of the earth at the time giving themselves over to the very kind of lifestyle advocated by these false teach-

Beware of False Teachers

ers. (See Genesis 6:5, 11-13; II Peter 2:5, 9-10, 12-14.) If God had intervened before to destroy those who lived in corruption, He would do so again (verses 7, 10-12).

Creation was accomplished "by the word of God." This is the consistent testimony of Scripture, beginning in Genesis 1:3. (See Genesis 1:6, 9, 11, 14, 20, 24.) Psalm 33 declares, "By the word of the LORD the heavens were made, and all the host of them by the breath of His mouth. . . . For He spoke, and it was done; He commanded, and it stood fast" (Psalm 33:6, 9, NKJV). After commanding several elements of the created realm to praise the LORD, Psalm 148:5 asserts, "For He commanded and they were created" (NKJV). John 1:1-3, 10 says, "In the beginning was the Word, and the Word was with God, and the Word was God. The same was in the beginning with God. All things were made by him; and without him was not any thing made that was made. . . . He was in the world, and the world was made by him, and the world knew him not." By faith "we understand that the worlds were framed by the word of God, so that the things which are seen were not made of things which do appear" (Hebrews 11:3).

We must understand all of these references to creation from the biblical, Hebraic concept of "word." If we use the perspective of Greek philosophy to interpret them, we will miss the point.[215] In Hebrew thought, the "word of God" is God's self-expression. Although in later Hellenistic Jewish thought the "word" was held to be divine but in some way distinct from God, the biblical record itself does not suggest this.[216]

Specifically, it is important for our understanding of the identity of Jesus Christ as the Word (John 1:1-3, 14;

Revelation 19:13) that we grasp the Hebrew underpinnings of this concept. If we view the "word" from the perspective of Greek philosophy, we will rob Jesus of His full deity. If we view the "word" from the perspective of late, Hellenistic Judaism, Jesus will become divine but distinct from God. A thorough study of the word of God in creation and the Word of God made flesh shows that Jesus Christ is the one true God revealed in human existence.[217]

In the creation account, water is significant. As the earth was formless and void, "the Spirit of God was hovering over the face of the waters" (Genesis 1:2, NKJV). On the second day of creation, God said, "Let there be a firmament in the midst of the waters, and let it divide the waters from the waters" (Genesis 1:6, NKJV). The firmament was the sky, which "divided the waters which were under the firmament from the waters which were above the firmament" (Genesis 1:7, NKJV).

The phrase translated "standing out of water [*ex hydatos*] and in the water [*dia hydatos*]" (NKJV) is somewhat of a puzzle. Since *dia* with the genitive essentially means "extension through," this phrase may mean something like "continuous land, rising out of and extending through water."[218]

Verse 6. Grammatically, the words "by which" could refer back to water, to the word of God, to the heavens, or to any combination of these. The content of verse 6 seems, however, to limit the possible referents to "water" or "water" and "word of God." The world that existed perished by being flooded with water, and this flood came by the word of God. (See Genesis 6:5-7, 13; 7:4.)

The "world" (*kosmos*) that perished was the human population of the earth, with the exception of Noah and his family, not the physical world itself.

God's intervention to destroy the wicked from the earth should have convinced the false teachers that all things had indeed not continued as they were from the beginning of creation. And it should have demonstrated to them that if He had intervened before, He could intervene again. (See verse 7.) But theirs was a willful forgetfulness. They did not want to believe that they would ever answer to God for their hedonistic lifestyle, so they "forgot" examples from the past which demonstrated that God does indeed call all to account for their deeds.

Verse 7. The NKJV translation is helpful here: "But the heavens and the earth which are now preserved by the same word, are reserved for fire until the day of judgment and perdition of ungodly men." It was the word of God that effected creation, that brought about the flood of Noah's day, and that presently preserves the heavens and the earth until they are destroyed by fire and "fervent heat." (See verses 10-12.)

Destruction by fire in the Day of the Lord is a common theme in the Old Testament. (See Psalm 97:1-5; Isaiah 66:15-16; Micah 1:3-4; Malachi 4:1.) At the revelation of the Lord Jesus, He will take vengeance "in flaming fire . . . and on those who do not obey the gospel of our Lord Jesus Christ" (II Thessalonians 1:8, NKJV).

This destruction by fire will precede "new heavens and a new earth" (II Peter 3:13). Since there will be "a new heaven and a new earth" after the "great white throne" judgment (Revelation 20:11; 21:1), which concludes the millennial era, the destruction by fire apparently occurs after the Millennium. The "day of judgment" in view here must be the "great white throne" judgment.

Second Peter

The "day of judgment" results in the "perdition [destruction] of ungodly men." Those whose names are not in the Book of Life when it is examined at the "great white throne" are "cast into the lake of fire" (Revelation 20:15).

IV

The Certainty of the Second Coming (3:8-14)

The false teachers were wrong in their assertion that the Lord would not return. Things were not as they claimed. All things had not remained the same since the creation; the flood of Noah's day was a dramatic example of God's intervention into the created realm. If He had intervened in past history to judge the rebellious population of the world, it was certain that He would do the same in the future. His greatest and final intervention in judgment will occur in conjunction with the Second Coming.

A. The Second Coming Will Be Unannounced (3:8-10)

(8) But, beloved, be not ignorant of this one thing, that one day is with the Lord as a thousand years, and a thousand years as one day. (9) The Lord is not slack concerning his promise, as some men count slackness; but is longsuffering to us-ward, not willing that any should perish, but that all should come to repentance. (10) But the day of the Lord will come as a thief in the night; in the which the heavens shall pass away with a great noise, and the elements shall melt with fervent heat, the earth also and the works that are therein shall be burned up.

Second Peter

One of the greatest mistakes we can make in studying eschatology is to think that God operates by a human calendar. Since He does not, all attempts to establish a date or a time frame for the Second Coming have failed and will continue to fail. The Scripture promises the Second Coming. The delay in this event is only apparent. Although we cannot know the time of the Second Coming—it will be "as a thief in the night"—we do know that it has not already occurred because God is extending His long-suffering due to His unwillingness for anyone to perish.

Verse 8. Appealing to the readers as "beloved," II Peter urges them not to make the mistake of the false teachers. It is essential that believers remember the many examples of God's direct intervention in His creation. Since God does not count time as we do, and since vast periods of time may seemingly go by without God's intervention to judge the wicked, we may believe that God is "slack concerning His promise" (verse 9). We may think it has been so long since God intervened that He will never do so.

The statement "with the Lord one day is as a thousand years, and a thousand years as one day" (NKJV) reflects Psalm 90:4: "For a thousand years in Your sight are like yesterday when it is past, and like a watch in the night" (NKJV). It is a mistake to think that this statement is some kind of prophetic "key" by which we can construct formulas to determine the time of the Second Coming. Neither this verse nor Psalm 90:4 says that with the Lord one day *is* a thousand years. The words "as" and "like" show that this is simply a figure of speech. Indeed, Psalm 90:4 uses two such figures—"a thousand years" and "a watch in the night." There is a vast difference between the

The Certainty of the Second Coming

two. The point is simply that God does not count time as we do. Since He does not, it would be a mistake for us to think that the length of time since His intervention says anything about how soon He will intervene again. God lives in the realm of eternity; He is not bound or even influenced by human calendars.

Interest in eschatology sometimes leads students of Scripture to link verses that do not address the same issues in an attempt to project at least an approximate time for the Second Coming. Sometimes people link II Peter 3:8 with Hosea 6:2: "After two days He will revive us; on the third day He will raise us up, that we may live in His sight" (NKJV). Hosea wrote of a future generation in Israel who would repent (6:1). They confidently expected that their repentance would result in the Lord reviving them "after two days" and raising them up "on the third day." Some have thought that these "two days" are two thousand years. Based on this assumption, some have predicted that Israel's restoration must occur on or about A.D. 2000.

There are several problems with this view: (1) The phrase "after two days," as used by the ancient Jews, simply meant "after a short time." It is somewhat similar to the American expression "after a couple of days." Few people would think this means precisely two days; this phrase simply means "after a little while." (2) The restoration envisioned by the repentant Israelites would occur "two days" *after* their repentance. Even if the phrase meant "two thousand years," their restoration would not occur for two thousand years after they returned to the Lord. They have not yet done this, so this view would put their restoration at least two thousand years in the future from this point. (3) Hosea wrote in the eighth century B.C., not in A.D. 1. If he meant the restoration would occur two thousand years from the time he wrote, it would have occurred in about A.D. 1200. It did not. And the people of Israel did not repent in A.D. 1; instead, they further rejected the Lord by spurning Jesus Christ the Messiah.

In the final analysis, it is impossible for us to know when the Second Coming will occur. (See Mark 13:32.) Not only can we not know the "day and hour," neither can we know the definite "times or seasons." (See Acts 1:6-7; I Thessalonians 5:1-2.) But if we are wise, we will recognize that God's direct intervention in the past is a guarantee that He will intervene in the future, and we will order our lives so as to be prepared whenever that event occurs. (See verses 11-14.)

Verse 9. The promise here is the promise of the Second Coming, the "day of the Lord" (verse 10). The phrase "day of the Lord" appears twenty times in the Old Testament. As with any other word or phrase in Scripture, the context determines its meaning. In general, the phrase has to do with cataclysmic events occurring in conjunction with the judgment of God upon nations who have rebelled against Him. In a number of specific contexts, it refers to the judgment of God at Christ's second coming upon those who have rebelled against Him. (See Isaiah 2:12; 13:6, 9; Joel 2:31; 3:14; Zechariah 14:1; Malachi 4:5.) The New Testament uses the phrase in the same way. (See I Thessalonians 5:2; II Thessalonians 2:2; II Peter 3:10.) The Bible also uses similar words and phrases that are apparently synonymous with "day of the Lord."[219]

The false teachers mocked "the promise of His com-

The Certainty of the Second Coming

ing" (verse 4), but their mockery denied a major stream of prophecy throughout Scripture. In order for their claims to be true, God would have to go back on His promise. This He will not do. The reason the Second Coming had not occurred when Peter wrote this letter—and the reason it has not yet occurred—is not that God is "slack concerning his promise." It is not any slackness on God's part but His long-suffering that lies behind the apparent delay in His coming.[220]

The word translated "slack" (*braduno*) has to do with being slow or loitering. The point is that the Lord is not in any way backing away from His promise. From the human perspective, the passage of what seems to be vast periods of time may indicate that He will never fulfill His promise. But if we adopt this attitude, we forget that God does not count time as we do (verse 8). What seems to be an interminable period of time to us is nothing to Him; God lives in the realm of eternity.

If we attempt to project a time frame for the coming of the Lord, we forget that it will be "as a thief in the night" (verse 10); He has not chosen to reveal to us when it will be.

The "some" who count God as being slack concerning His promise were no doubt the false teachers in view in this letter. Anyone today who concludes that the passing of time indicates that the Lord will never keep His promise to return has embraced the same error as those false teachers.

The real reason our Lord has not yet returned is His long-suffering. He does not want anyone to perish, so He continues to tolerate human rebellion in order to give people an opportunity to repent. (See Revelation 2:21.)

We also find this theme in the Old Testament. (See Ezekiel 18:23, 32; 33:11.)

The statement that the Lord is "not willing that any should perish but that all should come to repentance" has been the focus of debate between those of the Arminian and Calvinistic schools of thought. Arminians hold that "God genuinely and fully wills that all people come to repentance and faith. The reason that all people do not is because God gives people the freedom to decide either for or against him."[221] Certainly, on the face of it, the words of this verse support the Arminian view.

As Moo has pointed out, "this verse is troublesome to Calvinists, who believe that God has chosen only some people to be saved."[222] John Calvin offered an explanation of this verse:

> No mention is made here of the secret decree by God by which the wicked are doomed to their own ruin, but only of His loving-kindness as it is made known to us in the Gospel. There God stretches out His hand to all alike, but He only grasps (in such a way as to lead to Himself) whom He has chosen before the foundation of the world.[223]

Calvinism distinguishes "two 'wills' in God: his 'desiderative' will (what God desires to happen) and his 'effective' will. God desires and commands that all people repent, but he effectually makes it possible for only the elect to repent."[224]

The consistent testimony of Scripture is that God desires all people to be saved and enables all to repent. God "now commands all men everywhere to repent" (Acts

The Certainty of the Second Coming

17:30, NKJV). He "desires all men to be saved and to come to the knowledge of the truth" (I Timothy 2:4, NKJV). "God has committed . . . all to disobedience, that He might have mercy on all" (Romans 11:32, NKJV). If the "all" in the first part of the sentence is a reference to all humans—and it is—the "all" in the last part must also be. He is willing to have mercy on all those He counts as disobedient.

The Calvinistic view that only some can be saved imposes definitions on words like "willing" and "all" that are not contextually valid. Indeed, there would be no point in long-suffering if God has determined from eternity who will repent and who will not. If all those who have been eternally elected to repent will certainly do so, and if those who have not been so elected will not—regardless of how long it may be until the Second Coming—long-suffering becomes meaningless, because regardless of how long it is until the Second Coming, it will make no difference in any individual's salvation.

Those who hold to a Calvinistic view suggest that God is long-suffering only with believers.[225] But this idea also strips long-suffering of its meaning. If only those who have been unconditionally elected can repent, and if it is absolutely certain they will repent, long-suffering is an empty word. The purpose of God's long-suffering is to give people who have not already done so a legitimate opportunity to repent. If, as in Calvinism, the Second Coming has not occurred only because there are people whom God intends to regenerate but whom He has not yet regenerated, that cannot properly be called long-suffering.

Even though God is not willing for any to perish,

Second Peter

there will be some who do. The reason is that "some will exercise their God-given free will to exclude God. And this He cannot prevent unless He is to take away the very freedom of choice that marks us out as men."[226]

According to the final phrase in this verse, the only antidote to perishing is repentance. I Peter echoes the words of Jesus here. (See Luke 13:3, 5.) The word translated "repentance" (*metanoian*) means literally "to think again." In order to avoid the eternal consequences of sin, it is necessary to "think again" about Jesus and to place all of one's trust in Him for salvation. This also requires the rejection of errors such as those advanced by the false teachers who arose among first-century Christians.

Verse 10. Scripture frequently uses the phrase "the day of the Lord" to represent the judgment of God that comes upon unbelievers by surprise at various points in human history. It is also used of the Second Coming in connection with the specific judgment of God that will come upon unbelievers at that time. (See comments on verse 9.) The point is that, contrary to the claims of the false teachers, the Second Coming will occur.

Like Jesus, Paul, and John, Peter said the Second Coming would occur "as a thief." (See Matthew 24:42-51; Luke 12:35-40; I Thessalonians 5:2, 4; Revelation 3:3; 16:15.) In each occurrence of the thief imagery, the focus is on the surprise element. Although the coming of the Lord is certain, we cannot calculate the time of His coming. (See comments on verse 8.)

The Day of the Lord is not a twenty-four-hour day but the judgment of God upon unbelievers and the era and events that will commence at the Lord's coming. The events in this verse will occur at the end of the Millen-

The Certainty of the Second Coming

nium. At that time the heavens and earth will be destroyed, and in their place will come new heavens and a new earth (verse 13; see Revelation 20:11; 21:1).

The word translated "great noise" (*rhoizedon*) appears only here in the New Testament. Its meaning is probably something like "a roar of flames."[227] (See verse 7.) Although He did not describe the means of destruction, Jesus declared that "heaven and earth will pass away" (Mark 13:31). The statement here that "the heavens will pass away" reflects Christ's words.

The word translated "elements" (*stoicheia*) was used in the first century to refer to the elementary principles of a thing, a parallel in some ways to the American description of the ABC's of something. The New Testament uses the word in a variety of contexts and with a range of meanings. Paul described the "elements of the world" under which sinners are in bondage (Galatians 4:3, 9; Colossians 2:8, 20). The writer of Hebrews used the word to describe the ABC's of Christian doctrine (Hebrews 5:12). Here and in verse 12 the term refers to the physical components of the created realm, perhaps to earth, air, fire, and water—which people of the first century thought to be the elements of which all things are composed—or perhaps to the sun, moon, and stars. There may be some parallel to Jesus' statement in Mark 13:24-25 concerning the darkening of the sun and moon and the falling of the stars of heaven.[228]

The phrase "the earth and the works that are in it will be burned up" has been the subject of considerable debate because of uncertainty about the original text. It has been referred to as one of the most difficult textual problems in the New Testament.[229] Where the KJV and the

NKJV have "will be burned up," following the Byzantine textual tradition, other translations, following other textual evidence, have readings like "will be found," "will be laid bare," "will be disclosed," "will be brought to judgment," and even "will not be found." The first four of these alternate readings refer to a time when all obstacles will be removed so that humans will stand exposed before God for judgment. The final reading is another way of referring to the destruction of the earth and all the works of those who dwell on the earth.

We can understand all of these possibilities as referring in some way to the events accompanying the judgment of God, and we cannot resolve the textual problems here. The reading "burned up" is contextually satisfying (see verses 7, 12) and harmonizes with other descriptions of fire in the last days. (See Matthew 3:12; 13:40; Luke 12:49; Acts 2:19; II Thessalonians 1:8.)

B. Christian Conduct in View of the Second Coming (3:11-14)

(11) Seeing then that all these things shall be dissolved, what manner of persons ought ye to be in all holy conversation and godliness, (12) looking for and hasting unto the coming of the day of God, wherein the heavens being on fire shall be dissolved, and the elements shall melt with fervent heat? (13) Nevertheless we, according to his promise, look for new heavens and a new earth, wherein dwelleth righteousness. (14) Wherefore, beloved, seeing that ye look for such things, be diligent that ye may be found of him in peace, without spot, and blameless.

It is common for the Epistles to link the coming of the Lord to living in a way that honors Him.[230] II Peter develops that theme here, urging the readers to holy conduct, godliness, and diligence in the pursuit of peace and purity. Since all that we presently know will vanish, to be replaced by eternal things, it is only wise that we adopt eternal values now in preparation for that awesome event.

Verse 11. In view of the certainty of the Second Coming and the judgment that will come on those who have rebelled against God, believers "ought . . . to be holy [in] conduct and godliness" (NKJV).

The phrase "all these things will be dissolved," which refers back to the destruction described in verse 10, seems to support the reading "burned up" in verse 10 rather than the other textual variants. The word translated "dissolved" here (*luo*) appears again in verse 12, where it is translated in the same way. In verse 12, it is fire that dissolves the heavens. This further supports the reading of "burned up" in verse 10.

As much of the Western world over the past two centuries has rejected the belief that there is a divine purpose for life—and that human history is heading to a meaningful conclusion—hope has given way to hedonism, apathy, and despair.[231] If this life is all there is, and if death is the end, it is legitimate to merely "eat, drink, and be merry" (Ecclesiastes 8:15; see Luke 12:19). As Barclay pointed out, "without the truth, embodied in the second coming doctrine, that life is going somewhere, there is nothing left to live for."[232]

The word translated "what manner" (*potapous*) appears elsewhere in Matthew 8:27; Mark 13:1; Luke 1:29, 7:39; and I John 3:1. In view of the temporary

Second Peter

nature of the created realm as we presently know it, the people of God "should be outstanding in the quality of their lives."[233] Their lives should be characterized by, among other things in verses 12-14, holy conduct and godliness.

Holy conduct means a lifestyle that is separated unto God and from all that is unlike Him. II Peter does not specify the kind of conduct that is considered holy, as in I Peter 1:13-25; 2:1, 11-20; 3:1-17; 4:3-4, 7-9, 15-16. This letter does, however, describe what holiness is not. (See 2:10-19.)

The word translated "godliness" (*eusebeia*) was a favorite of Peter's. (See comments on 1:3, 6, 7.) Greek philosophers used the word in the first century, but Peter invested it with new meaning. In a Christian sense, godliness is reverence as "a very practical awareness of God in every aspect of life."[234]

Verse 12. Here is one of only two references in Scripture to "the day of God." The other one is Revelation 16:14, which mentions "the battle of that great day of God Almighty." Contextually, "the day of God" is closely allied with "the day of the Lord" (verse 10). It may be that "the day of God" refers more specifically to the final cataclysmic events at the conclusion of "the Day of the Lord," which introduce eternity, and also to eternity itself.

Believers should be "looking for" the Day of God. (See Luke 21:28; Philippians 3:20; II Timothy 4:8; Hebrews 9:28; II Peter 3:13-14.) This does not mean that it will be the next eschatological event, for the next event is the rapture of the church.[235] But since believers recognize that the Rapture will come before the Day of the Lord, which comes before the Day of God, they are in a sense

The Certainty of the Second Coming

looking for the Day of God through the lens of the Rapture. As they look for and anticipate the Rapture, they are in a sense looking for and anticipating all the events that will follow the Rapture.

The only way looking for the Day of God could be meaningful is if the rapture of the church is imminent. The doctrine of imminence means that, as far as we know, the Rapture could occur at any time. It does not mean there is any uncertainty in God's mind when this will be. If we knew that certain events had to occur before the church is caught up to be with Jesus, it would be difficult to see how believers living in the era before those events occurred could meaningfully look for the Rapture.

The KJV reads "hasting unto the coming of the day of God" where the NKJV has a reading much like most recent English translations: "hastening the coming of the day of God." The translation of the KJV indicates that believers should eagerly await the Day of God; other translations indicate that believers can actually do something to bring the Day of God closer.

The word translated "hasting" or "hastening" is *speudo*. The word can mean "strive, make an effort, or be eager,"[236] and II Peter uses a form of the word with that meaning in 1:5, 10, and 3:14. But the word can also mean "hastening," and it appears with that meaning in a variety of contexts. (See Luke 2:16; 19:5-6; Acts 20:16; 22:18.)

Ordinarily, we would say that the strong contextual influence in II Peter gives the meaning of eagerness to *speudo* here. The idea would be something like "be eager for the Day of God." But this interpretation is complicated by the word "unto," supplied by the KJV, which does not appear in any Greek text. The reading of the

NKJV is quite literal here: "hastening the coming of the day of God."

If we accept the literal translation, the implication is that there is something believers can do to speed the events leading to the Day of God. Since the rapture of the church must occur before the Day of God, this would indicate there is something believers can do to hasten the Rapture. Perhaps we can gain some insight from the biblical reference to the "fulness of the Gentiles" (Romans 11:25).[237] Since "blindness in part has happened to Israel until the fullness of the Gentiles has come in," after which "all Israel will be saved" (Romans 11:25-26, NKJV), perhaps anything we do to contribute to the fullness of the Gentiles will at the same time hasten the Rapture, which occurs after the fullness of the Gentiles has "come in" and before "all Israel" is saved. Thus, more energetic fulfillment of the great commission may hasten the rapture of the church. It is, of course, only God who knows the extent of the "fullness of the Gentiles."

The KJV translation "wherein the heavens being on fire shall be dissolved, and the elements shall melt with fervent heat" implies that the destruction of the present created realm will occur in the Day of God. This is problematic because the preposition *dia*, which occurs in all Greek texts here, ordinarily means "because of" or "on account of." Thus, the NKJV translates the phrase as "because of which the heavens will be dissolved. . . ." From this perspective, the "destruction takes place because God's 'day' has arrived."[238] (See Micah 1:4; Isaiah 34:4; 65:17; 66:22.)

Verse 13. The promise in view here is again the promise of the Second Coming, found in the Old Testament and

The Certainty of the Second Coming

reiterated by the New Testament writers. (See comments on 1:16; 3:4, 9.) Since Peter and those to whom he wrote ("we") were people of faith, they accepted the promise of the Second Coming as true, and they looked not only for the Second Coming but also for all of the events the prophets declared would accompany the Second Coming. This included the destruction of the present realm and the introduction of "new heavens" and a "new earth."

In this connection God said, "For behold, I create new heavens and a new earth; and the former shall not be remembered or come to mind" (Isaiah 65:17, NKJV). "For as the new heavens and the new earth which I will make shall remain before Me, says the LORD, so shall your descendants and your name remain" (Isaiah 66:22, NKJV).

It seems that Paul had in mind the same events as Peter, Isaiah, and John (Revelation 21:1) when he wrote, "For the earnest expectation of the creation eagerly waits for the revealing of the sons of God. For the creation was subjected to futility, not willingly, but because of Him who subjected it in hope; because the creation itself also will be delivered from the bondage of corruption into the glorious liberty of the children of God. For we know that the whole creation groans and labors with birth pangs together until now" (Romans 8:19-22, NKJV).

There is a distinction between the condition of the present heaven and earth during the Millennium and the new heaven and new earth that will follow. Although there will be radical changes during the Millennium as a consequence of the binding of Satan (Revelation 20:1-6; Isaiah 11:3-10), it seems clear from Revelation 21:1-10 that the new heaven and new earth follow the Great White Throne

Judgment, a judgment that occurs at the end of the Millennium. (See Revelation 20:2-15.)

Righteousness finds its home in the new heavens and the new earth.[239] The implication is that sin will be vanquished forever and that all who dwell in the new heavens and new earth will be righteous.[240] Prior to the new heavens and the new earth, all whose names were not written in the Book of Life will be cast into the lake of fire. (See Revelation 20:11-15.) These people are the "cowardly, unbelieving, abominable, murderers, sexually immoral, sorcerers, idolaters, and liars" (Revelation 21:8, NKJV).

Verse 14. Again, II Peter refers to the readers as "beloved." (See comments on verse 1.) Together with the conjunction "therefore" (*dio*), this seems to mark a kind of paragraph break in the flow of thought. The letter begins to reach its conclusion at this point, as demonstrated by the reiteration of themes found in the early part of the letter. Here is the exhortation to "be diligent," an exhortation first found in 1:5. The letter concludes with the exhortation to "grow in the grace and knowledge of our Lord and Savior Jesus Christ" (verse 18), which parallels the language of 1:3.[241]

As verse 11 indicates, the certainty of the Second Coming should provoke specific responses in believers. In verse 11, believers are to embrace "holy conduct and godliness." Here, they are to "be diligent to be found by Him in peace, without spot and blameless" (NKJV).

The same language of spotlessness and blamelessness appears in I Peter 1:19, describing Christ. Here the words connect the ideal Christian life with the character of Christ. That is, as we conform to His character, we are spotless and blameless. The specific qualities of character

The Certainty of the Second Coming

that we must develop are those in 1:5-7. The spotless and blameless character that Christians must develop stands in stark contrast to the character of the false teachers, who are "spots and blemishes" (2:13).

The life of abandonment to sin promoted by the false teachers (2:10-22) certainly does not result in peace with God or peace in any human relationship. By contrast, a focus on the certainty of the Second Coming and knowledge of the temporary nature of the present realm, coupled with the pursuit of a spotless and blameless life, will produce peace with God and with other people of faith. (See Romans 5:1-2; Hebrews 12:14.)

V

Exhortations in View of the Delay in the Second Coming (3:15-18)

As II Peter concludes, it reminds readers that the reason for the apparent delay in the Second Coming is that God is patiently waiting for people to prepare for that event. (See verse 9.) Paul also expressed the same truth. (See Romans 2:4.) Knowledge of the reason for the delay should lead believers to be steadfast in their faith rather than to join with false teachers in the error of thinking that the delay means the Second Coming will never occur. As they look toward the Second Coming, believers should grow in grace and in their knowledge of the Lord and Savior Jesus Christ.

A. The Reason for the Delay (3:15-16)

(15) And account that the longsuffering of our Lord is salvation; even as our beloved brother Paul also according to the wisdom given unto him hath written unto you; (16) as also in all his epistles, speaking in them of these things; in which are some things hard to be understood, which they that are unlearned and unstable wrest, as they do also the other scriptures, unto their own destruction.

That people may not immediately experience the full

Second Peter

consequences of their sin should never be interpreted to mean that God overlooks sin or that He will never hold people accountable. God suffered long with the wicked, violent people in the days before the Flood, with those who lived in Sodom and Gomorrah, and with the ancient Amorites. (See Genesis 15:16.) There may be occasions when God, for His own reasons, will allow people to experience severe consequences of sin more quickly (see Acts 5:1-11; I Corinthians 11:30-32; I John 5:16-17), but this does not seem to be the case ordinarily. In most cases, it seems that God delays judgment to allow time for repentance. (See Revelation 2:21.)

The apparent delay in the Second Coming does give people an opportunity for salvation. Peter and Paul agreed on this truth, because both were equally inspired in their teaching and writing. Some misinterpret Paul's letters to make them teach something he never endorsed, but Paul's perspective on eschatology was the same as Peter's.

Verse 15. Believers should "account" ("consider," NKJV) the long-suffering of the Lord, evident by the apparent delay in the Second Coming, as His extending the opportunity for salvation. II Peter frequently uses the word translated "account" (*hegeisthe*). It appears four times in this little letter, first in 1:13, where it is translated "think"; second in 2:13, where it is translated "count"; third in 3:9, where it is again translated "count"; and fourth here.

Here, the word describes the attitude believers are to have toward the apparent delay in the Second Coming as opposed to the attitude of the false teachers in verse 9. Whereas the false teachers considered the delay to be slackness, believers are to consider it to be salvation. As II Peter has already noted, the reason is that God is "not willing that any should perish but that all should come to repentance" (verse 9, NKJV).

Peter appealed to Paul's letters as an authoritative endorsement of the things he taught concerning the Second Coming. There is complete agreement in the New Testament, not only regarding the doctrine of salvation (see Galatians 2:1-10), but also regarding eschatology and all other teaching. Peter was the apostle to the Jewish community, and Paul was the apostle to the Gentile community (Galatians 2:8), and both proclaimed the same message. The reason for this was that the Holy Spirit led both of them in all they taught. (See comments on 3:2.)

Peter's reference to Paul as "our beloved brother" exposes as false any claim that there was continuing friction between the two from the time of their conflict in Antioch. (See Galatians 2:11-21.) Peter recognized the error of his own actions and received Paul's rebuke. Their perspective on Gentile freedom from the law of Moses was the same at the Jerusalem Council in A.D. 50. (See Acts 15:7-12.)

Paul wrote his letters by the "wisdom given to him." In verse 16 Peter placed Paul's letters on the same level as "the rest of the Scriptures," so the "wisdom" Paul had been given was the same as what had been given to "holy men of God" who "spoke as they were moved by the Holy Spirit" (1:21, NKJV). Because the words of the apostles are as authoritative as the "words which were spoken before by the holy prophets" (3:2, NKJV), believers must be "mindful" of them.

There is some uncertainty as to what Peter had in

mind when he indicated to his readers that Paul had written to them.[242] It seems most likely that he simply referred to letters written by Paul and circulated to all the churches. Since his letters are authoritative for all believers, and not just for their immediate audience, every epistle that Paul wrote is for all believers. (See I Corinthians 14:37; Colossians 4:16.)

Verse 16 contains a significant internal witness to the nature and authority of the New Testament. It compares all of Paul's letters—which together make up twenty-seven percent of the New Testament[243]—to "the rest of the Scriptures" (NKJV). The word translated "Scriptures" (*graphe*) is always used in the New Testament of inspired writings. In most cases, it is used of the Old Testament, but here and in I Timothy 5:18 it is used of the New Testament.[244] Since all Scripture is given by inspiration of God, the New Testament has the same authority as the Old Testament (II Timothy 3:16). Other indications of the authority of the New Testament include I Corinthians 14:37, II Peter 3:2, and Revelation 22:18-19.

In his letters, Paul spoke of the same things that Peter addressed in this letter. This is a reference specifically to the Second Coming, a subject Paul frequently addressed.[245] Like Peter, Paul taught "in all his letters about the need for holy, patient, steadfast, peaceable living (especially in the light of the parousia)."[246]

In Paul's letters, there are some things "hard to understand." Those who are "untaught and unstable" twist these things "to their own destruction" (NKJV). For the second time, this letter refers to those who are unstable (*asteriktos*). Previously, it described those who were enticed by the false teachers as "unstable souls" (2:14).

Exhortations in View of the Delay

The word translated "wrest" (*streblousin*, "twist," NKJV) is a vivid term that means "to twist, torture, dislocate the limbs on the rack."[247] Those who are unlearned and unstable "torture" Scripture by taking it out of context and giving it meaning that the original author never intended, as he wrote under the inspiration of the Holy Spirit. This is a serious and deadly error. Those who twist Scripture do so "to their own destruction." The premier consideration in interpreting Scripture is to do it in such a way as to receive the approval of God. (See II Timothy 2:15.)

Perhaps one of the things in Paul's letters that was hard to understand and that false teachers twisted, was his extended teaching on justification by faith. Paul acknowledged that on this subject, some slanderously reported that he said, "Let us do evil that good may come" (Romans 3:8, NKJV). This was, of course, contrary to his intent.

B. Remain Steadfast (3:17)

(17) Ye therefore, beloved, seeing ye know these things before, beware lest ye also, being led away with the error of the wicked, fall from your own stedfastness.

At this point, the attention shifts away from Paul's letters and back to the immediate audience. They were now prepared by means of this letter to avoid the snare of the false teachers, a snare that could potentially have cost them their salvation.

Verse 17. For the sixth time, II Peter uses the word

"beloved" (*agapetos*), and this is the fourth time it applies to the readers. (See 1:17; 3:1, 8, 14, 15.) Each time, it seems to be used for special effect. Here, coupled with the emphatic "ye" and "therefore," it contrasts the readers of the letter with the "untaught and unstable people" of the previous verse. Specifically, the word "beloved" indicates that the believers were beloved by God, just as Jesus was (1:17).[248] Although Peter warned his readers, he did not expect them to fall into the error of the false teachers.

By using the phrase, "you therefore, beloved," Peter turned his attention away from Paul's letters and back to the issues at hand throughout the letter: (1) the importance of resisting false teachers and (2) the necessity of spiritual growth.

Peter wrote this letter at least in part to prepare his readers in advance for false teaching that was sure to come (see comments on 3:1). It seems quite clear that false teaching had already infiltrated the believing community to which he wrote (see comments on 2:10-22), but it would certainly not be the last. The proper attitude for believers is to "beware," for lack of awareness and resistance can lead to a loss of "steadfastness" or stability. The steadfastness in view here is the believer's security in salvation. If there were no possibility of losing salvation, this warning would be pointless.

The word translated "steadfastness" (*sterigmos*) has a meaning opposite to "unstable" (*asteriktos*) in verse 16. A related word appears in I Peter 5:10 (translated "stablish") and II Peter 1:12 (translated "established"). Contextually, the word refers to the steadfastness or stability that comes from embracing the truth as opposed to "being led away with the error of the wicked."

False teaching is always dangerous, and believers must always be on the alert to detect, expose, and reject it. Regardless of the form it takes, error is destructive. (See comments on verse 16.) Error can be subtle, and believers must be especially alert to any teaching that in any way compromises the fundamental truths of the deity of Christ, the sufficiency of the Cross, and the bodily resurrection and second coming of Jesus.

C. Grow in Grace and Knowledge (3:18)

(18) But grow in grace, and in the knowledge of our Lord and Saviour Jesus Christ. To him be glory both now and for ever. Amen.

The final verse of II Peter reminds us of the opening section. (See 1:5-7.) The Christian life is about growth; one cannot be spiritually stagnant and be a healthy, stable Christian. In a much-repeated statement, someone said that the Christian life is like riding a bicycle: We must keep moving or fall off![249]

The final verse is one of the places in the New Testament that specifically identify Jesus as the recipient of glory. Other places ascribe glory to God. The phrase here underscores the deity of Christ. If He were not God, He would not be worthy of glory. (Compare Revelation 1:4-6 with 4:8-11.)

Verse 18. Christian growth is in view here—no doubt the maturing process of 1:5-8. It is not quite so clear, however, whether we should translate *chariti kai gnosei* as "in grace, and in the knowledge" (KJV) or "in the grace and knowledge" (NKJV and other modern English translations). The definite article ("the") does not appear before either word in the Greek text, but either translation would be accurate.

There is a subtle but significant difference in meaning depending on the placement of the definite article. If we translate "in the grace and knowledge," the point is that Christians mature as they receive the gift of grace from Christ. With this translation, it would be most natural to understand "knowledge" as the knowledge that Christ gives. (See 1:5-6.) Even with this translation, it would be possible, however, to understand "knowledge" as coming to know Jesus more intimately and personally.[250] If we translate "in grace, and in the knowledge," the reference to grace is generic with no specific reference to Christ as the source, and "the knowledge" is specifically the knowledge that Christ gives.

II Peter proclaims Jesus as both Lord and Savior. (See comments on 1:2.) For a Jewish author to identify Jesus in this way indicates his conviction that Jesus is truly God. Peter's inspired conviction of this truth is further underscored here by the doxology: "To Him be the glory both now and forever" (NKJV). Blum pointed out that "for a Jew who has learned the great words in Isaiah 42:8—'I am the LORD; that is my name! I will not give my glory to another'—this doxology is a clear confession of Christ."[251] There can be no separation of God, to whom the New Testament ascribes glory, and Jesus, to whom it ascribes the same glory.[252]

The last three words of the sentence in the Greek text (*eis hemeran aionos*), translated "forever," mean literally "unto the day of the age."[253] The phrase refers back to

Exhortations in View of the Delay

"the day" or "the day of the Lord" or "the day of God" (verses 7, 10, 12). The point is that glory belongs to Jesus Christ now and up until and through the eternal "day." (See Revelation 4:11.)

"Amen" is the English transliteration of the Greek transliteration of the Hebrew word that means something like, "So be it!" Thus concludes a letter that warns of the dangers of false teaching and that proclaims the only sure antidote to being deceived—continual Christian growth.

JUDE

BEWARE OF FALSE TEACHERS

Introduction to Jude

Jude shares with II Peter a concern about false teachers infiltrating the church. Because we still see the same errors taught by early heretics, these books are particularly relevant for the church of the twenty-first century.[254] If it were possible for heresy to creep into the church well before the end of the first century, it is certainly possible that heresy could be present today. Christians are not to be of this world, but they do live in a world that constantly seeks to influence them in ways inherently opposed to biblical values. Not only do believers wrestle with the continuing influence of the fallen nature (see Galatians 5:17) but also with the pressure of living among those who do not share their faith. More than wishful thinking is required to maintain a godly lifestyle and to maintain doctrinal integrity.

Although it was Jude's wish to write a joyous treatise concerning the salvation shared by all believers, he found it necessary instead to encourage his readers to "contend earnestly for the faith" (3). This illustrates that Scripture was not written by the will of men, but by the influence of the Holy Spirit. (See II Peter 1:21.) There is a time to focus on the good news of the gospel, but there is also a time to defend the faith against the efforts of some to reinterpret it. (See II Peter 3:16.)

At least in some places, false teachers had infiltrated the community of believers so cleverly that people had not even noticed them (4a). They misinterpreted the grace of God so as to promote lewdness, and they also denied the lordship of Jesus Christ (4b).

Jude

How is to possible for false teachers to filter into the church unnoticed? It seems this would be possible only if they claimed to be genuine Christians, only if they gave lip service to Jesus Christ and to Christian doctrine, and only if they used the vocabulary of Christianity. If they blatantly denied Jesus Christ, rejected any identity with the Christian community, and openly contradicted biblical doctrine, the fellowship of believers would have summarily rejected them.

This is a sobering concern for the present-day church. Though there is certainly room in the church for differences of opinion on nonessential issues (see Romans 14), there is no room for a radical reinterpretation of what Christianity is all about. The false teachers of Jude's day had turned the grace of God into lewdness and taught a doctrine that somehow compromised the identity of the Lord Jesus (4). These have been traits of false teachers from that day until ours.

By illustrations from the Old Testament, the Epistle of Jude points out that the judgment of God upon sin is certain (5-7). The error of the first-century heretics was really nothing new. They were proponents of the same kinds of sins as Cain, Balaam, and Korah (8-13). Enoch had foretold the judgment of God upon people like these (14-15). The apostles foretold that there would be false teachers (17-18).

Jude offers an antidote to the false teachers' deception. The antidote includes contending for the faith "once for all delivered to the saints" (3, NKJV), remembering the warnings of the apostles (17), building oneself up in the faith, praying in the Spirit (20), keeping oneself in the love of God, and focusing on the Lord's mercy (21).

Introduction to Jude

Jude encourages proactive involvement with those who have been seduced by the false teachers. This includes responding with compassion or fear, as appropriate (22-23). Although it may be painful and challenging to confront those who have been seduced by error, the Christian response is never to ignore error. (See Galatians 6:1; James 5:19-20.)

Regardless of the influence of the false teachers, Jude assures its readers that God is able to preserve them from deception; their salvation is sure (24).

The letter concludes with a remarkable doxology (25).

Although, taken as a whole, Jude's letter seems essentially negative, it begins by identifying its recipients as called, sanctified, and preserved (1). It concludes with the assurance that, due to God's ability, believers can avoid falling, and they can be faultless (24). If the letter did not include verses 1-2 and 20-25, it might seem to present an almost hopeless problem. But the good news of Jude is that no matter how cleverly false teachers disguise their heresy, and no matter how perverse are those who proclaim it, the truth will prevail and people of faith will be steadfast.

The faith to which Jude refers in verse 3 is the body of doctrine that constitutes new covenant truth. The word "faith," like all words, is defined by its context. In some cases it refers to the faith in God that is necessary for salvation (e.g., Hebrews 11:6). In some cases it refers to the fruit of the Spirit (Galatians 5:22). There is even a gift of faith in the nine supernatural spiritual gifts (I Corinthians 12:9). Here, however, "the faith" refers to the actual content of the new covenant instituted by Jesus Christ. This faith has been "once for all delivered to the saints"

(NKJV). This means there is no room for variation in the body of doctrine as it existed in the first century.

Inspiration and Place in the Canon

Jude's appeal to noncanonical sources (*Assumption of Moses* and *I Enoch*) is the apparent reason that some early Christians questioned its value. For this reason, early Christian writers rarely cited it.[255] The use of pseudepigraphical material seems to have been more of a problem for Christians in the east than in the west.

Ultimately, the church universally recognized the value of Jude. It was included in the Muratorian Canon (mid to late second century) and the Syriac Canon. Other prominent Christian teachers such as Tertullian, Clement of Alexandria, and Origen recognized it as inspired. Eusebius wrote that most churches used Jude along with the rest of the general letters.[256] Didymus of Alexandria's defense of Jude's inspiration and canonicity largely silenced all opposition by the close of the fourth century.

Author

The letter was written by "Jude, the servant of Jesus Christ, and brother of James" (verse 1). The Greek word translated "Jude" (*Ioudas*) appears over forty times in the New Testament, translated variously as Judas, Juda, and Jude. The meaning of the name is "he shall be praised." Of the various people named *Ioudas* in the New Testament, only a few could be authors of this letter. They include a prophet of the church at Jerusalem who ministered with Silas (Acts 15:22, 27, 32); one of the twelve apostles, not Iscariot (John 14:22); and a half-brother of Jesus (Matthew 13:55). Of these possibilities, it is almost certain that Jesus' half-brother wrote the letter.

The Jude who wrote this letter identified himself as the brother of James. This seems to eliminate the Judas who was one of the twelve apostles, for he was the son of James. (See Luke 6:16; Acts 1:13). This Judas could have had a brother named James as well as a father named James, but it seems unlikely that he would mention this relationship as a way of identifying himself if it is not mentioned elsewhere in the New Testament. The same reasoning applies to the prophet Judas, who is never identified as a brother of James.

The identification of Jude as the brother of James indicates that this James was widely known among those to whom Jude wrote. The best-known James was a recognized leader of the church in Jerusalem. (See Acts 15:13; 21:17-18; Galatians 1:18-19; 2:9, 12.) This James was the author of the letter bearing his name[257] and the half-brother of the Lord Jesus. (See Mark 6:3; Matthew 13:55; Galatians 1:19.) Another of Jesus' half-brothers was Judas. (See Mark 6:3; Matthew 13:55.) Jesus' brothers did not believe on Him prior to His resurrection. (See John 7:5.) But after His resurrection, Jesus appeared to James (not one of the Twelve, I Corinthians 15:5, 7). His post-resurrection appearances apparently resulted in the conversion of all Jesus' brothers. (See Acts 1:14; I Corinthians 9:5.)

A further indication that Jude was the half-brother of the Lord Jesus is "the deeply Jewish colouring of the letter, especially the love for Jewish apocalypses and the Aramaic sentence structure with its triple arrangements, coupled with the good Greek that one might expect from a native of bilingual Galilee."[258] There was general

Jude

agreement in the early church that the letter was written by Jesus' half-brother.

If Jude was the half-brother of Jesus, why did he not say so? It is possible that humility prevented him from doing this. Jesus' brothers became believers only after His resurrection. How did they feel about their steadfast refusal to believe on Him so long as He was associated so closely with them? It could also be that Jude, like his brother James in his letter, saw "no point in claiming a physical relationship to Jesus that brought him no spiritual benefit and that did not give to him any special authority."[259]

Date of Composition

Any attempt to establish the date for the composition of Jude is tied to the apparent relationship between Jude and II Peter. The best evidence indicates that II Peter was written in late A.D. 64 or early A.D. 65. If Jude influenced II Peter, this would require an earlier date for Jude. If II Peter influenced Jude, this would require a later date for Jude. If an unknown third source influenced both II Peter and Jude, it would be impossible to know which letter was written first.

Although we cannot finally resolve the nature of the relationship between II Peter and Jude, a clue in Jude 17-18 indicates that II Peter influenced Jude. If these verses refer to the warning of II Peter 3:3, they certainly indicate the priority of II Peter. In this case, Jude would have been written after II Peter but probably before the destruction of Jerusalem in A.D. 70. In view of the Jewishness of the letter, Jude surely would have mentioned the destruction of Jerusalem if had it already occurred.[260]

Place of Origin

There is no internal clue as to where Jude was when he wrote this letter. We can only guess, and common guesses include Egypt and Palestine. If Jude remained in Jerusalem to minister with his brother James, then he probably wrote in Palestine. On the other hand, I Corinthians 9:5 may indicate that Jude had an itinerant ministry in various locations in the eastern Mediterranean world; if so, he could have written this letter at any point in his travels.

Original Audience

Jude identified his original recipients simply as those who "are sanctified by God the Father, and preserved in Jesus Christ, and called" (verse 1). Because of this, it is impossible to know precisely who they were and where they were.

It is evident that the original readers of this letter were familiar with the Old Testament and with various noncanonical Jewish writings, including the *Assumption of Moses* and *I Enoch*. The pervasive Jewish flavor of the letter indicates a Jewish-Christian audience, but the nature of the false teachings addressed may suggest that Gentile heretics had infiltrated this Jewish-Christian audience.

Purpose

The purpose of Jude's letter is to warn of false teachers who had infiltrated the community of believers. He had originally intended to write concerning the "common salvation," but he found it necessary to exhort the believers "to contend earnestly for the faith which was once for all delivered to the saints" (verse 3, NKJV).

As a secondary purpose, Jude encouraged his readers

Jude

to grow spiritually (verses 20-21) and to rescue those who had been seduced by the false teachers (verses 22-23).

Style and Structure

In general, Jude is a "letter-essay, a letter used as a sermon."[261] It was common in the first century to use letters as substitutes for speeches or for the personal presence of the writer.[262]

Commentators have often noted that Jude makes extensive use of triple expressions. The following chart illustrates this point:[263]

```
Verse 1  . . . . Jude, servant, brother
Verse 1  . . . . sanctified, preserved, called
Verse 2  . . . . mercy, peace, love
Verse 4  . . . . ungodly, lascivious, deniers of Christ
Verses 5-7 . . Israel, angels, Sodom and Gomorrah
Verse 8  . . . . defile the flesh, reject authority, speak
                 evil of dignitaries
Verse 11 . . . Cain, Balaam, Korah
Verse 19 . . . sensual, divisive, unspiritual
```

Again, the letter has a pervasively Jewish perspective, seen in the references to Jewish noncanonical literature and the Aramaic sentence structure. Jude's Greek is good, as we would expect of a Jew who was a native of bilingual Galilee.[264]

Summary of Content

Jude was James's brother, and he considered himself to be a slave of Jesus Christ. The original recipients of the letter had been called and sanctified, and their salvation was sure (verse 1). Jude wished for them abundant mercy, peace, and love (verse 2).

Though he wished to write concerning the salvation all believers share, Jude found it necessary instead to address the danger of heresy creeping in among the believers. The purpose of the letter is to urge readers to resist heresy by earnestly contending for the body of faith that had been delivered to the saints and that would never change (verse 3). The nature of the heresy was twofold: (1) It claimed that the grace of God gave people the freedom to practice lewdness. (2) It compromised in some way the lordship of Jesus Christ (verse 4).

Three historical examples show the certainty of God's judgment upon those who promote heresy: (1) the destruction of those who refused to believe they could possess the Promised Land, even after God had delivered them from Egypt (verse 5); (2) the imprisonment in everlasting chains under darkness of the angels who did not keep their proper domain (verse 6); and (3) the destruction of Sodom and Gomorrah and surrounding cities that had abandoned themselves to sexual immorality (verse 7).

Evidence of the heretics' depravity included their sexual immorality, rejection of authority, and speaking evil of dignitaries (verse 8).

An example drawn apparently from the *Assumption of Moses* demonstrates that faithful angels do not speak evil of dignitaries even when those dignitaries are themselves rebels against God (verse 9). The heretics, however, carelessly spoke evil even when they did not know what they were talking about, and they corrupted themselves like beasts in things about which they had natural knowledge (verse 10).

Jude

The spiritual predecessors of the heretics included Cain, Balaam, and Korah (verse 11).

The false teachers were so empty of reverence for God that they fearlessly participated in the love feasts (fellowship meals) of early Christians (verses 12-13). The arrival of such teachers had been long anticipated by the prophets and apostles, and their judgment was certain (verses 14-19).

The antidote to seduction by heresy is spiritual growth, accomplished by strengthening faith, spiritual prayer, remaining in God's love, and focusing on the Lord's mercy (verses 20-21).

Not only are believers to develop their own spiritual life, they are also to take whatever steps necessary and appropriate to prevent people from being deceived and to rescue those who are lost (verses 22-23).

The letter's doxology focuses on the assurance of salvation and the wisdom, glory, majesty, dominion, and power of God (verses 24-25).

I

Salutation
(1-2)

A. Author (1a)

(1a) Jude, the servant of Jesus Christ, and brother of James.

Verse 1a. The author of the letter identifies himself first of all as Jude, a name by which at least six different men mentioned in the New Testament are known. This Jude, however, is the "brother of James." There would have been little point in mentioning this relationship unless it was meaningful to the original recipients of this letter. The "James" to whom Jude referred must have been well-known to the readers.

The available evidence suggests strongly that Jude and James were brothers of Jesus, who did not believe on Him until after His resurrection. The well-known James was the spiritual leader of the church in Jerusalem.[265]

Like James, Jude did not mention his physical relationship to Jesus. This could have been due to humility. Neither could boast that they had gained any significant spiritual insight or authority from living in the same family with Jesus. Not only had they not believed on Him until after His resurrection, they had at one point thought Him to be insane. (See Mark 3:21, 31; John 7:5.)

Jude

Instead of calling attention to his physical relationship with Jesus, Jude, like James, declared himself to be "a servant . . . of Jesus Christ." (See James 1:1.) Others in the Epistles who identified themselves as the servants of Jesus Christ were Paul, Timothy, and Peter. (See Romans 1:1; Philippians 1:1; II Peter 1:1.)

We are so far removed from Hebrew thought that we may overlook the significance of a Jewish writer identifying himself as the servant (*doulos*, "slave") of Jesus Christ. The background of this term comes from the Old Testament, where devout Jews were identified as servants of God.[266]

When New Testament writers, like Jude, put "Jesus Christ" in this formulaic title where the Old Testament has "God" or "the LORD," it is significant. As Douglas J. Moo has pointed out, it is in "this transfer of language about God in the Old Testament to Jesus that we find some of the best New Testament evidence for Jesus' deity."[267] Specific verses that identify Jesus Christ as God are important (e.g., John 1:1; 20:28; Romans 9:5; II Peter 1:1; Titus 2:13). However:

> Even more impressive is the abundant New Testament evidence that the early Christians, most from rigidly monotheistic backgrounds, came to act toward Jesus and to speak of him as if he were God. They worshiped him (e.g., Matt. 14:33; 28:9, 17, cf. Heb. 1:6); they applied Old Testament verses about Yahweh to him (e.g., Rom. 10:13); they prayed to him (e.g., Acts 7:59).[268]

In addition, devout and strictly monotheistic Jews refused to acknowledge that they were the servants of anyone but God. This was due to the command in the law of Moses that they were to serve God only. (Compare Deuteronomy 6:13; 10:20 with Matthew 4:10; Luke 4:8.[269]) Due to the nature of slavery, "no man can serve two masters" (Matthew 6:24; Luke 16:13).[270]

As Moo has pointed out, that Jude believed Jesus was God does not mean that he was "at the point of formulating the doctrine of the Trinity."[271] Later Christians did appeal to statements such as these as they "hammered out the concept of the Trinity,"[272] but this was far from Jude's mind. As a devout, monotheistic Jew (see Deuteronomy 6:4), Jude had come to believe that the brother with whom he grew up was in some marvelous and miraculous way God Himself. There is no hint in this letter that Jude thought Jesus was a person distinct from God. Although later Greek manuscripts insert "God" (*theon*) into verse 4, thus introducing the possibility that God and Jesus Christ are in some way distinct, the abundance of earlier manuscript evidence indicates that false teachers had turned against "our only Master and Lord, Jesus Christ" (*ton monon despoten kai kurion hemon Iesoun Christon*).

Most textual critics (but not all) view shorter readings as more likely to represent the original text. They make an exception, however, in verse 25. Here, the text upon which the KJV is based reads, "To the only wise God our Saviour, be glory and majesty, dominion and power, both now and ever. Amen." In the larger context of the entire letter, this reading indicates that Jesus is "the only wise God." The longer reading says, "To the only God our Savior be glory, majesty, power and authority, through Jesus Christ our Lord, before all ages, now and forevermore! Amen" (NIV).

Jude

In some cases, issues concerning textual criticism may never be finally settled to the satisfaction of everyone. But in this case, the most natural meaning of the longer reading is that we can ascribe glory, majesty, power, and authority to God only through Jesus Christ, and this is the case not only now and forever but also "before all ages." Here it seems better to adopt the shorter reading, because it would seem curious to say we can ascribe all of these virtues to God only through Jesus Christ "before all ages," that is, even before the Incarnation occurred and thus before Christ was revealed. It would be difficult to know how people of faith who lived before written revelation (e.g., Enoch, Noah, Job, Abraham, Isaac, Jacob) could ascribe glory to God through Jesus Christ. Indeed, how could Moses and those after him do so, since the Incarnation was still very much a mystery? (See I Timothy 3:16.)

As in verse 4, the shorter reading is simpler and more direct. In both verses, the shorter readings identify Jesus Christ as God. (Verse 25 does so because Jesus Christ is the Savior in Matthew 1:21; Luke 2:11.) Thus they accord well with Jude's confession that he was a servant of Jesus Christ.

B. Recipients (1b)

(1b) To them that are sanctified by God the Father, and preserved in Jesus Christ, and called.

Verse 1b. Here is the only identification of the original recipients of Jude's letter. They are sanctified, preserved, and called. Both "sanctified" and "preserved" are

Salutation

perfect passive participles, indicating that the sanctification and preservation occurred in the past with effects continuing into the present. The word "called" is an adjective functioning as a noun. Those who are "the called" have been and are sanctified and preserved.

Instead of "sanctified," the oldest Greek manuscripts have "beloved." In Greek, the two words are somewhat similar in appearance. Some scholars believe that the reading of "sanctified," found in later manuscripts, "was introduced by copyists in order to avoid the difficult and unusual combination [beloved by God the Father]."[273] Christians are sanctified by the Holy Spirit (Romans 15:16; II Thessalonians 2:13; I Peter 1:2.) They "are sanctified in Christ Jesus" (I Corinthians 1:2). (The preposition *en* is translated "in," whereas in Jude 1 the KJV translates it as "by.") Jesus prayed that the Father would sanctify His disciples through (*en*) the truth (John 17:17). In Ephesians 5:26, it is Christ who sanctifies and cleanses the church "with the washing of water by the word." Paul prayed that "the God of peace" would sanctify believers completely (I Thessalonians 5:23). Jesus sanctifies "the people with his own blood" (Hebrews 13:12). Believers are sanctified, as well as justified, "in the name of the Lord Jesus, and by the Spirit of our God" (I Corinthians 6:11). In Hebrews 2:11, it is the Messiah who sanctifies. (See Hebrews 9:13-14; 10:10, 14.)

Sanctification means to be "set apart" unto God and from all that is unlike Him. The Greek word translated "sanctification" is related to the word translated "holy." In one sense, sanctification is complete at the moment of salvation. (See Hebrews 10:10; I Corinthians 1:2, 30; 6:11; Acts 20:32; 26:18.) At the moment believers obey

Jude

the gospel and are born again, they are fully children of God, separated unto God and from their sins. We can call this positional sanctification.

In another sense, sanctification is a process by which believers daily come into greater conformity with the character of Christ. This occurs as they seek, by the strength of the Holy Spirit, to internalize Christ's character. (See I Thessalonians 4:4; 5:23; II Corinthians 7:1; Hebrews 10:14, NKJV; 12:10, 14.)

There is another sense in which final sanctification will occur when Christ presents the church to Himself as a spotless bride free of any wrinkle or blemish (Ephesians 5:26-27).[274]

If the original reading here is "beloved by [or "in"] God the Father," it is the only place in the New Testament to read precisely this way. Elsewhere, believers are said to be "beloved of God" (Romans 1:7) and "beloved of the Lord" (II Thessalonians 2:13). The statement in verse 21 that believers are to keep themselves "in the love of God" may support the idea that the original reading of verse 1 is "beloved" rather than "sanctified."

Not only are believers sanctified by God the Father (or beloved by or in Him), they are also "preserved in Jesus Christ." The Greek word *tereo*, a form of which is translated "preserved" here, appears four more times in Jude. In verse 6, it describes the angels who "kept not" their first estate and points out that God has "reserved" them in everlasting chains. Verse 13 describes the false teachers as "wandering stars" to whom the blackness of darkness is "reserved." In verse 21, the word describes the responsibility of believers to "keep" themselves in the love of God.

In His high priestly prayer, Jesus prayed, "Holy Father, keep [*tereo*] through Your name those whom You have given Me" (John 17:11, NKJV).

The promise that believers are preserved or kept means that God has done everything needed to assure salvation to believers. There is nothing lacking in His provision, desire, or ability to prevent the loss of salvation. (See verse 24 and I Peter 1:5.[275]) This promise does not mean that believers have no responsibility, however. Verse 21 uses the same word translated "preserved" in this verse to admonish believers to "keep" themselves in the love of God. On God's part, He will preserve the believer; but on the believers' part, they must keep themselves. It seems evident that verses 22-23 describe those who have not kept themselves and who thus must be rescued from destruction. Even though God is able to keep believers from stumbling (verse 24), some do stumble due to neglect of their spiritual well-being or to intentional rebellion. (See James 5:19-20.)

The word translated "called" (*kletos*) essentially involves an invitation.[276] In connection with salvation, the word alludes to the universal nature of the call. Jesus said, "Many are called, but few are chosen" (Matthew 22:14). In a Jewish context, "many" is a reference to the entire human population, including Gentiles, as opposed to the nation of Israel alone. To say "many are called" means that the call is not limited to Israel alone.[277]

What is the significance of the reference to "God the Father" and "Jesus Christ"? The first and most obvious significance is to proclaim the full deity of Christ. No devout Jew would ever refer to God the Father together with someone less than God in a grammatical structure

Jude

implying complete equality. Since the verse connects sanctification with God the Father and preservation with Jesus Christ, it indicates the equality of God the Father and Jesus Christ. Thus, Jesus Christ is just as truly God as the Father is; indeed He is the true God (the Father) manifested in the flesh. (See comments on verse 1a.)

But what does this reference tell us about the divine essence or about the relationship between the Father and Jesus Christ? When the concept of the trinity developed in the third and fourth centuries, references like this were cited as evidence that the Father was a person distinct from the Son.[278] But as F. W. Beare pointed out in his discussion of Matthew 28:19, references like these are "not, properly speaking, 'trinitarian'; there is no element of speculation about the divine essence or the relations between Father, Son, and Holy Spirit. It reflects the modes in which the divine is manifested in Christian faith."[279] Moo observed:

> We must not imagine that [Jude] had worked out all the theological implications inherent in speaking of Jesus in these terms. Jude was not at the point of formulating the doctrine of the Trinity! But when later Christians hammered out the concept of the Trinity, they built their theology on the almost casual kinds of indications that we find in this verse. Early Christians had an experience of Jesus that led them to begin applying to him language they had in the past reserved for God.[280]

The question remains, however, whether the formulations of the third and fourth centuries accurately understand these references. It did not and would not have occurred to believing Jewish writers of Scripture in the first century to think of God in terms of "persons." That formulation arose, not from Hebrew theology, but from the Greek perspective of the second-century apologists. Certainly, first-century Christians knew God as their Father, they knew Him as He was manifest in human existence in the person of Jesus Christ, and they knew Him through their experience with His Holy Spirit, but there is no indisputable evidence in the New Testament that they thought of God as more than one "person." To them, there was one God (see James 2:19), known as Father, Son, and Holy Spirit (Matthew 28:19; II Corinthians 13:14). When they thought of the Father, they thought of God transcendent, above and beyond the created realm. When they thought of the Son, Jesus Christ, they thought of God incarnate, God made known in genuine and full humanity, entering experientially into His own creation. When they thought of the Holy Spirit, they thought of God immanent, among and in His people. But they did not think of the Father, Son, and Holy Spirit as distinct "persons" in any meaningful sense of the word. To think of God as persons immediately introduces questions that cannot be resolved concerning the nature of the relationship between the persons and how they can be genuinely distinct and yet one.

As Beare has pointed out, to speak of the Father, Son, and Holy Spirit is to reflect "the modes in which the divine is manifested in Christian faith." This is not so-called Sabellian modalism, with a changing God going through a metamorphosis, changing from Father to Son and again to the Holy Spirit. Instead, it is the one God, the

Jude

Father of all (Ephesians 4:6), who is an eternal Spirit-being and who is revealed in human existence in Jesus Christ.

The writers of the New Testament accepted without question the deity of Jesus Christ, and they never speculated about a plurality of persons in God. All speculation occurred in the postbiblical era, relying on formulas and words not in Scripture. Obfuscation usually results from human attempts to go beyond what Scripture has proclaimed. It is sufficient to believe the testimony of Scripture, and we should be content to express our faith in the same words as our first-century ancestors.

C. Greetings (2)

(2) Mercy unto you, and peace, and love, be multiplied.

It is unusual for the writer of a New Testament letter to wish "mercy" for his readers. The more common wish is "grace."[281] When mercy appears in a greeting (sometimes together with grace), it seems contextually significant that the letter addresses the threat of false teaching, as here in Jude. (See I Timothy 1:2; II Timothy 1:2; Titus 1:4; II John 3.) This is not to say that only those letters including a wish for mercy in the greeting deal with the problem of false teaching. But even Galatians, which does not include a wish for mercy in the greeting and which forcibly deals with the problem of false teachers, includes a wish for mercy elsewhere (Galatians 6:16).

We could say that the meanings of mercy and grace are essentially the same.[282] But when the greetings include

Salutation

mercy in addition to grace, the letters deal with the problem of false teaching. Thus, the inclusion of mercy with grace or instead of grace may be significant. The point may be that those who confront the destructive danger of false teaching are especially in need of mercy. Generally, mercy signifies that people are saved as God extends clemency to them. Rather than giving us what we deserve, which is death, God gives us what we do not deserve, which is life. (See Ephesians 2:4-5; Titus 3:5; I Peter 1:3; Jude 21.) Those who are in danger from false teaching are, in the final analysis, in danger of losing their faith and thus their salvation. They are in need of mercy to avoid this loss.

Jude also wished peace for his readers. This is common in the New Testament letters; the only letters that do not include it are Hebrews, James, and I John. Hebrews does not include the traditional salutation and greeting either. James simply wrote, "Greetings" (James 1:1), with no reference to the common formula. The opening verses of I John are in many ways parallel to the opening verses of the gospel of John.

The wish for peace, especially in a letter written by such a thoroughly Jewish author, reflects the Hebrew idea of *shalom*. This word, which occurs over two hundred times in the Old Testament, and which is still the common greeting among those who speak Hebrew, means much more than the mere absence of conflict. *Shalom* includes a broad range of meaning. The idea is essentially that of well-being in every relationship and in all aspects of life. It includes physical well-being, social (relational) well-being, and spiritual well-being.

Jude's third wish for his readers is love. This is the

Jude

only New Testament letter to include love in its greeting, although love is mentioned 112 times in the Epistles. The love here is apparently the love of God for His people.[283]

Jude wished that mercy, peace, and love might "be multiplied" (*plethyntheie*). The same word appears in I Peter 1:2 and II Peter 1:2. The idea is that the readers might enjoy these virtues to their fullest capacity.[284] When it comes to the development of our spiritual life—our relationship with God—there is always room for growth.

II

Purpose for the Letter (3-4)

It is typical of Paul's letters that immediately after his salutations and greetings he commended his readers and offered a prayer for them.[285] This was not Jude's approach. Jude went immediately from the salutation and greeting to a clear statement of the purpose of the letter.

Jude intended to write concerning the "common salvation," but he was somehow redirected in his purpose. False teachers had "crept in" among the believers so that Jude found it necessary to encourage his readers to earnestly contend for the unchanging body of faith that had already been delivered to the saints. He hoped to help his readers avoid the seduction of false teaching that would have caused them to stumble in their relationship with God. (See verse 24.)

A. Contend for the Faith (3)

(3) Beloved, when I gave all diligence to write unto you of the common salvation, it was needful for me to write unto you, and exhort you that ye should earnestly contend for the faith which was once delivered unto the saints.

Verse 3. Jude referred to his readers as "beloved" three times. (See verses 17 and 20.) Here, the term simply

Jude

indicates Jude's love for his readers. In the other two instances, "beloved" seems to contrast the readers with the false teachers. In both of those cases, *humeis de* is best translated "but you." While Jude showed the depth of his love for his readers by his choice of words, he actually showed rejection of the false teachers in the same way. To say "certain men" (verse 4) is a way of showing disapproval,[286] as it is to say "ungodly men" (verse 4), "these dreamers" (verse 8), and "like brute beasts" (verse 10). This little letter uses many other negative terms for those who would infiltrate the body of believers to introduce destructive teaching. (See 12-13, 15-16, 18-19).

Translators differ on whether the phrase *pasan spouden poioumenos graphein* means "while I was very diligent to write" (NKJV) or "although I was very eager to write" (NIV). The KJV translates the phrase as "when I gave all diligence to write." Neither "while" nor "although" nor "when" are in the Greek text. *Pasan* means "all," as the KJV literally translates. The NKJV and many other recent translations understand *pasan* contextually to mean "very" as it modifies *spouden* (which could have to do with diligence, eagerness, haste, or carefulness). The NKJV, for example, understands "all diligence" to mean "very diligent." *Poioumenos* is a participle that means "making." *Graphein* is the infinitive "to write." A very literal, but rough, translation of the phrase would be "making very [or "all"] diligence to write." To introduce a word like "while," "when," or "although" is an interpretive effort to capture the sense of this participial phrase.[287]

The significance of the translation is that it determines whether Jude wrote the letter he intended to write or whether he intended to write on one topic and ended

Purpose of the Letter

up writing on another. If we translate "while" or "when," it suggests that Jude wrote the letter he intended to write. That is, to warn his readers against false teachers is the same thing as to write to them of the common salvation. By warning them against error, Jude encouraged them to retain the common salvation. But if we translate "although," it suggests that Jude intended to write on the topic of the salvation all believers share, but that he instead wrote a polemic against false doctrine that sought to corrupt the content of "the faith."

Since inspired utterances or writings do not come by the "will of man" (II Peter 1:21), it is certainly possible that Jude intended to write on one theme but that the Holy Spirit prompted him to write on another. The repetition of "to write" later in the verse argues in favor of translating the phrase something like "although I was eager to write." Jude set out to write on the joys of the salvation he shared with his readers, but the Holy Spirit instead guided him to urge his readers not to deviate from the content of the faith once delivered.

The idea of "common salvation" means that all are saved on the same basis and with the same experience. There is no difference in the salvation of Jews and Gentiles, men and women, and freemen and slaves. It makes no difference about one's ethnicity, gender, or social status. There is only one salvation; it is common to all. (See Acts 4:12; Romans 3:1, 22, 29-30; 4:11-12, 16; Galatians 3:26-29; Ephesians 2:8-19; 4:1-6; Colossians 3:11.)

Beyond what Jude said here, we can only speculate on what he would have written had he not been divinely interrupted. As a thoroughly Jewish believer, perhaps he

Jude

intended to address the unity between Jews and Gentiles in Christ, as Paul often did. But this was not to be. The very faith of his readers was in jeopardy, and the Holy Spirit directed him to address this pressing crisis.

The word translated "exhort" (*parakalon*) means something like "to call alongside." It expresses the idea of calling someone to one's side to encourage, to comfort, to entreat, or to urge to do something. In this case, the last idea is most appropriate. Jude wanted to impress upon his readers the urgency of being proactive in defending the faith.

The word translated "earnestly contend" (*epagonizesthai*) is formed by compounding the preposition *epi* with *agonizomai* (from which comes the English "agonize"). The word is used in the context of athletics to describe the agonizing struggle to win. (See I Corinthians 9:25; Colossians 1:29; I Timothy 4:10; 6:12; II Timothy 4:7.) The essential idea is strenuous zeal. Believers are not to be passive in their response to false teaching that could destroy true faith. They are to be energetically, actively, and determinedly involved in standing for the true faith.

The word "faith" appears well over two hundred times in the New Testament, but "the faith" appears only forty-two times.[288] In many cases where the definite article precedes "faith," the reference is to the actual body of belief, or the propositions that make up the content of Christian faith. The meaning of "faith" in verse 20 is the same. The definite article is in the Greek text even though it is not translated.

Although Jude did not elaborate here on the content of "the faith," the New Testament is quite clear that those who have faith in Christ will affirm a body of propositional truth. (See Acts 2:42; Romans 6:17; Galatians 1:23.) The word translated "delivered" (*paradotheise*) has to do with authorized, and therefore authoritative, tradition. (See I Corinthians 15:1-3; II Thessalonians 3:6.) This body of truth was delivered to the saints—the holy, believing community—"once for all" (NKJV). The "once for all" idea is contained in the aorist tense. That is, once delivered, there is no room for any change in the content of the faith. (See Galatians 1:6-9.) Those who attempt to introduce change must be resisted. (See II John 7-11.)

What is the content of the faith "once delivered"? It includes "such things as Jesus' atoning death and resurrection, the indwelling of the Holy Spirit, salvation by grace through faith, and (especially in Jude's situation) the holy lifestyle that flows from God's grace in Christ."[289]

B. Beware of False Teachers (4)

(4) For there are certain men crept in unawares, who were before of old ordained to this condemnation, ungodly men, turning the grace of our God into lasciviousness, and denying the only Lord God, and our Lord Jesus Christ.

Verse 4. This verse explains why Jude had to urge his readers "to contend earnestly for the faith which was once for all delivered to the saints" (verse 3, NKJV). Ungodly men had "crept in unnoticed" (NKJV), who perverted a fundamental of the Christian faith—the grace of God—and who in some way denied the Lord. Jude was concerned about the corrupting influence these false teachers would have on the believing community.

Jude

This is the first of eleven verses in Jude that have close parallels in II Peter.[290] Peter wrote, "But there were also false prophets among the people, even as there will be false teachers among you, who will secretly bring in destructive heresies, even denying the Lord who bought them, and bring on themselves swift destruction" (II Peter 2:1, NKJV). In II Peter, the false teachers introduced destructive heresies "secretly." In Jude, they "crept in unnoticed."

No person intent on introducing heresy would work in such a blatant way that his intention and error would be obvious. That would defeat his purpose. Instead, he would do his best to conceal his aim and apostasy. He would do this, no doubt, by pretending to be something he is not: he would wear a cloak of respectability, orthodoxy, and faith. He would use the right vocabulary and conduct himself in such a way as to gain a position of influence. He would be, in short, a wolf in sheep's clothing. (See Matthew 7:15.) Indeed, the more successful he would be in appearing to share the faith of those around him, the more devastating would be his destructive influence. This was the case for Jude's first-century readers, for false teachers had crept in "unnoticed." They had been so successful in passing themselves off as genuine believers who embraced "the faith" (see comments on verse 3) that those who were indeed genuine believers had not even noticed that heretics had infiltrated the community of believers.

These false teachers had been "long ago . . . marked out for this condemnation" (NKJV). "Ordained" is not the best translation for *progegrammenoi*, a word that means "foretold in writing."[291] (See Romans 15:4; Galatians 3:1;

Purpose of the Letter

Ephesians 3:3, where the same word is translated variously as "were written aforetime," "hath been evidently set forth," and "wrote afore.") The English word "ordained" could imply that these false teachers were in some way predestined to their sin and punishment. That is not the point. The simplest meaning of the phrase *hoi palai progegrammenoi eis touto to krima* is that these teachers were those whose judgment had been foretold in writing.

When was the judgment of these false teachers foretold in writing? If II Peter preceded Jude, and if II Peter influenced Jude, the reference here could be to the judgment of false teachers described in II Peter.[292] (See II Peter 2.) This may seem unlikely in view of the translation "before of old" or "long ago" (NKJV). It is possible, however, for the word so translated (*palai*) refers to something that previously happened, with no regard to the length of time since the event occurred. (See, for example, Mark 15:44, where *palai* is translated "any while" [KJV] or "some time" [NKJV].) Or it could be, in light of Jude 14-15, that the previous writing is *I Enoch*. But the "simplest explanation . . . is that Jude introduces the evidence for the false teachers' condemnation that he will adduce in the rest of the letter."[293] This includes references to judgment in the Old Testament (verses 5-8, 11), in Jewish tradition (verses 9, 14-16), and in the apostolic teaching (verses 17-18).

These false teachers are "ungodly men." The word translated "ungodly" (*asebeis*) is a key word in Jude. It appears in some form six times in this short letter. (See verses 15 and 18.) It indicates a complete lack of reverence for God. It may even result in condemning God. Paul used the noun or verbal form of the word in Romans 1:18; 4:5; 5:6; 11:26; I Timothy 1:9; II Timothy 2:16; Titus 2:12, and Peter used it in I Peter 4:18; II Peter 2:5; 3:7. Hellenistic Jews used it in the first century to mean "irreverence in an ethical sense: 'not theoretical atheism, but practical godlessness.'"[294]

One error promoted by these false teachers was to "turn the grace of our God into lewdness" (NKJV). Jude does not explain precisely how they did this, but the general tenor of the letter suggests that they misinterpreted the doctrine of grace. They claimed that since grace means salvation is a free gift (Ephesians 2:8-9), which cannot be earned or deserved, it makes no difference how we live. We can almost hear their reasoning now: "Salvation is a free gift. We do not earn it by good works. Therefore, we cannot lose it for a lack of good works. Therefore, it doesn't matter how we live." What this kind of reasoning misses is the connection between genuine faith and transformed behavior.

It is true that we are not saved because of good works. Nonetheless, the kind of faith that saves results in a transformed life. A person of genuine faith will give evidence of that faith by good works. And a person who has no faith or who has lost his faith will give evidence of that by a lack of good works.

Works alone do not prove conclusively that a person has saving faith, however. A person with no faith in God may do some good works, but he is not thereby saved. Nevertheless, a person with faith in God will do good works. Thus, a person who does no good works is simply displaying to the world his lack of faith in God.[295] If we are saved, we will demonstrate our status by our works. If we

Purpose of the Letter

are not saved, we will demonstrate that status by our works as well. (See Titus 1:16; James 2:14, 20, 26.)

These false teachers "turn[ed] the grace of our God into lewdness" (NKJV), or "lasciviousness" (KJV), which indicates that they were sexually immoral. This was also the case with the false teachers in II Peter 2:14. Jude's example of the people of Sodom and Gomorrah, who gave themselves over to sexual immorality and went after "strange flesh" (verse 7), suggests that these teachers were sexually immoral. Hedonism is soundly condemned throughout the New Testament. (See Romans 13:13; II Corinthians 12:21; Galatians 5:19; Ephesians 4:19; I Peter 4:3; II Peter 2:14, 18.)

The text from which the KJV is translated has a longer reading in the latter part of this verse: *kai ton monon despoten theon kai kurion hemon Iesoun christon arnoumenoi*. The KJV translates the phrase: "and denying the only Lord God, and our Lord Jesus Christ." This introduces the grammatical possibility that the Lord God and the Lord Jesus Christ are in some way distinct. But it is the later Greek manuscripts that include the word "God" (*theon*) in verse 4. The earlier manuscript evidence indicates that false teachers have turned against "our only Master and Lord, Jesus Christ" (*ton monon despoten kai kurion hemon Iesoun Christon*). Where there is only one definite article (e.g., *ton*) preceding two nouns linked by *kai*, and the nouns are the same gender, case, and number, as here, only one is indicated.[296] *Despoten* ("master") is used of Jesus also in II Peter 2:1.

How did these false teachers deny Jesus? Although the Scripture does not explain here, the contextual indication is that they denied His rights as the sovereign Lord by their flagrant disregard for His commands. By their abandonment to hedonism, they behaved as if they thought they would never stand before the Lord Jesus to give an account. They set themselves up as their own authority. They usurped the Lord's place in their lives. This is the essence of humanism.

III

Warnings from History
(5-7)

To illustrate the certainty of the judgment of God upon the false teachers who had crept in among the believers, the Epistle of Jude offers three historical accounts of God's judgment. The first was God's judgment upon the Israelites who did not believe He would enable them to possess the land He promised to Abraham. The second was the judgment of God upon sinning angels. The third was the judgment of God upon Sodom and Gomorrah and some surrounding cities. These three examples describe three sins: (1) unbelief; (2) rebellion; (3) sexual immorality.

All three examples were especially meaningful to Jewish readers. Since the letter reminds the readers of things they had once known (verse 5), it seems evident that it was originally written to a Jewish audience. Gentiles would have had little interest in or knowledge of these events.

A. The Destruction of the Israelites (5)

(5) I will therefore put you in remembrance, though ye once knew this, how that the Lord, having saved the people out of the land of Egypt, afterward destroyed them that believed not.

Verse 5. In many cases, New Testament letters seek to remind their readers of things they already know or may

Jude

have forgotten.[297] Forgetfulness is spiritually dangerous. The feasts and holy days of ancient Israel—including the Passover—regularly reminded the nation of significant events when God had intervened in their national life.[298] In the new covenant, the Lord's Supper reminds believers of the broken body and shed blood of Jesus. (See I Corinthians 11:24-26.) If we forget the points at which God intervened in our lives in the past, we are cut loose from any sense of destiny, purpose, and responsibility. Those who have no meaningful past have no future.

The specific event about which Jude reminds its readers is the exodus of Israel from Egyptian captivity and the subsequent destruction of all those who were thus "saved"—with the exception of Joshua and Caleb and those who were under twenty years old. Although God saved the people from slavery and bondage, He destroyed the same people because of their unbelief. God had promised them the land of Canaan, but the Israelites could not believe—due to the large, fortified cities and the giants who inhabited the land—that He would enable them to possess it. (See Numbers 13-14.) This tragedy became a common theme in warning the church about the consequences of unbelief. (See Acts 7:39; I Corinthians 10:1-11; Hebrews 3:12-19.)

This illustration indicates that the false teachers had once been people of genuine faith—just as the Israelites were upon their deliverance from Egypt—but had drifted into unbelief. For this warning to be meaningful, it must be possible to be genuinely saved and to lose salvation through unbelief. As Green pointed out, "Even the redeemed can backslide to a fate like this. . . . [Jude] argues from the fate of apostate Israel to the fate which could overtake apostate Christians."[299] If there were no real danger of the loss of salvation, warnings such as these would have little impact, for they would warn of something that could not happen.

B. The Judgment of Angels (6)

(6) And the angels which kept not their first estate, but left their own habitation, he hath reserved in everlasting chains under darkness unto the judgment of the great day.

Verse 6. The judgment of God is certain, not only for sinning humans like the ancient Israelites (verse 5) and the inhabitants of Sodom and Gomorrah and the surrounding cities (verse 7), but also for sinning angels. It is evident from this statement that God created angels for a specific purpose, with a designated realm of existence. They did not keep "their proper domain" but "left their own abode" (NKJV).

Biblical references to some kind of an angelic fall include Isaiah 14:12-17; 24:21-22; Matthew 25:41; Luke 10:18; Revelation 12:7-10. Speculation about the time of this fall and the circumstances surrounding it has led to a rich lore going far beyond the information of Scripture. Some students of Scripture have suggested that there were two occasions when angels defected from their loyalty to God. The first was when Lucifer rebelled and took perhaps one-third of the angels with him. (See Revelation 12:3-4, 7-10.) The second was when angels allegedly took human women for wives. (See Genesis 6:1-4.) Others see only one fall and reject the view that the "sons of God" of Genesis 6 were angels.

Jude

What does Jude have in view? We should first note the parallel of this verse with II Peter 2:4: "For if God did not spare the angels who sinned, but cast them down to hell and delivered them into chains of darkness, to be reserved for judgment" (NKJV). Neither II Peter nor Jude identifies the time of this sin.

"Most Jews during the intertestamental period thought that these 'sons of God' [of Genesis 6] were angels."[300] And Jude 14-15 apparently refers to *I Enoch*, a book that popularized the idea that Genesis 6 described angels marrying women. *I Enoch* 7:1-2, 7, 10-15 says:

> It happened after the sons of men had multiplied in those days, that daughters were born to them, elegant and beautiful. And when the angels, the sons of heaven, beheld them, they became enamoured of them, saying to each other, Come, let us select for ourselves wives from the progeny of men, and let us beget children. . . . Their whole number was two hundred. . . . Then they took wives, each choosing for himself; whom they began to approach, and with whom they cohabited; teaching them sorcery, incantations, and the dividing of roots and trees. And the women conceiving brought forth giants, whose stature was each three hundred cubits. These devoured all which the labour of men produced; until it became impossible to feed them; when they turned themselves against men, in order to devour them; and began to injure birds, beasts, reptiles, and fishes, to eat their flesh one after another, and to drink their blood. Then the earth reproved the unrighteous.[301]

According to this account, two hundred angels selected human women as their wives. These women conceived and gave birth to giants 437.5 feet tall.[302]

Does the Epistle of Jude endorse this account?

On the face of it, the account in *I Enoch*—part of the pseudepigrapha (false writings)—seems fantastic. The best information suggests that *I Enoch* was written "in or soon after the year 95 [B.C.]."[303] It reflects Jewish legends current at the time, including the idea of two Messiahs, "well known to the Jewish eschatology of the last centuries B.C."[304]

Even if Jude did quote from *I Enoch* in verses 14-15, and it is by no means certain that he did, this does not mean that Jude endorsed all of the content of *I Enoch*. Just as Paul quoted pagan poets without endorsing everything the poets said, so Jude could have quoted from current literature without endorsing the full content of the book. And it may be that Jude did not quote from *I Enoch* at all; he may simply have referred to well-known oral tradition in the Jewish community that was also included in *I Enoch*. We could explain other apparent similarities between Jude and *I Enoch* on the same basis.

The argument for the idea that angels married women goes something like this:

1. The "sons of God" must have been angels, because Job identifies angels as "sons of God." (See Job 1:6; 2:1; 38:7.)

2. The wives taken by the "sons of God" bore giants, so "the sons of God" must not have been ordinary men. Ordinary men do not have giants for offspring.

3. Jewish tradition viewed the "sons of God" as angels.

4. The reference to the sexual sin of the inhabitants of Sodom and Gomorrah (verse 7) is a contextual indicator that the sin of the angels was also sexual. The grammatical agreement of "these" in the phrase "in a similar manner to these" (NKJV) in verse 7 with "the angels" of verse 6 indicates that the sin of the angels was the same as the sin of the people of Sodom and Gomorrah.

The objection to the idea that angels married women goes something like this:

1. Job is the only Old Testament book to identify angels as "sons of God," with the possible exception of Daniel 3:25, where the pagan King Nebuchadnezzar identified the fourth man in the fire as "like the Son of God."[305] The context of Job is far removed from the context of Genesis. We ordinarily look for definitions in immediate contexts.

2. Angels are spirits. (See Hebrews 1:7.) How could a spirit cohabit with a human being and produce offspring? The Incarnation provides no support for the idea that spirit beings can have sexual intercourse with humans. The Incarnation occurred not by a sexual relationship but by a miracle. If God created everything to reproduce after its kind (see Genesis 1:24-25), so that species cannot be crossed, then the same must hold true throughout creation. (See I Corinthians 15:39.)

3. A careful reading of Genesis 6:1-4 does not indicate that the giants were the offspring of the union of angels and women. The text simply says that "there were giants on the earth in those days, and also afterward, when the sons of God came into the daughters of men and they bore children to them. Those [giants] were the mighty men who were of old, men of renown" (Genesis 6:4,

NKJV). The text does not say that the children born by the daughters of men to the sons of God were giants; it merely says there were giants on the earth at that time who were "men of renown."

4. Nor does a careful reading of Genesis 6:1-4 indicate that the judgment of God came on the earth as a result of the union of sons of God and daughters of men. Genesis 6:1-2 could fit contextually as the final two verses of Genesis 5,[306] as a simple statement of fact. The first clue of the coming judgment appears in Genesis 6:3. Genesis 6:4 is another simple statement of fact: there were giants on the earth at that time. We find the reason for the coming judgment in Genesis 6:5, and it is not connected with the marriage of the sons of God with the daughters of men. It would seem strange, indeed, to blame human beings alone for sins conceived and perpetrated by angels. Would human women have been able to resist the advances of "superhuman" men who had once been angels?

5. There is no reason the "sons of God" could not have been human descendants of Seth. When Eve gave birth to Seth, she said, "For God has appointed another seed for me instead of Abel, whom Cain killed" (Genesis 4:25, NKJV). If Seth was a seed appointed by God, he was in a sense the son of God and so were his descendants. Scripture describes Adam as having been made "in the image of God" (Genesis 1:26-27). Adam was thus the "son of God" (Luke 3:38). The Bible takes care to describe Seth as having been in Adam's "own likeness, after his image" (Genesis 5:3, NKJV). If Adam was the son of God, so was Seth (Luke 3:38). The point may simply be that descendants of Seth married women who were not

Jude

the descendants of Seth. The implication may be that Seth's descendants had a godly heritage while the women they married did not.

6. Angels do not marry. (See Matthew 22:30.) Some may say that only angels "in heaven" do not marry, but this assumes something that Jesus did not intend. The point is that angels are spirit-beings, and spirit-beings do not marry. Nothing in their defection from heaven would make angels anything other than spirit-beings. Descriptions of angels as "men" do not mean they are male. This is simply a description based on what is observable to the human senses. These descriptions are of godly angels who appeared to people at various times and places to communicate a divine message. As faithful angels, they still had a place "in heaven" and thus did not marry, even though the Bible describes them as "men."

7. Concerning the grammatical agreement of "these" (*toutois*) of verse 7 with the angels of verse 6, we can make the following observations: (a) The agreement may actually be with the "men" of verse 4 and "these dreamers" of verse 8. (b) Even if the antecedent of "these" is the angels of verse 6, the point may be that both the angels and the cities of Sodom and Gommorah are examples of God's judgment rather than examples of the same kind of sin.

8. The account in *I Enoch* seems to be a "Jewish fable." (See I Timothy 1:4; 4:7; II Timothy 4:4; Titus 1:14.) Without question, it reflects Jewish speculations from the era just before Christ. It has all the ingredients that might make a good science fiction story: angels becoming human, cohabiting with women, producing children over four hundred feet tall, and teaching all forms of magic and sorcery to the world. Could such a

thing happen again? If this were really the reason God destroyed the earth with a flood, and if it is the purpose of Satan and his angels to see the human race destroyed, why is this not happening today?

Whenever the sin of these angels occurred, the Epistle of Jude points it out to assure readers of the certainty of God's judgment upon false teachers. The sinning angels are "reserved in everlasting chains under darkness for the judgment of the great day" (NKJV). This is not a reference to literal chains. To qualify as "everlasting" the "chains" must be metaphorical; they describe the finality of the judgment. Nor are the fallen angels locked in a dark dungeon. The "darkness" in which they exist is spiritual darkness as opposed to the light of truth in which they formerly existed. (See comments on II Peter 2:4.)

The "great day" is a reference to the Day of the Lord, a term that refers to all of the events transpiring in conjunction with the second coming of Jesus. (See comments on II Peter 1:19.) In some way, believers will participate in judging fallen angels (I Corinthians 6:3).

C. The Judgment of Sodom and Gomorrah (7)

(7) Even as Sodom and Gomorrha, and the cities about them in like manner, giving themselves over to fornication, and going after strange flesh, are set forth for an example, suffering the vengeance of eternal fire.

Verse 7. The last of the three examples of the certainty of God's judgment on the false teachers is the destruction of Sodom and Gomorrah. It may be that Jude

Jude

intentionally arranges these examples out of chronological order to create an ascending scale: (1) physical death (verse 5); (2) darkness awaiting judgment (verse 6); (3) the finality of eternal fire (verse 7).[307]

The destruction of Sodom and Gomorrah was such a remarkable event that it became one of the most common examples of the judgment of God in biblical and apocryphal literature.[308] "The LORD rained brimstone and fire on Sodom and Gomorrah, from the LORD out of the heavens. So He overthrew those cities, all the plain, all the inhabitants of the cities, and what grew on the ground" (Genesis 19:24-25, NKJV). Jude does not mention Lot's escape from the destruction. (See, however, II Peter 2:6-8.)

Sodom and Gomorrah are usually the primary focus in this event, but other cities shared their fate. Jude refers to them as the cities around Sodom and Gomorrah. (See Jeremiah 49:18; 50:40.) These cities included Admah and Zeboiim (Deuteronomy 29:23). Another small city nearby, Zoar, was spared from destruction at Lot's request (Genesis 19:17-23).

When we consider the cause of the destruction of Sodom and Gomorrah, we usually focus on the rampant sexual immorality of the inhabitants of these cities. This is a legitimate observation, and it is, in fact, Jude's emphasis. But Sodom's sin was not limited to sexual immorality. It also included "pride, fullness of food, and abundance of idleness; neither did she strengthen the hand of the poor and needy" (Ezekiel 16:49, NKJV).

It is quite common today to focus almost exclusively on Sodom's sexual immorality, especially to draw parallels between the sin of this ancient community and the growing acceptance of the same sin in our day. But people often overlook the parallels between the broader scope of Sodom's sin and our day—especially when such sins arise within the community of believers. Somehow many do not perceive pride, excess, idleness, and a lack of concern for the economically deprived to be as significant as sexual perversion.

It is quite clear, however, that pride is a grievous sin. (See Proverbs 6:17; 8:13; 16:5, 18; Isaiah 28:1; James 4:6; I Peter 5:5; I John 2:16). The word translated "fullness of food" (*sib'ah*) includes the idea of being satiated or indulging to excess. It occurs also in Ecclesiastes in a condemnation of the rich whose abundance rules their lives to the extent they cannot sleep but who still refuse to share with others. (See Ecclesiastes 5:12-13.) Ezekiel's connection of "abundance" (*shalvah*) with "idleness" (*shaqat*) indicates that the people of Sodom were at ease in their prosperity. Oppression of the poor and needy is an abomination to God. (See Ezekiel 18:7, 12-13, 16.) What God desires far more than asceticism is that people would limit their personal consumption so as to be able to feed the hungry, house the homeless, and provide adequate clothing for those in need. (See Isaiah 58:7; Luke 16:19-31; I Timothy 5:8; James 2:15-16; 5:1-5.) God's hatred for the oppression of the poor is a frequent theme in Scripture.[309]

People of faith should vigorously resist the sin of sexual immorality, but they should not be apathetic toward the sins of pride, greed, materialism, excess, idleness, and neglect for the poor and needy. These, too, were the sins of Sodom.

The people of Sodom and Gomorrah and the surrounding cities abandoned themselves to sexual immorality. The word translated "giving themselves over to fornication" (*ekporneuo*) appears only here in the New Testament. It is

Jude

a compound word formed from the preposition *ek* and the more common *porneuo*. This rare word may suggest, by the addition of *ek* ("out of"), the meaning of "against the course of nature."[310] This idea is certainly contained in the statement that they went "after strange flesh." The word translated "strange" (*heteras*) means "a different kind." The idea here is a different kind than God intended."

The sexual sin of the Sodomites was a perversion that went beyond heterosexual immorality. The Sodomites lusted for homosexual encounters. This is apparent in their attempt to force Lot to hand over to them the angels (the Sodomites did not recognize them as angels) whom Lot was sheltering in his house.

Genesis 19:5-11 (NKJV) records the sordid account: "And they called to Lot and said to him, 'Where are the men who came to you tonight? Bring them out to us that we may know them carnally.' So Lot went out to them through the doorway, shut the door behind him, and said, 'Please, my brethren, do not do so wickedly! See now, I have two daughters who have not known a man; please, let me bring them out to you, and you may do to them as you wish; only do nothing to these men, since this is the reason they have come under the shadow of my roof.' And they said, 'Stand back!' Then they said, 'This one came in to stay here, and he keeps acting as a judge; now we will deal worse with you than with them.' So they pressed hard against the man Lot, and came near to break down the door. But the men reached out their hands and pulled Lot into the house with them, and shut the door. And they struck the men who were at the doorway of the house with blindness, both small and great, so that they became weary trying to find the door."

Homosexuality has been practiced from the early days of human history, but Scripture always identifies it as a sinful perversion. Scriptural evidence and historical records indicate that it thrives especially where there is great material prosperity and excess leisure time accompanied by self-centered arrogance. (See comments above on Ezekiel 16:49.)

Lot, a righteous man (II Peter 2:6-9), identified the sin of the Sodomites as wickedness (Genesis 19:7). He was willing to release his virgin daughters to these men for heterosexual abuse rather than to release his angelic visitors for homosexual abuse. Either would have been wrong, but Lot's offer indicates a hierarchy of values. He viewed homosexual activity as worse than heterosexual immorality.

The law of Moses identified homosexual behavior as an abomination: "You shall not lie with a male as with a woman. It is an abomination" (Leviticus 18:22, NKJV). Homosexual activity called for the death penalty: "If a man lies with a male as he lies with a woman, both of them have committed an abomination. They shall surely be put to death. Their blood shall be upon them" (Leviticus 20:13, NKJV). Although the death penalties of the Law of Moses ended with the termination of the Law, the seriousness of the sins that called for the death penalty has not diminished.

Homosexual conduct is an abomination (*to'ebah*, "detestable") because it runs counter to the order of creation. When God created the first two humans, He created them as male and female (Genesis 1:27). When God saw that it was not good for the man to be alone, He created a woman to complement him (Genesis 2:18, 22). God's purpose in this relationship included the man and woman being joined together to become "one flesh" (Genesis 2:24), a reference to the sexual relationship (I Corinthians 6:16). The word translated "woman" (*'ishshah*) is the feminine form of the word translated "man" (*'iysh*) in Genesis 2:23. God designed the male and female bodies to uniquely complement each other and enabled them to reproduce and perpetuate humanity. None of this is possible in a homosexual relationship.

The Old Testament is not alone in identifying homosexual behavior as a sin. In a discussion of the consequences of turning away from the knowledge of God, Romans 1:26-28 says, "For this reason God gave them up to vile passions. For even their women exchanged the natural use for what is against nature. Likewise also the men, leaving the natural use of the woman, burned in their lust for one another, men with men committing what is shameful, and receiving in themselves the penalty of their error which was due. And even as they did not like to retain God in their knowledge, God gave them over to a debased mind, to do those things which are not fitting" (NKJV). Some attempt to blunt the impact of this passage by suggesting that it is not a condemnation of homosexual behavior but only of promiscuous homosexual conduct. In other words, they do not believe it identifies a monogamous homosexual relationship as sinful. But this is simply not the meaning of the text. The Scripture condemns what is "against nature." This involves men "leaving the natural use of the woman" to burn in their lust for one another. It also involves women changing their "natural use." The heterosexual relationship is natural; the homosexual relationship is unnatural.

I Corinthians 6:9-10 identifies homosexual behavior as unrighteousness: "Do you not know that the unrighteous

Warnings from History

will not inherit the kingdom of God? Do not be deceived. Neither fornicators, nor idolaters, nor adulterers, nor homosexuals, nor sodomites, nor thieves, nor covetous, nor drunkards, nor revilers, nor extortioners will inherit the kingdom of God" (NKJV). The word "homosexuals" here comes from *malakos*. It denotes a boy kept for homosexual relations with a man, or a male who submits his body to unnatural lewdness; the idea is some kind of male prostitution. The word translated "sodomites" (*arsenokoites*) deals with homosexual behavior in the broadest sense. (See I Timothy 1:10, where the NKJV translates *arsenokoites* as "sodomites.") *Arsenokoites* reflects the language of the Septuagint in the prohibition of homosexual behavior. (See Leviticus 18:22; 20:13.)

Jude's use of the Sodom and Gomorrah account may suggest that the false teachers were, like those ancient people, practicing homosexuals. The phrase "in a similar manner to these" (NKJV) may refer to the false teachers rather than to the angels (verse 6), and Sodom and Gomorrah is "set forth as an example" (NKJV). But regardless of whether the false teachers practiced homosexuality, they definitely engaged in sexual immorality. (See verses 4, 8.)

The term "eternal fire" ordinarily refers to the final fate of the wicked. (See Matthew 18:8; 25:41; Revelation 14:10-11; 20:10; 14-15.) Here, it obviously does not mean the fires that destroyed Sodom and Gomorrah are still burning and that they will continue to burn for eternity; rather, "eternal fire" refers to the finality of the judgment that came on these cities. Moreover, this fire was a precursor of the judgment the inhabitants of those cities will suffer eternally.

Jude

It is true that homosexual behavior is a sin, but it is a sin from which people can be redeemed. Therefore, the Bible reveals that those who are inclined toward homosexual behavior can experience a radical change so that they are no longer so inclined. Following the identification of homosexual behavior as unrighteousness that will bar a person from the kingdom of God, Scripture continues, "And such were some of you. But you were washed, but you were sanctified, but you were justified in the name of the Lord Jesus and by the Spirit of our God" (I Corinthians 6:11, NKJV). The divine solution for the sin of homosexual conduct is the same as for every other sin: it is the redemption provided by Christ Jesus.

Believers who understand the sinfulness of homosexual conduct must not hate, or appear to hate, those who are caught in this destructive behavior. Nor should they imply that it is the worst possible sin that one could commit, or that there is no hope for those who are involved with it. Although the idea of homosexual behavior is no doubt repulsive to most heterosexuals, we must remember that God loves all people, regardless of their sin (John 3:16) and that the blood of Jesus provides redemption for the sin of the whole world, which certainly includes homosexuals (I John 2:2).

Those who are passionately opposed to homosexuality sometimes say, "If God does not judge America, He will have to apologize to Sodom and Gomorrah." We should keep in mind, however, that God would have spared Sodom and Gomorrah—as sinful as their conduct was—if only ten righteous people dwelt there (Genesis 18:26-32). Are there ten righteous people in America today? Even in cities where homosexual behavior is most rampant, are there ten righteous people?

We should also keep in mind that, according to Jesus, some people who did not engage in homosexual conduct will experience more severe judgment than those who did. Of those who rejected the preaching of the gospel in the first century, Jesus said, "Assuredly, I say to you, it will be more tolerable for the land of Sodom and Gomorrah in the day of judgment than for that city!" (Matthew 10:15, NKJV). (See Matthew 11:24; Mark 6:11; Luke 10:12). These statements indicate that there will be degrees of punishment based on degrees of revelation. Although sin cannot be overlooked in any case, those who had greater opportunity and who received greater revelation will be judged differently from those with less opportunity and less revelation. As Jesus said, "And that servant who knew his master's will, and did not prepare himself or do according to his will, shall be beaten with many stripes. But he who did not know, yet committed things deserving of stripes, shall be beaten with few. For everyone to whom much is given, from him much will be required; and to whom much has been committed, of him they will ask the more" (Luke 12:47-48, NKJV).

We cannot excuse homosexual behavior. But rather than lashing out in anger, fear, or ridicule against homosexuals, it is more appropriate to respond to the growing acceptance of this sin in the culture around us by examining ourselves for signs that we might have compromised our own integrity by condoning pride, greed, materialism, and oppression. Once we have examined ourselves, it is then appropriate to reach out in love to share the good news of the gospel with those who are trapped in the destructive bondage of a homosexual lifestyle.

IV

Characteristics of False Teachers (8-19)

The Epistle of Jude is quite specific in identifying the characteristics of the false teachers. Jesus taught concerning false prophets, "By their fruits you will know them" (Matthew 7:20, NKJV). Therefore, whenever we see any of these characteristics, we must assume that those who exhibit these traits are spiritually corrupt, and we must avoid their influence.

The false teachers of whom Jude wrote practiced sexual immorality, rebelled against authority, and spoke evil of glorious beings (8-10). Greedy and rebellious (11), they were empty of spiritual life (12-13). Their judgment was certain, having been foretold by Enoch (14-15). They grumbled, complained, did whatever they wanted, and flattered others to get what they wanted from them (16). The apostles had previously warned of this kind of people (17). They practiced mockery and did whatever their ungodly desires prompted them to do (18). They were sensual, not spiritual, and the result of their influence was division among believers (19).

A. They Defile the Flesh (8a)

(8a) Likewise also these filthy dreamers defile the flesh.

Jude

Verse 8a. The three previous examples of the certainty of God's judgment (verses 5-7) were appropriate for comparison with the sins of the false teachers. "Likewise" (*homoios*) indicates that the false teachers were guilty of the same kinds of sins as the Israelites who were destroyed for their unbelief (verse 5), the angels who rebelled against God (verse 6), and the inhabitants of Sodom, Gomorrah, and the surrounding cities who practiced sexual immorality (verse 7).

Neither the KJV nor the NKJV picks up the full force of the phrase *homoios mentoi kai*, translated "likewise also." *Homoios* does mean "likewise," and *kai* means "also," but *mentoi* indicates that the false teachers engaged in their sins in spite of having such clear historical examples of the certainty of God's judgment on those who do such things. *Mentoi* means something like "but yet." The full sense of the verse, including the significance of *mentoi*, would be: "Yet these dreamers also likewise defile the flesh, despise authority, and speak evil of glorious beings."[311]

The KJV inserts the word "filthy"—which is not in the Greek text—to describe the "dreamers." The translators may have been influenced by the contextual reference to the inhabitants of Sodom, Gomorrah, and the surrounding cities who were sexually immorality (verse 7).

The reference to the false teachers as "dreamers" (from *enupniazomai*) could suggest that they entertained impure fantasies, but that seems unlikely since these dreamers not only defiled the flesh but they also rejected authority and spoke evil of glorious beings. If their dreams were about immorality, they were also about the rejection of authority and speaking evil.[312] The only other time the word translated "dreamers" appears in the

Characteristics of False Teachers

New Testament is in Acts 2:17, where it describes old men who dream under the influence of the Holy Spirit. The Septuagint uses the word to refer to false prophets who claim to have divinely inspired dreams. (See Deuteronomy 13:1-2, 5-6; Jeremiah 23:25.)

It seems better to understand the description of the false teachers as "dreamers" to allude to their erroneous claim to divine authority for their doctrine. That is, like the false prophets of the Old Testament, they pretended to dream under divine influence.

Apparently these false teachers appealed to their "dreams" as justification for their sexual immorality. They "defile[d] the flesh." The contextual reference may mean that they engaged in homosexual conduct, like the people of Sodom, Gomorrah, and the surrounding cities (verse 7). Although we may not be sure that their sexual immorality was the same as that of the Sodomites, it is certain that they—like their counterparts in II Peter 2:10, 14, 18—"pollute[d] their own bodies" (NIV). Such pollution occurs when people engage in sexual activity outside the covenant bonds of marriage. (See Hebrews 13:4.[313])

B. They Reject Authority (8b)

(8b) Despise dominion.

Verse 8b. The words translated "despise dominion" (*kurioteta de athetousin*) suggest that the false teachers rejected the lordship of Jesus Christ. The word *kurioteta* is related to *kurios*, which means "Lord" and is used of Jesus in verse 4, where the false teachers are said to deny Him. Some commentators have suggested that the false teachers despised civil authority, religious authority, angelic authority, or authority in general—and all of that is no doubt true—but the contextual indication is that they specifically rejected any claim of Jesus to be the Lord of their lives. Their rejection of His authority was evident in the hedonistic, self-indulgent lifestyle they embraced.

C. They Speak Evil of Dignitaries (8c-10)

(8c) And speak evil of dignities. (9) Yet Michael the archangel, when contending with the devil he disputed about the body of Moses, durst not bring against him a railing accusation, but said, The Lord rebuke thee. (10) But these speak evil of those things which they know not: but what they know naturally, as brute beasts, in those things they corrupt themselves.

Verse 8c. "Dignities" is translated from *doxas*, a word that means "glories." The NIV translates the word as "celestial beings." The NLT translates it as "glorious ones," indicating in a footnote that these "*glorious ones* are probably evil angels." It may seem strange to think of fallen angels (as in verse 6) as "glorious ones," but the contextual influence of verse 9 is an indicator that this is the case. (See II Peter 2:10, where *doxas* is translated "dignities," as here.) Though fallen, "evil angels still bear the impress of their glorious creation and original status, and they should not be treated lightly."[314] If the false teachers were not speaking evil of fallen angels, they might have been mocking the idea of angels altogether, like the Sadducees (Acts 23:8); or they may have claimed that angels served an inferior god, like some Gnostics; or

Characteristics of False Teachers

they may have minimized the idea of a coming judgment in which angels had an important role, as taught in the Old Testament and in Jewish tradition.[315] Another view suggests that by rejecting God's moral order, the false teachers' slander of angels "probably relates to the angels' function as mediators of the law of Moses."[316] But all of these possibilities seem unlikely in view of the connection between verses 8 and 9.

The word translated "speak evil" (*blasphemousin*) is a form of the word sometimes transliterated "blasphemy" or "blaspheme." As indicated here, the word means "to speak evil." (See Matthew 9:3; 26:65; 27:39 [where it is translated "reviled"]; Mark 3:28-29; Acts 13:45; 18:6; 26:11; Romans 2:24; 3:8 [where it is translated "slanderously reported"]; 14:16; I Timothy 1:20.) Verse 9 provides an example of how Michael the archangel avoided blasphemy.

Verse 9. Here is the fascinating account of an event not recorded in the Old Testament but preserved in Jewish tradition and in the pseudepigraphical *Assumption of Moses*, a first-century work that exists today only in a corrupt and incomplete version.[317] In the story, after Moses' death and burial (see Deuteronomy 34:5-6), Satan asserted his right to the body since Moses had murdered a man, thus making him a murderer in spite of all the good he did later in life, and because of Satan's supposed ownership of all material things. Satan, the accuser of God's people (Revelation 12:10), sought to prove his right to Moses' body. Hillyer pointed out:

> The terms used in this passage are forensic, the language of the courtroom. . . . Satan . . . "slandered" . . . Moses by accusing him of murder. Michael, in his

Jude

> capacity as a legal advocate, refuted the slander . . . and appealed to God for judgment against Satan. . . . Michael refused to take it upon himself to pronounce judgment, for that was God's prerogative.[318]

We may question whether the Epistle of Jude presents this account as actual history or whether it simply draws an illustration from popular folklore.[319] We should note, however, that it tells the story as an actual historical account, and this is at the direction of the Holy Spirit. We should also note that some events in the history of Israel were not recorded in the Old Testament but that were passed down by oral tradition, tradition proven accurate by the New Testament. An example is the tradition that the law of Moses was given on Sinai by angels. The Old Testament never mentions this, but the New Testament confirms it. (See Acts 7:38; Galatians 3:19; Hebrews 2:2.) There is no reason that this account could not fall into the same category.

Whatever we may think of the story itself, we must not miss the reason for its inclusion at this point. The story serves as a deterrent to the practice of the false teachers, who spoke evil of glorious beings, apparently angels. (See comments on verse 8.) Since Michael, an angel of the highest rank (*archangelos* means "top angel" or "head angel"), did not dare speak evil (*blasphemias*) of the devil and instead deferred the devil's judgment to the Lord, how much more should humans refrain from speaking evil of angels, including even those that are fallen. (See verse 10.) As Barclay has pointed out, "If the greatest of the good angels refused to speak evil of the greatest of the evil angels, even in circumstances like that, surely no human being may speak evil of any

Characteristics of False Teachers

angel."[320] This view finds support in the parallel reference in II Peter 2:10-11. For a similar account where the angel of the Lord deferred the judgment of Satan to the Lord Himself, see Zechariah 3:1-2.

One reason it is always inappropriate for humans to pass judgment is that judgment is God's prerogative. (See John 5:22; Romans 1:32; 14:10; Hebrews 6:2; II Peter 2:4; Jude 6.) Although believers will somehow participate in judging angels (I Corinthians 6:3), that event is yet future and it will be under God's direction. Although judgment may very well be deserved, when a human presumes to pass judgment he is usurping a divine right. A claim to be qualified to judge is a claim to deity, a claim to be God. The only one qualified to judge is one who is completely innocent, and God alone is in that category.

We may wonder what significance Jude's warning has for believers involved in spiritual warfare, including the casting out of evil spirits. A review of all of the references to Satan, the devil, or demons in the New Testament indicates that spiritual warfare is not characterized by believers speaking evil of Satan or demons. Even in His encounter with Satan following his forty days of fasting, Jesus did not speak evil of Satan. Instead, He countered Satan's temptations with truth, with the written Scriptures. (See Matthew 4:1-11; Luke 4:1-13.)

This is the pattern for spiritual warfare. Believers resist Satan by rejecting his lies and by relying on truth. (See II Corinthians 10:4-5; Ephesians 6:12-18.) When they cast out evil spirits, believers do so in the name of Jesus, which means they do it only by His authority and in His stead. (See Luke 10:17-19; Mark 16:17.) Believers are not to rejoice because spirits are subject to them; this

Jude

would be the wrong focus. They are to rejoice because their names are written in heaven (Luke 10:20). Anyone who would cast out spirits must be sure he does so on the basis of his personal relationship with Jesus and at His direction. (See Acts 19:13-16.)

Michael is the only archangel identified in Scripture. (See I Thessalonians 4:16; Revelation 12:7.) The Book of Daniel describes Michael as "one of the chief princes" and the prince of the people of Israel (Daniel 10:13, 21; 12:1). His name means "who is like God?" The existence of an archangel indicates some kind of hierarchy in the angelic realm, a hierarchy that could extend even to the realm of fallen angels.

The devil's interest in the body of Moses indicates the holistic biblical view of human existence. The biblical mind, unlike the Greek perspective that has so influenced the Western world, did not divide the material and immaterial realms of human existence so sharply as to render the material insignificant. This is reflected in the biblical teaching of the bodily resurrection. Satan understood the significance of the human body and was willing to contend with Michael, the most powerful of the faithful angels, for his alleged right to it. He was refused, of course, demonstrating that even the inanimate body is of great significance to God, for it awaits reunion with the human spirit on the great resurrection day.[321]

Verse 10. A close parallel to this verse occurs in II Peter 2:12: "But these, as natural brute beasts, made to be taken and destroyed, speak evil of the things that they understand not; and shall utterly perish in their own corruption." Both Jude and II Peter begin with "but these" (*houtoi de*), contrasting the false teachers, who speak evil, with the

Characteristics of False Teachers

angels and specifically Michael, who refuse to speak evil. Both Jude and II Peter compare the false teachers to "brute beasts" (*aloga zoa*). Both letters describe the corruption that false teachers bring on themselves.

These false teachers "speak evil of those things which they know not." The immediate context suggests that what they do not understand is the role of angels in the divine economy. It may seem strange that anyone associated with first-century believers would have a flawed view of the angelic realm, but perhaps this should not be surprising, for some in the Corinthian church denied such a fundamental of the Christian faith as the resurrection of the dead. (See I Corinthians 15:12.) Other professing Christians said the resurrection had already occurred. (See II Timothy 2:18.) It is just as likely that there would be error concerning the spiritual realm in the first century as today.

The only knowledge these false teachers possessed—natural knowledge—failed to lift them above the realm of "brute beasts," or unreasoning animals. They had no more sense of virtue and morality than an animal does. But since they were humans, not animals, their animalistic behavior would destroy them.

Spiritual truth is beyond the grasp of those who are merely "natural." (I Corinthians 2:14-16.) And in spite of their claims to dreams and special knowledge, these false teachers were merely natural, for they were without the Spirit (verse 19).

D. They Are Greedy and Rebellious (11)

(11) Woe unto them! for they have gone in the way of Cain, and ran greedily after the error of Balaam

Jude

for reward, and perished in the gainsaying of Core.

Verse 11. The use of "woe" to pronounce judgment has its origins with the Old Testament prophets. (See Isaiah 3:11.) Jesus also used it in His denunciation of those who rejected His messianic claims. (See Matthew 11:21.) The English "woe" is transliterated from the Greek *ouai,* which is in turn transliterated from the Hebrew *'owy*. The Hebrew word is probably derived from *'avah,* which can include the meaning "to sigh." "Woe" indicates dismay and resignation to the certainty of judgment.

Just as Jude offers three examples of the certainty of judgment upon these false teachers (see verses 5-7), so it offers three examples of the kind of sins in which they engaged. First, "they have gone in the way of Cain." This statement brings to mind the murder of Abel by his brother, Cain. (See Genesis 4:3-16.) Since Jude does not specify what is the "way of Cain," we may speculate from various statements about Cain in Scripture or Jewish tradition.

The "way of Cain" may refer to Cain's murderous act, driven by his apparent envy for his brother. (See I John 3:12.) In this case, the false teachers are murderers of the souls of people of faith.[322]

Or perhaps the reference is to Cain's inferior sacrifice, a consequence of his lack of faith. (See Hebrews 11:4.) Just as Cain invented his own religion, a "religion of his own works without faith,"[323] so these false teachers "manufacture[d] religion, and kill[ed] the souls of men by error."[324]

Another possibility is that the "way of Cain" comes

Characteristics of False Teachers

from Jewish tradition in the first century, similar to the references to events recorded in *Assumption of Moses* and *I Enoch*. In one Jewish tradition, "Cain became a classic example of an ungodly skeptic."[325] In its Aramaic paraphrase of the Pentateuch, the Jerusalem Targum has Cain saying, "There is no judgment, no judge, no future life; no reward will be given to the righteous, and no judgment will be imposed on the wicked."[326] In this case, Jude may have cited Cain "to reinforce his accusation of the false teachers as being rejecters of authority and blasphemers."[327]

Josephus recorded another Jewish tradition about Cain as one who "incited to luxury and pillage all whom he met, and became their instructor in wicked practices."[328] In this case, Jude's focus is on the content of the teaching given by the false teachers.

Regardless of which, if any, of these ideas is the primary meaning of the "way of Cain," "one who takes the attitude of a Cain feels free to do as he or she likes, and Cain's example misleads others: Cain is the archetypal false teacher."[329]

Second, these false teachers "ran greedily after the error of Balaam for reward." II Peter does not mention Cain or Korah, but it does compare false teachers to Balaam: "Which have forsaken the right way, and are gone astray, following the way of Balaam the son of Bosor, who loved the wages of unrighteousness" (II Peter 2:15).

It may be possible to distinguish between the "way of Balaam," the "error of Balaam," and the "doctrine of Balaam" (Revelation 2:14). It may be that the "way of Balaam" is the way of a hireling prophet who seeks to

245

Jude

profit from his gift.[330] The "error of Balaam" may be that he reasoned from natural morality and supposed God would have to curse Israel because of the evil among the people.[331] The "doctrine of Balaam" seems to be "his teaching Balak to corrupt the people who could not be cursed."[332] By his teaching, Balaam was able to set in motion a chain of events that would lead to God's judgment of Israel for their sin. (See Numbers 22-25; 31:16.)

If it is possible to distinguish between Balaam's "way," his "error" and his "doctrine," it is nevertheless true that these false teachers "ran greedily" (i.e., "they were poured out" or "they plunged"[333]) after the error of Balaam "for profit." It was not uncommon in the first century for traveling teachers to teach whatever they could be paid to teach.[334] It was not unknown for false teachers to infiltrate the Christian community for the purpose of profiting from their teaching. (See Titus 1:10-11.)

As Westcott pointed out, the word translated "error" (*plane*) always has the idea of "straying from the one way; not of misconception in itself but of misconduct (as in Rom. 1. 27). Such going astray is essentially ruinous."[335] (See also Ephesians 4:14, where *plane* is translated "cunning"; I Thessalonians 2:3, where it is translated "deceit"; James 5:20; II Peter 2:18; 3:17.) As Blum has pointed out, "Balaam was the prototype of all greedy religionists who lead God's people into false religion and immorality."[336]

The third comparison Jude makes with the false teachers has to do with Korah, a Levite who rose up in a conspiracy against Moses and Aaron. (See Numbers 16.) The essence of Korah's rebellion was his discontentment with his responsibilities as a Levite and his desire to intrude into the priesthood. (See Numbers 16:10.) The priesthood was an honor that no one could take unto himself (Hebrews 5:4). The judgment of God upon Korah and his co-conspirators was swift: the earth opened beneath their feet, swallowing them. God destroyed by fire 250 others who had identified with them in their rebellion. (See Numbers 26:9-10; Psalm 106:16-18.)

This reference to Korah may illustrate that the false teachers had been discontent with their place in the life of the church and had rejected God-ordained authority in an attempt to exalt themselves to a position for which they were not gifted. If so, they were not the only ones in the first century to practice self-promotion. John wrote of Diotrephes, "who loves to have the preeminence" (III John 9, NKJV). Self-promotion is always wrong; God resists the proud, but He gives grace to the humble (James 4:6).

It may be, on the other hand, that Jude was influenced here, as elsewhere, by Jewish tradition circulating in the first century. If so, it may refer to Korah as "the classic example of the antinomian [one who is against law] heretic."[337] As one who rejected God's ordained ruler, Korah was in essence rejecting God Himself, and thus the law given by God through Moses. The false teachers had rejected any external authority; they were a law unto themselves.

Jude describes the false teachers as already having perished. This may reflect the prophetic perfect in the Hebrew language, in which prophesied events are spoken of as having already occurred to emphasize their certainty.[338] There was no question: since the false teachers had embarked on a destructive path, they would be destroyed.

Jude

E. They Are Spiritually Empty (12-13)

(12) These are spots in your feasts of charity, when they feast with you, feeding themselves without fear: clouds they are without water, carried about of winds; trees whose fruit withereth, without fruit, twice dead, plucked up by the roots; (13) raging waves of the sea, foaming out their own shame; wandering stars, to whom is reserved the blackness of darkness for ever.

Verse 12. A parallel to this verse appears in II Peter 2:13b: "They are spots and blemishes, carousing in their own deceptions while they feast with you" (NKJV). (See comments on II Peter 2:13.) Jude uses the word "these" six times as a kind of derogatory way to describe the false teachers. (See verses 8, 10, 14, 16, 19.)

The house churches of the first century commonly held "feasts of charity," or "love feasts" as a prelude to the Lord's Supper. Believers would bring food to share with others, as is still often the practice at the social events of today's church. These feasts were to be uplifting events where all believers, regardless of social standing, shared equally in the celebration of Christian love.

The abuse of the love feasts began early (see I Corinthians 11:17-22, 33-34), as arrogant, self-centered, and drunken people infiltrated the celebrations. Among these were false teachers, like those in Jude and II Peter, whose agenda included more than merely satisfying their physical hunger. It was their intent to introduce error and to persuade believers to follow them.

The word translated "spots" in the KJV (*spilades*)

Characteristics of False Teachers

appears only here in the New Testament. It is a different word from what appears in II Peter 2:13 (*spiloi*), which means "spots." Translators are divided on whether *spilades* here means "rocks" or "sunken rocks," as in secular Greek, or "spots," as used at least by the fourth century.[339] Regardless of whether the false teachers were dangerous reefs that could shipwreck the unwary (see I Timothy 1:19) or blemishes in an otherwise holy celebration, the image is a powerful warning. If they were sunken rocks, the believers needed to steer clear of them. If they were blemishes on the love feasts, they needed to be purged from the feasts.

The description of the false teachers as "feeding themselves" evokes the idea of a shepherd who has betrayed his trust. The word translated "feeding" (*poimainontes*) is from a word frequently translated "shepherd" and, in Ephesians 4:11, "pastor" (*poimen*). The shepherd's responsibility is to "feed [*poimanate*] the flock of God" (I Peter 5:2). The implication is that these false teachers were renegade shepherds, or pastors; God had called them to provide nourishment for the people of God by feeding them good, wholesome spiritual food, but they had deserted their duty and were now engaged in self-indulgence.

At this point, Jude may reflect Ezekiel's warning to the faithless shepherds of Israel: "Therefore, you shepherds, hear the word of the LORD: 'As I live,' says the Lord GOD, 'surely because My flock became a prey, and My flock became food for every beast of the field, because there was no shepherd, nor did My shepherds search for My flock, but the shepherds fed themselves and did not feed My flock'—therefore, O shepherds, hear the word of

Jude

the LORD! Thus says the Lord GOD: 'Behold, I am against the shepherds, and I will require My flock at their hand; I will cause them to cease feeding the sheep, and the shepherds shall feed themselves no more; for I will deliver My flock from their mouths, that they may no longer be food for them'" (Ezekiel 34:7-10, NKJV). Just as the shepherds in Ezekiel's day fed themselves while neglecting the flock, so the false teachers in the first century turned inward, caring only for themselves and nothing for the people of God.

The Greek text here could be translated "feeding themselves without fear," as in the KJV, or "feast[ing] with you without fear," as in the NKJV. The latter translation is probably preferable. These false teachers had no fear of engaging in the love feasts. They were so spiritually dull that the danger of their hypocrisy did not occur to them. The love feasts portrayed the purity, love, and solidarity of the Christian community. Everything the false teachers did and taught was contrary to this. It apparently did not occur to them that their abuse of a sacred practice put them in danger—as it did those who practiced similar abuse in Corinth—of weakness, sickness, and even premature death. (See I Corinthians 11:30.)

Beginning in this verse and continuing through verse 13, Jude portrays the false teachers by a series of four negative examples drawn from the natural realm. These examples are the sky ("clouds they are without water, carried about of winds"), the earth ("trees whose fruit withereth, without fruit, twice dead, plucked up by the roots"), the sea ("raging waves of the sea, foaming out their own shame"), and the heavens ("wandering stars, to whom is reserved the blackness of darkness for ever").

These examples indicate the emptiness of the false teachers' promise of spiritual nourishment, their spiritual deadness, their spiritual instability, and the certainty of their eternal destiny.

To describe the false teachers as "clouds without water, carried about by the winds" (NKJV) suggests that they promise something they do not deliver. In a parallel description, II Peter 2:17 says, "These are wells without water, clouds carried by a tempest, for whom is reserved the blackness of darkness forever" (NKJV). Apparently continuing further with this imagery, II Peter 2:18 continues, "For when they speak great swelling words of emptiness . . ." (NKJV). Like clouds that give the farmer the promise of rain, the false teachers "speak great swelling words." But these words turn out to be empty; there is no rain in the clouds. Instead of providing the moisture needed to produce a crop, these empty clouds blow on by.

This description may an allusion to a proverb: "Whoever falsely boasts of giving is like clouds and wind without rain" (Proverbs 25:14, NKJV). Green's comment at this point is perceptive: "Here is a graphic example of the uselessness of teaching which is supposedly 'advanced' and 'enlightened' but has nothing to offer the ordinary Christian for the nourishment of his spiritual life."[340] False teachers who make great boasts about receiving new revelations or about having discovered "deeper truths" have ever been the bane of Christianity. Something about human nature is intrigued by the idea of secret information and about the prospect of being part of an elite group that has been favored with superior knowledge. It is this kind of deception that gave rise to the Gnostic movements in early Christianity and that has

Jude

continued to fuel destructive error to this day.

The KJV translates the next description of the false teachers as "trees whose fruit withereth, without fruit, twice dead, plucked up by the roots." Uncertainty about the meaning of *phthinoporina*, translated "whose fruit withereth" by the KJV, has given rise to alternate translations like the NKJV's "late autumn trees without fruit." The word is from a derivative of *phthino*, which means "to wane," and *opora*, which has to do with the autumn season. The point may be that these trees have had the entire season for produce; their branches should be heavy with fruit, but they are barren. This illustration is like the previous one: the false teachers are not only clouds without water, they are also trees without fruit.

But not only are these "trees" fruitless, they are also "twice dead, plucked up by the roots." Because they are barren, they have been uprooted. This description implies that these trees had once been rooted. They had the opportunity to produce fruit. As those who had once been shepherds (see comments above), they had once had, in a different metaphor, spiritual life surging through their branches. Because they had neglected the kind of spiritual growth described in II Peter 1:5-7, they had become "barren [and] unfruitful" (II Peter 1:8). As Green pointed out, "They are called *twice dead* and *plucked up by the roots* because they had once been 'dead in trespasses and sins' (Eph. ii. 1) and were now dead again, in the sense that they were cut off from their life-giving root, Jesus Christ."[341]

Moo recognized the possibility of this meaning: "They were once 'dead' in their transgressions and sins (Eph. 2:1) but were made alive in Christ. Now, however, by

Characteristics of False Teachers

rebelling against the Lord, they have slid back into the state of spiritual death (see, e.g., Heb. 6:4-8; 2 Peter 2:18-22)."[342] He suggested, however, that the first death of these false teachers is their physical death and their second death is the one at the final judgment. (See Revelation 2:11; 20:6, 14; 21:8.) The first view recognizes that it is possible for a person to lose his salvation; the second view is favored by those who think it is impossible for a person to lose his salvation.

The first view is correct, for Jude describes the condition of the false teachers as something that already exists, not as something that will happen in the future. At the writing of Jude, the false teachers were already "twice dead" and "plucked up by the roots." Like the false teachers in II Peter, these false teachers had once "escaped the pollutions of the world through the knowledge of the Lord and Savior Jesus Christ," but they were "again entangled in them and overcome" (II Peter 2:20, NKJV). It "would have been better for them not to have known the way of righteousness, than having known it, to turn from the holy commandment delivered to them" (II Peter 2:21, NKJV).

The uprooting of trees is a metaphor for judgment in the Old Testament. (See Psalm 52:5; Proverbs 2:22.) On the other hand, a tree whose roots grow deep is a metaphor for spiritual health. (See Psalm 1:3.)

Verse 13. In another metaphor, the false teachers were "raging waves of the sea, foaming out their own shame." These words remind us of Isaiah's description of the wicked: "But the wicked are like the troubled sea, when it cannot rest, whose waters cast up mire and dirt" (Isaiah 57:20). James used the image of "a wave of the sea driven and tossed by the wind" to describe those who

Jude

are double-minded and unstable (James 1:6-8).[343] Jude's use of this image indicates the false teachers' dangerous instability. As Blum pointed out, "For modern man, the sea is often a thing of beauty; to ancient man, less able to cope with the sea's fury, it was a terror."[344] Just as a sailor would want to avoid the sea in the midst of a violent storm, so believers should avoid the influence of false teachers.

The word translated "foam out" (*epaphrizo*) appears only here in the New Testament. It is a rare word used in secular Greek "of the seaweed and other rubbish borne on the crest of the wave and then deposited on the beach."[345] The result of the false teachers' apostasy in their lifestyle and teaching was like filthy scum washed up on the seashore; it shamed them. The word translated "shame" (*aischunas*) is plural; they were guilty of a broad spectrum of shameful deeds and doctrines.

The final image Jude uses here describes the false teachers as "wandering stars, to whom is reserved the blackness of darkness for ever." II Peter 2:17 has a virtually identical phrase, although it does not use the star imagery. To say that the false teachers were "wandering stars" reflects the ancient view of the planets as wandering through the heavens with no discernible pattern of movement. In a word, they were unpredictable.[346] Since their movements were—so far as they could tell—unpredictable, sailors could not safely chart their course by them. This metaphor builds on the previous image of the false teachers as "raging waves of the sea" and possibly on the meaning of "sunken rocks" for *spilades* in verse 12. When we compare the Christian life to the life of a seafarer, the false teachers are as dangerous as hidden

Characteristics of False Teachers

rocks, as unstable as raging waves, and as unhelpful as wandering stars.

The eternal doom of the false teachers is certain. To them "is reserved the blackness of darkness for ever." (See comments on II Peter 2:17.) Darkness is often an image of the destiny awaiting those who have rebelled against God (see Matthew 8:12; 22:13), as is the better known "everlasting fire" or "lake of fire." (See Matthew 25:30, 41; Revelation 20:10, 15.) Although we may not be able to know the precise significance of the images of "darkness" and "fire," we may be sure they accurately reflect the unspeakable horror of an eternity without God. "The Lord Jesus [will be] revealed from heaven with His mighty angels, in flaming fire taking vengeance on those who do not know God, and on those who do not obey the gospel of our Lord Jesus Christ. These shall be punished with everlasting destruction from the presence of the Lord and from the glory of His power" (II Thessalonians 1:7-9, NKJV).

F. They Face Certain Judgment (14-15)

(14) And Enoch also, the seventh from Adam, prophesied of these, saying, Behold, the Lord cometh with ten thousands of his saints, (15) to execute judgment upon all, and to convince all that are ungodly among them of all their ungodly deeds which they have ungodly committed, and of all their hard speeches which ungodly sinners have spoken against him.

Verse 14. At this point, commentators generally conclude that Jude quoted from the pseudepigraphical book,

I Enoch, written during the early first century B.C. (c. 95 B.C.). *I Enoch* was well-known among the Jewish people during the first century A.D. (See comments on verse 6 and under "Inspiration and Place in the Canon" and "Original Audience.") This may be the case, although Jude could simply have referred to a common oral tradition that was included in *I Enoch*. In some cases, Jewish tradition accurately preserved information not found in the Old Testament Scriptures.

This would not be the only place where the New Testament legitimizes Jewish traditions not found in the Old Testament. Another example is the tradition that angels were involved in the giving of the law, an idea not found in the Old Testament, but endorsed three times in the New Testament. (See Acts 7:38; Galatians 3:19; Hebrews 2:2). Other instances of the New Testament lending credibility to Jewish traditions include Paul's allusion to rabbinic midrash (typological interpretation) in I Corinthians 10:4; the identification in II Timothy 3:8 of the Egyptian magicians who opposed Moses as Jannes and Jambres—from Jewish *haggadah* on Exodus 7:11; the reference to Moses in Acts 7:22; the reference to Elijah in James 5:17; and the identification of persecuted believers in Hebrews 11:37.[347]

Not only did Paul endorse Jewish tradition when it was true and suited his purpose; he also quoted pagan poets when their statements were true and useful. In Acts 17:28, Paul quoted Cleanthes and Aratus. In I Corinthians 15:33, he quoted Menander. In Titus 1:12, Paul quoted Epimenides.[348]

It is not problematic that inspired writers would quote uninspired writers. Neither should we think that by quot-

Characteristics of False Teachers

ing someone, inspired writers conferred inspiration on the person they quoted. The writers of Scripture, though inspired by God, were people of their times. They used illustrations and information well-known to their readers to make a point, just as writers and speakers do today. Inspiration means that what they wrote has authoritative status; even if it includes material from noninspired sources, it is accurate and trustworthy.

I Enoch was originally written in the Aramaic language, but only fragments remain in that language today. The entire text is found in the Ethiopic language, with portions in Greek and Latin translations. Whatever version existed in Jude's day, he apparently did his own translation into Greek.[349] As translated by Laurence, the relevant verse reads as follows: "Behold, he comes with ten thousands of his saints, to execute judgment upon them, and destroy the wicked, and reprove all the carnal for everything which the sinful and ungodly have done, and committed against him."[350]

Enoch was a man of faith who "walked with God" and "was not; for God took him" (Genesis 5:24). As the writer of Hebrews described this event, "Enoch was taken away so that he did not see death, 'and was not found, because God had taken him'; for before he was taken he had this testimony, that he pleased God" (Hebrews 11:5, NKJV). Luke 3:37 also mentions Enoch in the lineage of Christ.

Enoch was "the seventh from Adam." It was the Jewish custom to count inclusively, so that beginning with Adam as the first and including Enoch, Enoch is the seventh. (See Genesis 5:1-19; I Chronicles 1:1-3; Luke 3:37-38.) In Jewish thought, the number seven was the number of perfect completion. Enoch's status as the seventh

Jude

thus gave added weight to his prophecy.[351]

Although Jude never identifies *I Enoch* as Scripture, it does declare that Enoch prophesied. To prophesy is to speak authoritatively on behalf of God. (See Exodus 7:1.) Holy men uttered many prophecies during the Old Testament era that were never written down by those who uttered them; this is one of them.

When Jude declares that Enoch "prophesied of these," it obviously means "prophesied of these false teachers." Did Enoch have these specific false teachers in mind, or does Enoch's prophecy simply include all who will one day stand before God to give an account for their rebellious words and deeds? Apparently Enoch's prophecy reaches to all who fit his description in any age.

In its original form, Enoch's prophecy no doubt had "God" or "LORD" (*Yahweh*) as the subject; Jude sees this as fulfilled in the second coming of Jesus.[352] The "saints" with whom He is coming are "holy ones" (*hagiais*). This is a reference to the angelic host. (See Matthew 16:27; 25:31; Mark 8:38; Luke 9:26; II Thessalonians 1:7.) The word translated "ten thousands" (*myriasin*) does not refer to a literal number. It is translated variously in the KJV as "ten thousand times ten thousand," "innumerable multitude," "innumerable company," and "thousands." As the word from which the English "myriad" is derived, *myrias* refers to a vast host that is, from a human perspective, innumerable.

Verse 15. Included in the purpose of the Lord's coming is to "execute judgment on all" and to "convict all" (NKJV) who are ungodly. For emphasis, Jude uses a form of the word "ungodly" (*asebeia*) four times in this verse. *Asebeia* indicates a lack of reverence for God. The judgment of God upon these irreverent people will be not only for their ungodly deeds but also for their ungodly words. Jude agrees with the general teaching of Scripture on this subject: there is coming a day when every person will stand before God for judgment. Those who have done evil will be condemned; those who have done well will enter into eternal life. (See John 5:25-29; Acts 24:15.) All people will die. And after death, all will face judgment. (See Hebrews 9:27.)[353]

G. They Are Grumblers and Complainers (16a)

(16a) These are murmurers, complainers.

Verse 16a. The word translated "murmurers" (*goggustai*) occurs only here in the New Testament. The word does appear in the Septuagint to describe the murmuring of the Israelites against God for having brought them out of Egypt into the desert. (See Exodus 15:24; 16:7-12; 17:3; Numbers 14:27-29; 17:5, 10.) Paul used a related word to describe the same event. (See I Corinthians 10:10.) The use of the word elsewhere indicates that it specifically involves murmuring against God. Just as the Israelites were delivered from Egypt, so these false teachers had been redeemed. But just as the Israelites grew discontent with their deliverance, so these false teachers found fault with their new life and turned against the Lord who had saved them.

Not only were the false teachers murmurers; they were also complainers. In the first-century world, the complainer (*mempsimoiros*) was a standard Greek character who was always cursing his lot in life, somewhat like

Jude

The Born Loser in American comics.[354] Rather than learning contentment (see Philippians 4:11; I Timothy 6:8; Hebrews 13:5), these false teachers continually bemoaned their fate. Nothing ever turned out right for them.

H. They Walk according to Their Own Lusts (16b)

(16b) Walking after their own lusts.

Verse 16b. The false teachers went where their desires took them. This phrase could be translated "they live by their passions."[355] The contextual indication is that these passions include both lust and greed.[356] (See verses 8, 10-11.) These were first-century examples of those who did as they pleased; no one could tell them what to do. This is no different from the twenty-first century's tendency for radical individualism, at least in the Western world. Where individualism prevails, hedonism is not far behind. And self-indulgence is a sure path to self-destruction.

I. They Practice Flattery (16c)

(16c) And their mouth speaketh great swelling words, having men's persons in admiration because of advantage.

Verse 16c. One possible translation of this phrase is "their mouth talks big."[357] This is a wonderful way to describe the arrogant boasting of the false teachers. The context suggests that their boasting is against God Himself.[358] They may have grumbled and complained, but they had no shortage of words to declare their personal greatness and their lofty intentions. II Peter 2:18 uses the same terminology, stating that false teachers "speak great swelling words of emptiness" (NKJV). The word translated "great swelling" (*hyperonka*) means "of excessive bulk" or "swollen beyond natural size."[359] The false teachers were quite creative at knowing how to elicit sympathy by bemoaning their fate while at the same time puffing themselves up into something they were not.

The final description Jude gives of the false teachers is that of "flattering people to gain advantage" (NKJV). This is a sin that Scripture repeatedly condemns. (See Leviticus 19:15; Deuteronomy 10:17; Proverbs 24:23; Amos 5:12; James 2:1.) Flattery is always seen in a negative light. (See Proverbs 2:16; 6:24; 7:5; 20:19; 28:23; 29:5.) Flattery may appeal to the fallen nature with its craving for stature and admiration, but the problem with flattery is the same as always: those who flatter seek to take advantage of those they puff up. Flattery is simply a way of breaking down natural defenses against deception and loss. For this reason, the false teachers used flattery as a part of their arsenal in an attempt to win people to their side.

J. They Are Sensual (17-18)

(17) But, beloved, remember ye the words which were spoken before of the apostles of our Lord Jesus Christ; (18) how that they told you there should be mockers in the last time, who should walk after their own ungodly lusts.

Jude

Verse 17. This verse represents a sharp turn from a concern about false teachers to a concern for the readers. The first two words in the Greek text, *hymeis de* ("but you"), signal this transition. The nominative personal pronoun *hymeis* ("you") is usually used for emphasis.[360] The word "but" (*de*) is emphatic, contrasting Jude's "beloved" (*agapetoi*) with the false teachers.[361]

There is a parallel in form between verses 17-19 and 5-16. Both sections begin with:

> an exhortation to remember; in each case Jude begins by addressing himself to the faithful in warning and ends by addressing the heretics in condemnation. But the tenor of the passages is different. Verses 5-16 expose and condemn the sin of the heretics . . . whereas verses 17-19, while laying bare once again the character of the opposition, have a different purpose, to encourage and reassure the faithful.[362]

Like II Peter, Jude urges upon its readers the importance of remembrance.[363] The goal is not merely remembering as a mental exercise; the words they recall are to help them avoid the seduction of false teaching and to cement their loyalty to the true faith. Specifically, the readers are to remember "the words which were spoken before by the apostles of our Lord Jesus Christ" (NKJV). Verse 17 records these words.

Verse 18. There is a close parallel between this verse and II Peter 3:3: "Knowing this first: that scoffers will come in the last days, walking according to their own lusts" (NKJV). There is also a contextual parallel. Jude

Characteristics of False Teachers

couches its words, which it attributes to "the apostles," in terms of remembering. II Peter stirs up its readers' "pure minds" by way of "remembrance" (II Peter 3:1). It admonishes them to "be mindful" not only of the words spoken before by the holy prophets, but also of "the commandment" of the apostles of the Lord and Savior (II Peter 3:2). This "commandment" is connected with the warning about last-day scoffers who will live according to their own perverse desires.[364] The word translated "mockers" (*empaiktai*) in Jude is precisely the same as the word in II Peter that is translated "scoffers." These are the only two times this word appears in the New Testament. Both Jude and II Peter are concerned about the "last" days or time.[365]

But there are also differences between Jude and II Peter at this point. II Peter's concern is about scoffers who deny the Second Coming. Jude makes no mention of the Second Coming in this immediate context; by its reiteration of the word "ungodly" and by the contextual description of the false teachers' errors, it demonstrates a concern about their theological error that results in casting off moral restraint. (See comments on verses 4, 8, 10, 15-16.)

This verse provides an indication that Jude was written after II Peter, for this reference could easily include II Peter 3:3. Many scholars suggest that II Peter and Jude were both influenced by a common source, a written document circulating among Christians in the first century that included the warnings reflected in both letters. This is not impossible, but it is not necessary. We can explain the similarities between the two letters by saying that II Peter preceded the Epistle of Jude and that the Holy Spirit inspired Jude to adapt some of the content of II Peter for his own similar purposes. If Jude

Jude

could incorporate into his letter the words of Enoch—and possibly words from the *Assumption of Moses*—whether he was quoting from the actual documents or from oral tradition preserved in the documents, he could certainly quote from or allude to an inspired letter like II Peter. (See the comments on verses 9, 14-15.)

Warnings of future apostasy are common in the New Testament. (See Mark 13:5-6, 21-22; Acts 20:29-30; I Timothy 4:1-3; II Timothy 3:1-9.) No doubt, the apostles also gave many oral warnings that were never included in Scripture. These warnings would have circulated by word-of-mouth among the believing communities in the first century, much as Christians all over the world today share with one another the words of preachers and teachers. (See Acts 2:40; 5:25; 15:35; 18:11; 28:30-31.) Indeed, Jude's reference here may include oral warnings, for it says, "They told you" (*elegon hymin*), an imperfect active indicative form indicating the repeated nature of the warnings.[366]

K. They Cause Divisions (19a)

(19a) These be they who separate themselves.

Verse 19a. The word "themselves" is not in the Greek text.[367] A more literal translation would be, "These are the ones making divisions." The translation of the NKJV is, "These are sensual persons, who cause divisions, not having the Spirit."

It is possible that the false teachers made "theoretical distinctions between two kinds of Christians."[368] They may have embraced an incipient form of Gnosticism with its emphasis on those who had special knowledge as opposed to those who did not have it. But this may be reading more into "making divisions" than is warranted. The idea could be that the false teachers, like the Pharisees (whose name comes from a word probably meaning "separated") thought of themselves as spiritually elite because of their supposed superior knowledge. Because they perceived themselves superior to "common" Christians, they separated from them, perhaps forming their own elite circle of fellowship at the love feasts (verse 12), rejecting recognized authority (verse 8), and currying favor with those who could in some way advance their cause (verse 16).[369]

On the other hand, the reference to the false teachers as "making divisions" could simply speak of the way that false teaching always divides people. By introducing error, the false teachers created division where there had been unity. This is a sin that God detests. (See Proverbs 6:16-19.)

L. They Do Not Have the Spirit (19b)

(19b) Sensual, having not the Spirit.

Verse 19b. Here is the essential problem with the false teachers: They do not have the Holy Spirit. (See Romans 8:9.) They are "sensual" (*psychikoi*). They may make great boasts about their spirituality, including their dreams and visions and superior revelations, but it is all a sham. They are completely out of touch with the reality of New Testament Christianity. They have no grasp on the meaning of grace (verse 4), and thus their theology is

Jude

flawed at its foundation. The simplest believer who has genuine faith in God and is filled with the Spirit is far more spiritually perceptive than these false teachers, even if he never makes loud boasts about his spirituality and revelations.

I Corinthians 2:14 uses the same word here translated as "sensual" to describe the person who cannot receive spiritual things. This is the "natural man." James 3:15 also uses the word to describe "wisdom" that is not from above and uses it in parallel with the words "earthly" and "demonic."

Since these false teachers did not have the Spirit, they were not believers. (See John 7:37-39.) Since they had once been rooted in faith (see comments on verses 5, 12), the Spirit had departed from them, even as from the false teachers of whom Peter wrote. (See II Peter 2:20-22.)

V

Exhortations to Believers (20-23)

To this point, the Epistle of Jude is concerned primarily with exposing the dangerous influence of false teachers. Now, in verses 20-21, it gives four specific commands to enable the readers to avoid the contamination of heresy. Verses 22-23 explain how to deal with believers who are wavering under the influence of false teaching, those who are on the very brink of deception, and those who have been deceived—an apparent reference to the false teachers themselves.

A. Build Yourselves Up in Your Most Holy Faith (20a)

(20a) But ye, beloved, building up yourselves on your most holy faith.

Verse 20a. Verse 17 signals an emphatic change by the Greek *hymeis de* ("but you") as Jude turns from its almost single-minded focus on the false teachers to a focus on the readers themselves. But even after that, Jude turns again to a brief discussion of the false teachers (verses 18-19). Now, by another use of *hymeis de*, the letter returns to a primary focus on the readers, confining to verse 23 any reference to the false teachers.

One of the steps the community of believers must take

Jude

to avoid seduction by false teaching is to build itself up in its "most holy faith." This is not a reference to saving faith, the faith that is part of the fruit of the Spirit (Galatians 5:22), or the gift of faith that is one of the nine spiritual gifts (I Corinthians 12:9). It is, instead, a reference to the body of doctrine—the content of the faith—once for all delivered to the saints. (See comments on verse 3.) This meaning is indicated by the definite article that specifies the precise faith in view.

The faith once for all delivered to the saints is the same in content as "the apostles' doctrine" (Acts 2:42), upon which the church was built from the beginning. Christ is the chief cornerstone of the church (Ephesians 2:20), but the church is built on the foundation of the apostles and prophets, for they were the recipients of foundational revelation. Any variance from the teachings of Christ and the apostles is spiritually deadly. (See Romans 6:17.)

The word translated "building up" (*epoikodomountes*) is a participial imperative. It is not merely an individualistic command; it is given to the community of believers. The Western ideal of rugged individualism is largely missing from biblical thought. Although, in the final analysis, salvation is a matter of an individual's relationship with God, Scripture sees this relationship as existing in a communal context. This is true in God's dealings with the people of faith in the Old Testament—Abraham, Isaac, Jacob, and their descendants, the nation of Israel—and it is true in the New Testament church. Many of the images of the church are images of community: a flock, a growing temple made up of individual stones, a vine and branches, the people of God, the body of Christ made up of individual members. We also see the communal nature of faith in the second-greatest commandment: "Thou shalt love thy neighbour as thyself" (Matthew 22:39).

The believing community builds itself up on its most holy faith through the study of the Scriptures under the direction of faithful spiritual leaders. (See Ephesians 4:11-16; Colossians 2:6-7; II Timothy 4:1-4; Titus 1:9; Hebrews 5:12-14; 6:1-2.) Polycarp wrote to the Philippians, "If you study the Epistles of the blessed apostle Paul you can be built up in the faith given to you."[370]

The faith once for all delivered to the saints is "most holy" because it is "utterly different."[371] It is like no other teaching, no other religion in the world.

B. Pray in the Holy Spirit (20b)

(20b) Praying in the Holy Ghost.

Verse 20b. The word translated "praying" (*proseuchomenoi*) is a participial imperative, as is "building up" in the first part of the verse. But there may be a suggestion here that "the second injunction is a means by which the first can be carried out—that is, by 'praying in the Holy Spirit' we can build one another up in the faith."[372] This certainly does not denigrate the importance of Bible study, as noted previously, but prayer motivated, empowered, and led by the Holy Spirit can strengthen the believer in the faith.

Whether or not there is a grammatical connection between this command and the other three imperatives in verses 20-21, there is great value in Spirit-led prayer. Moo

Jude

pointed out that "many commentators think that Jude is enjoining believers here to engage in distinctly 'charismatic' praying, including, though not limited to, speaking in tongues. They suggest that this praying is a praying in which the Spirit himself supplies the words."[373] This is Hillyer's understanding. He pointed out that the command to pray in the Holy Spirit is "an expression that includes, but is not confined to, praying in tongues (1 Cor. 14:15-16)."[374]

When compared with other references to the role of the Holy Spirit in prayer, it seems certain that to pray "in the Holy Spirit" includes praying in tongues. When a person speaks with tongues, the Holy Spirit gives utterance to the words. (See Acts 2:4.) Paul wrote, "If I pray in a tongue, my spirit prays" (I Corinthians 14:14, NKJV). He distinguished between prayer where the Holy Spirit provides the actual words and prayer where the person praying provides the words: "I will pray with the spirit, and I will also pray with the understanding" (I Corinthians 14:15, NKJV). Although believers must always rely on the Holy Spirit for direction in prayer (Romans 8:26; Ephesians 6:18), there is a dimension of prayer that surpasses the realm of human understanding, which we can only call "praying in the Holy Spirit."[375]

C. Keep Yourselves in the Love of God (21a)

(21a) Keep yourselves in the love of God.

Verse 21a. The third thing believers must do to avoid deception by false teachers is to keep (*teresate*) themselves in the love of God. Although God's ability to keep the believer is without limit (see verse 1, where a form of the same word is translated "preserved"), believers have a responsibility to cooperate with Him. (See verse 24.)

There are at least two aspects to keeping oneself in the love of God. First, since God has made known His love in Jesus Christ, "those who depart from Christ depart from the love of God."[376] (See John 3:16.) The false teachers were guilty of this. (See comments on verse 4.)

Second, believers must obey the commands of Christ. When Jude wrote this verse, he may have had in mind the words of Jesus: "As the Father loved Me, I also have loved you; abide in My love" (John 15:9, NKJV). Then, Jesus explained how believers are to keep themselves in His love: "If you keep My commandments, you will abide in My love, just as I have kept My Father's commandments and abide in His love" (John 15:10, NKJV). Again, the false teachers certainly were not keeping Christ's commandments. (See also John 13:34-35; 15:11-17.)

D. Look for the Mercy of Our Lord to Bring You to Eternal Life (21b)

(21b) Looking for the mercy of our Lord Jesus Christ unto eternal life.

Verse 21b. The fourth command in this series is translated "looking" (*prosdechomenoi*, a participial imperative). This is an apparent reference to the need for believers to stay focused on the hope of the Second Coming. The sentiment here seems to be the same as in I Peter 1:3-5. I Peter ties mercy together with the "living hope" that involves an "incorruptible and undefiled" inheritance "reserved in

Jude

heaven" and "ready to be revealed in the last time."

The common meaning of *prosdechomai* is "awaiting." (See Mark 15:43; Luke 2:25, 38; 12:36; 23:51; Acts 23:21; Titus 2:13.) It relates to the thing for which one waits. It is, in that sense, the thing for which one is looking. II Peter twice uses a form of the word in an eschatological context. (See II Peter 3:12-14.)

Jude recognizes that eternal life is a consequence of mercy. It is not something one deserves, earns, or merits. Since it is an expression of mercy, it is something one does not deserve.

Elsewhere, as in I Peter 1:3, Scripture presents mercy as an attribute of the Father. (See Romans 9:16; 11:32; 15:9; Ephesians 2:4; Philippians 2:27.) But in some references, as here, mercy is an attribute of our Lord Jesus. Jesus is, of course, God, and thus He possesses all divine attributes, but here the reference to His mercy is doubtless "an allusion to the atonement He wrought upon the cross."[377] This is the basis of eternal life. Eternal life already resides in believers, but they will not fully experience it until the return of Christ.

Verses 20-21 connect spiritual maturity with faith, hope (hope is bound up in "looking"), and love, just as many of Paul's letters do. (See I Corinthians 13:13.)[378]

E. Be Merciful to Those Who Doubt (22)

(22) And of some have compassion, making a difference.

Verse 22. The Greek text of verses 22-23 exists in at least six different variants.[379] In a broad sense, these variants fall within two general categories: Some of the readings present two clauses (e.g., KJV, NKJV, TEV, NEB); other readings present three clauses (e.g., RSV, NRSV, NASB, NJB). There are reasonable defenses for each of the readings as original, but we will here comment on the three-clause reading for the following reasons: (1) The majority of manuscripts read three clauses.[380] (2) It follows Jude's tendency to use triads.[381] (3) It best explains the other readings.[382]

Following the three-clause reading, the first clause says "and be merciful to some who are wavering." The word translated "wavering" (*diakrinomenous*) is a present middle participle. The Textus Receptus has *diakrinomenoi* at this point, which we would translate something like "making a distinction" or "making a difference." If we read *diakrinomenous*, the idea is that the people in view are questioning; they are not fully convinced of the ideas of the false teachers, but they are wondering. They are in somewhat the same position as those who waver like a wave of the sea; they are double-minded. (See James 1:6-8.)

If we read *diakrinomenoi*, the idea is that believers are to exercise discernment in dealing with these people. Not everyone is to be dealt with in the same way. How we deal with those who are in danger of being seduced by false teaching depends on the degree of their involvement with the error. (See Galatians 6:1; James 5:19-20.)

Jude's overriding concern is for its readers to "earnestly contend for the faith which was once delivered unto the saints" (verse 3). The false teaching had had a range of impact on those who heard it: (1) Some were questioning their faith, as here. (2) Some were at

Jude

the point of departing from the faith, as in verse 23a. (3) Some had departed from the faith, as in verse 23b.

Those who are questioning are at a critical point in their spiritual journey. We must treat them gently, with kindness and love. We must not condemn them for having questions. It is acceptable to have questions. Great heroes of biblical fame sometimes questioned God and their understanding of His ways and words. The Psalms are especially rich in the candid accounts of a struggling soul.

Neither must we give pat answers to those who are at this point. Those who would rescue the wavering must be willing to invest the time and effort to deal with hard questions and to give thoughtful, biblically consistent answers.

F. Snatch from the Fire Those on the Verge of Deception (23a)

(23a) And others save with fear, pulling them out of the fire.

Verse 23a. Some who encounter persuasive heretics will be unable to answer their arguments. They may not be quite ready to depart from the faith, but they are in danger of losing their salvation unless someone intervenes and pulls them "out of the fire."

This phrase and the next (verse 23b) are couched in Old Testament imagery. (See Zechariah 3:1-4.) Joshua, the high priest, was a burning stick snatched from the fire. He was "retrieved for God's future purpose."[383]

When a person is at this point in his spiritual journey,

he must be forcibly confronted by someone who is able and willing to clearly point out error and the danger of the loss of salvation. Still, the person giving the correction must do it in a spirit of gentleness with full awareness that he could someday need correction himself. (See Galatians 6:1.) But he should also give it with the urgency born of mindfulness that a failure to rescue the "burning stick" will certainly result in a soul's death. (See James 5:19-20.)

In the text we are following at this point, the word "fear" (*phobos*) is located in the third clause, as follows.

G. Show Mercy to the Deceived While Hating Deception's Effects (23b)

(23b) Hating even the garment spotted by the flesh.

Verse 23b. Following the longer text, this clause reads "to others show mercy, mixed with fear—hating even the clothing stained by corrupted flesh" (NIV). This seems to be a reference to the false teachers themselves or to those who have been fully convinced by the false teachers. They are in need of mercy, but those who show mercy to them must do so "with fear," that is, with full awareness of the danger associated with the false teaching. Even to be close enough to heretics to show them mercy is to be in a certain amount of spiritual danger.

Zechariah 3:1-4 apparently also influenced the reference to stained clothing. (See comments on verse 23a.) In the scene from Zechariah, the high priest Joshua was clothed with filthy garments. The Lord said, "Take away

Jude

the filthy garments from him" (Zechariah 3:4, NKJV).

Jude seems to use the word translated "spotted" or "stained" (*espilomenon*) as the equivalent of the Hebrew *tsow'*, translated "filthy" in Zechariah. The Hebrew word refers to human excrement.[384] The word in Jude that is translated "garment" (*chiton*) refers to the garment worn closest to the body. To associate these words makes for strong language, but the letter makes us acutely aware of the corruption and far-reaching danger of false teaching. It "pictures the sinful teaching and practices of these people as underclothes fouled by feces."[385]

In a number of places, Scripture employs language that is not used in polite company in the Western world, in order to provide emphasis. (See Philippians 3:8.) Although we may not use such descriptions on a regular basis, we should be fully aware of the stark message that Scripture intends: false teaching is repulsive and dangerous. Anyone who harbors fond feelings for heresy is misguided.

Even though believers must extend mercy to all, they must remember that mercy is for the person caught in the trap of error; it is not for the error itself. There must be zero tolerance for false teaching. (See Galatians 1:8-9; 2:4-5; 5:12; Philippians 3:2.) The New Living Translation offers a helpful dynamic-equivalent translation: "There are still others to whom you need to show mercy, but be careful that you aren't contaminated by their sins."

VI

Benediction
(24-25)

The final two verses of Jude form a striking doxology. Doxologies appear frequently in the New Testament at the conclusion of letters or major sections within letters.[386] The word "doxology" comes from the Greek *doxa* ("glory") and *logos* ("word"). We use it here because in this literary form, *doxa* typically appears, as in verse 25, attributing glory to God. The ancient Jewish people often used doxologies, sometimes to conclude prayers and sermons.[387]

There are four basic elements in New Testament doxologies: (1) the person praised; (2) a word of praise (usually including *doxa*); (3) an indication of time (e.g., "forever" or "forever and ever"); and (4) amen.[388]

There is a textual variant in Jude's doxology that we will discuss in the comments on verse 25. In this case, the Textus Receptus follows the shorter reading.

A. The Believer's Security (24)

(24) Now unto him that is able to keep you from falling, and to present you faultless before the presence of his glory with exceeding joy.

Verse 24. Believers have personal responsibility to respond to the grace of God (see Galatians 2:21; 5:4;

Jude

Hebrews 12:15; II Peter 3:18; Jude 4) and to live in such a way as to keep themselves in the love of God (see comments on verse 21). But in the final analysis it is only God who is able to preserve them (see comments on verse 1). Even the ability to believe is a gift of God. (See Acts 11:18.)

Even though Jude and II Peter describe false teachers as people who were once saved (see comments on verse 12 and II Peter 2:15, 20-22), we cannot blame God for the loss of their salvation. He is able to keep believers from falling. (See John 10:28-29; Romans 14:4; II Timothy 1:12; Hebrews 7:25; I Peter 1:5.) Only those who reject Jesus Christ fall (see Romans 11:11), and this was the case with the false teachers. (See verse 4.)

In one sense, the Epistle of Jude is bleak. As many as seventeen verses out of twenty-five discuss the devastating effects of false doctrine. But the letter does not lack good news altogether. In spite of the deceptive danger of heresy, God is able to keep believers from falling. Not only that, He is also able to present believers faultless before the presence of His glory—that is, before His throne on the Day of Judgment—with exceeding joy! Truth is more powerful than a lie. (See John 8:32.) In the end, good overcomes evil. (See Romans 12:21.)

The word translated "falling" (*aptaistous*) appears only here in the New Testament. In secular Greek, the word refers to a surefooted horse that does not stumble, of the steady falling of snow, and of a man without moral lapses.[389]

The New Testament uses the word translated "faultless" (*amomous*) in a sacrificial context, that is, to describe the sacrifices without blemish that were offered

Benediction

to God. (See Hebrews 9:14; I Peter 1:19.) It is also used elsewhere, as here in Jude, to describe the perfection of believers as they stand before God in the last day. (See Ephesians 5:26-27; Colossians 1:21-23.) Revelation 14:5 uses it to describe the faultlessness of the 144,000 sealed ones.

Although believers are always to conform more closely to the character of Christ, their faultlessness, as they stand before God, will not be due to their ability to live without sin. It will be due to the cleansing effect of the blood of Jesus (Ephesians 5:26-27; Colossians 1:21-23; Hebrews 10:10, 14, 16-19) and to the imputation of His righteousness to their accounts (Romans 4:11, 23-24).

The New Testament elsewhere uses the word translated "exceeding joy" (*agalliasei*) for joyous events connected with the promise of the Messiah and the outpouring of the Holy Spirit. (See Luke 1:14, 44; Acts 2:46; Hebrews 1:9.) The judgment of believers will be a joyous event, not one of sadness and regret. Of course this would not be possible if the judgment focused on the failures of believers. It is possible only because the judgment will finally and fully reveal the eternal consequences of trusting in Christ Jesus alone for salvation. It will not be just a happy time; it will be an experience of "exceeding joy."

The "presence of his glory" reflects the Old Testament concept of the presence (*paniym*) of the Lord representing the Lord Himself. (See Genesis 3:8; 4:16; Psalm 97:5; 114:7; Zephaniah 1:7.) The word often translated "presence" in the Old Testament means "face." It is actually a plural form, but the Hebrew language uses plurals not only to indicate more than one of something, but also to indicate intensity or fullness. Since both meanings cannot be intended simultaneously, *paniym* is always translated with the singular "face." The "face" of God is a Hebraism for the presence of God, not a reference to a literal face.

B. The Worthiness of God (25)

(25) To the only wise God our Saviour, be glory and majesty, dominion and power, both now and ever. Amen.

Verse 25. A textual variant introduces a longer reading into the final verse of the doxology: "to the only God our Savior be glory, majesty, power and authority, through Jesus Christ our Lord, before all ages, now and forevermore! Amen" (NIV). Although the Textus Receptus, upon which the King James Version is based, generally represents a longer text, there are cases where it does not. This is one of them. (Compare I Peter 2:2.)

The word "wise" is absent from the longer reading; many textual critics think it is borrowed from Romans 16:27.[390] The additional words are "through Jesus Christ our Lord, before all ages."

There is undisputed textual evidence for attributing divine attributes to God and approaching God "through Jesus Christ." (See Romans 1:8; 6:11, 23; 7:25; 16:27; Hebrews 13:21; I Peter 4:11.) From a Jewish perspective, such a phrase indicates the deity of Jesus Christ. No devout Jew would ascribe glory to God through a mere human being. It would be blasphemous to speak of "God" and "Jesus Christ" in the same breath in this manner unless Jesus is God. These phrases indicate an understanding that Jesus Christ is the way to God and that it is

Benediction

impossible to approach God except through Jesus, the Messiah. (See John 14:6.) Since the Incarnation, the only way we can properly glorify God is through the person of Jesus Christ, who is Himself God manifested in genuine human existence. (See I Timothy 3:16; John 1:1, 14.)

In view of the identification of God here as the "only . . . God," Douglas Moo offered a warning to trinitarians: "Many of us probably need to be more guarded about the way we talk of the Father, Son, and Holy Spirit in light of this truth; we are often perilously close to 'tritheism,' the belief in three different gods."[391] If the original text did read "through Jesus Christ," it is certainly no indication that Jesus is a person in the Godhead distinct from the Father. (See comments on verse 1.) Jude's letter presents Jesus as God Himself. (See comments on verse 4.) From his monotheistic perspective, Jude did not imagine God to consist of "persons," as in the theological speculations of the Greek apologists and church councils. He knew, as we see here, that there was only one God, and he was convinced after the resurrection of Jesus—his half-brother—that Jesus was in some marvelous way the Messiah (i.e., "Christ," verses 1, 4, 17, 21). Based on the Hebrew prophets, this meant that Jesus was God Himself made known in human existence. (See Isaiah 9:6; Micah 5:2; John 1:1, 14, 18.)

But the question remains whether the longer reading represents the original text in this verse. There is textual evidence for both readings. Although there has been a tendency to reduce textual criticism to a system of rules to apply to each variant in the attempt to reconstruct the original text, it seems doubtful that we can count on any system of rules to provide without question the original

Jude

reading in every instance. Can we always be certain the reading in the oldest manuscripts is the original reading? Is it not possible that later manuscripts could preserve readings even older than any manuscript currently known? Can we say with certainty that we can discover the original reading simply by counting the manuscript evidence? Is it not possible that the majority of copies have preserved a later reading in a specific text? Can we say for sure that the reading that presents more grammatical difficulties is the original text? Does a smoother reading guarantee that copyists corrected grammatical difficulties? And can we always be certain in identifying the reading that gave birth to other readings?[392]

Because any system of rules cannot guarantee consistent results, many modern textual critics are more flexible in their approach to determining the original reading among the existing variants. One significant matter that we must not overlook is the influence of the context in determining the most authentic variant. This factor seems to be important here.

If we adopt the longer reading, we are at a loss to understand the phrase "before all ages" in the clause "through Jesus Christ our Lord, before all ages." Because of the difficulty in saying that "glory was only given to God through Christ 'before all time,'" Green interpreted the phrase to mean that "through Christ . . . God saves man."[393] The more natural interpretation of these words, however, is to ascribe "glory, majesty, power and authority" to God "through Jesus Christ . . . before all ages." The theological difficulty is to know how these divine attributes could be ascribed to God through Christ "before all ages" even though the Incarnation had not yet occurred.

Benediction

Since there is substantial evidence for the shorter reading as well as for the longer, since no other doxology contains the words "before all ages . . . through Jesus Christ,"[394] and since the introduction of this phrase introduces theological difficulties, it seems best to accept the shorter reading here as original.

Many New Testament references identify Jesus as Savior.[395] A fewer number of references identify God as Savior. (See I Timothy 1:1; 2:3; 4:10; Titus 1:3; 2:10; 3:4.) This designation does not indicate a bifurcation within God. God is the only Savior (Isaiah 43:11). Jesus is Immanuel, God with us (Matthew 1:23), God made known in human existence (John 1:14; I Timothy 3:16; I John 1:1-2; 2:22-23; 3:1). Since Jesus is God, whatever we may say of God, we may say of Jesus. Since God is the Savior, Jesus is the Savior.

The identification of Jesus as the "only . . . God" reinforces the strict monotheism of Scripture. There is no other God but one (Deuteronomy 6:4; I Corinthians 8:4, 6), so Jesus is that God who has come among us to redeem us from our sins. Even the name God has taken in His incarnation indicates His mission. (See Matthew 1:21.)

The four virtues here are frequently identified as divine attributes. "Glory" relates to God's "weighty and majestic presence."[396] "Majesty" has to do with His kingly status.[397] (Compare Hebrews 1:3; 8:1.) "Dominion" describes His control over all created things.[398] "Power" refers to His intrinsic right to rule.[399]

The Majority Text and the Textus Receptus include "wise" in the description of "the only wise God." Even if the critical text is correct in omitting it—and that is by no

Jude

means certain—we do know that all the treasures of wisdom and knowledge are hidden in Christ (Colossians 2:3). He is the supreme and final ("both now and ever") revelation of God's person. (See Hebrews 1:1-3.)

"Amen" transliterates the Greek *amen*, which comes from the Hebrew *'amen*. The word means something like "so be it!" It is a common and fitting conclusion to New Testament doxologies. What the doxology has declared is eternal truth; this is the way it is. Nothing will change it, not even the passing of time. The declared truth will endure for all eternity.

Endnotes

[1]See Acts 15:1-2, 5; 20:29-30; Romans 2:1-6, 17-24; I Corinthians 1:10-11; 3:3-4; 4:18-21; 5:1-13; 11:17-22; 15:12, 32; 16:22; II Corinthians 2:17; 10:12; 11:3-4, 12-15, 18-23; Galatians 1:6-9; 2:4-5; 3:1; 4:9-11, 17, 21; 5:4, 7, 12; 6:12-13; Ephesians 4:14; Philippians 3:2; Colossians 2:8, 16, 18-22; II Thessalonians 2:2-3; I Timothy 1:3-7, 19-20; 4:7; 6:3-5; II Timothy 1:15; 2:14, 16-18, 23-26; 3:6-8, 13; 4:3-4; Titus 1:9-16; 3:9-11; Hebrews 3:12; 10:26, 29, 35, 39; 12:14-16; 13:9; James 1:13-14, 26; 2:1, 14, 19-20; 3:14-16; 4:1-4, 11, 16; 5:19-20; I John 2:4, 9, 11, 18-19, 22-23; 3:10, 15, 17; 4:1-3, 6, 20; II John 7, 9-11; III John 4, 9-11; Revelation 2:2, 9, 14-15, 20; 3:9, 17.

[2]Douglas J. Moo, *2 Peter, Jude, The NIV Application Commentary* (Grand Rapids, MI: Zondervan Publishing House, 1996), 21.

[3]See Daniel L. Segraves, *I Peter: Standing Fast in the Grace of God* (Hazelwood, MO: Word Aflame Press, 1999).

[4]See Edwin A. Blum in Frank E. Gaebelein, gen. ed., *The Expositor's Bible Commentary* (Grand Rapids, MI: Zondervan Publishing House, 1981) 12:257-61.

[5]See Michael Green, *2 Peter and Jude, Tyndale New Testament Commentaries* (Grand Rapids, MI: William B. Eerdmans Publishing Company, 1968) 18:13-14. Green discusses the full range of evidence and affirms Peter to be the author (see 13-35).

[6]See discussion in Blum, 258.

[7]Blum cites Morton as asserting on the basis of a

Second Peter & Jude

computer analysis that I and II Peter are "linguistically indistinguishable." Ibid., 258-59. Green is "impressed by the similarities between 2 Peter and 1 Peter both in diction and doctrine, and also to some extent with the reported Petrine speeches in Acts." Green, 34.

[8]Blum, 261.

[9]Blum has a thorough discussion of the arguments against accepting Peter as the author of the letter and responses to those arguments; he concludes that Peter was the author.

[10]Moo, 24.

[11]See discussion under "Date of Composition" in Segraves, *I Peter*.

[12]See discussion under "Place of Origin" in Segraves, *I Peter*.

[13]See discussion under "Original Audience" in Segraves, *I Peter*.

[14]See comments in Green, 18-19.

[15]See Norman Hillyer, *1 and 2 Peter, Jude, New International Biblical Commentary* (Peabody, MA: Hendrickson Publishers, 1992), 13.

[16]See discussion in Blum, 264.

[17]Note that Paul's quote is without specific citation.

[18]See discussion in Green, 169-70. Also note that Jude did not cite his source in this case.

[19]Green, 18.

[20]Ibid., 17, n. 4.

[21]Ibid., n. 8. Also, Hillyer offers a chart showing the similarities in vocabularies and ideas between I Peter and II Peter. See Hillyer, 15.

[22]See discussion under "Author, Inspiration, and Place in the Canon."

[23]See discussion on I Peter 1:1a in Segraves, *I Peter*.

[24]For further information on Peter, see comments on I Peter 1:1a in Segraves, *I Peter*.

[25]The epistles identifying the author as a slave of Jesus are Romans, Philippians, James, II Peter, and Jude. The common denominator among these letters could be that they were addressed to an audience that was primarily Jewish or at least had a significant Jewish component. Romans is clearly addressed to both Jewish and Gentile believers (Romans 2:17; 11:13). The church at Philippi was founded among devout Jews who met at a riverside for prayer on the Sabbath (Acts 16:11-13).

James was written to a Jewish audience described as "the twelve tribes scattered abroad" (James 1:1). There is strong evidence that II Peter was written to a primarily Jewish audience. (See discussion under "Original Audience" in the Introduction.) The obvious familiarity of Jude's readers with the Hebrew Scriptures and the Apocrypha indicates a Jewish audience.

There also appears to be a common denominator among those letters that do not identify the author as a slave of Jesus Christ. They are I Corinthians, II Corinthians, Galatians, Ephesians, Colossians, I Thessalonians, II Thessalonians, I Timothy, II Timothy, Titus, Philemon, Hebrews, I Peter, I John, II John, and III John.

Paul wrote his Corinthian letters primarily to the Gentile believers in the Corinthian church. Though there was an apparent Jewish component in the churches of Galatia, Paul, again, wrote primarily to the Gentile believers in Galatia who were in danger of being seduced into Judaism. Paul apparently intended his letter to the Ephesians to circulate among the numerous churches he founded in Ephesus and in the surrounding cities; thus it does not address a specific ethnic audience. Paul also indirectly founded the church in Colossae (Colossians 2:1); it apparently was primarily Gentile. When Paul first went to Thessalonica, he ministered to the Jewish population but was rejected (Acts 17:1-9). Many Gentiles believed, however, and to them Paul addressed I and II Thessalonians (I Thessalonians 1:9). Though Timothy had a Jewish mother, his father was a Gentile, and Timothy was uncircumcised until Paul's influence entered his life. (See Acts 16:1-3.) At least by the second century, Jewish law recognized the offspring of a Jewish-Gentile marriage as Jewish if the mother was Jewish. In Timothy's case, however, he would not have been recognized as Jewish because he had not been circumcised on the eighth day as prescribed by the law of Moses. See discussion in Craig S. Keener, *The Bible Background Commentary, New Testament* (Downers Grove, IL: InterVarsity Press, 1993), 366. Even if Timothy were considered Jewish, Paul's letters to him were personal letters written for different purposes than Paul's letters to specific churches. Titus was a Gentile—in his letter to Titus, Paul identified himself as a slave of God (Titus 1:1)—as was Philemon.

Although the letter to the Hebrews is written to a Jewish audience, the author does not identify himself, so the letter does not fit the pattern of the other epistles.

There is substantial evidence that I Peter was written to a Jewish audience. (See I Peter 1:1 and the comments in Segraves, *I Peter*.) In it, Peter did not identify himself as a servant of Jesus Christ. But he did so identify himself in his second letter to the same recipients (II Peter 3:1). We can only speculate as to why Peter did not identify

Endnotes

himself as a servant of Jesus Christ in his first letter; it may be that in his second letter he focused more purposefully on the deity of Christ than in his first letter. In his first letter, Peter identified Jesus as Lord only once (I Peter 1:3). In his second letter, though shorter, Peter identified Jesus as Lord seven times (II Peter 1:2, 8, 11, 14, 16; 2:20; 3:18). Also in the second letter, he identified Jesus as God (II Peter 1:1).

I John contains no information about the identity of the original recipients other than that they were Christians wrestling with false teaching concerning the nature of the Incarnation. The nature of this heresy seems to indicate a Gentile audience, since Jews rejected the dualism inherent in the error confronting John's readers. Nothing specific in II John indicates the original audience, but false teaching similar to that exposed in I John confronted the recipients, suggesting a Gentile audience. (Compare II John 7 with I John 2:22-23; 4:1-3.) III John is a personal letter written to Gaius, a Gentile believer.

[26] Walter Bauer, *A Greek-English Lexicon of the New Testament and Other Early Christian Literature*, trans. William F. Arndt and F. Wilbur Gingrich, revised and augmented by F. Wilbur Gingrich and Frederick W. Danker, 2nd ed. (Chicago: University of Chicago Press, 1979) (hereafter BAGD), 436.

[27] See Green, 60; Hillyer, 158; Blum, 267.

[28] See Moo, 35.

[29] BAGD, 196.

[30] See H. E. Dana and Julius R. Mantey, *A Manual Grammar of the Greek New Testament* (New York: Macmillan Publishing Co., 1955), 147.

[31] Moo, 35.

[32]Ibid., 35-36.

[33]Green, 61.

[34]Luke 2:11; John 4:42; Acts 5:31; 13:23; Ephesians 5:23; Philippians 3:20; II Timothy 1:10; Titus 1:4; 2:13; 3:6; I John 4:14.

[35]Luke 1:47; I Timothy 1:1; 2:3; 4:10; Titus 1:3; 2:10; 3:4; Jude 25.

[36]Green, 61.

[37]See Daniel L. Segraves, *The Messiah's Name: JESUS, Not Yahshua* (Kearney, NE: Morris Publishing, 1997), 32-34.

[38]For Paul's insight on grace, see Romans 1:5; 3:24; 4:4; 5:15, 17; 11:6; 12:3, 6; I Corinthians 3:10; 15:10; II Corinthians 9:8; 12:9; Galatians 2:21; Philippians 2:13.

[39]See Green, 62; Hillyer, 159.

[40]Green, 62.

[41]Quoted in C. Kuehne, "The Greek Article and the Doctrine of Christ's Deity," *Journal of Theology: Church of the Lutheran Confession*, vol. 13, no. 3: 19-20, brackets in original.

[42]Ibid., 21, emphasis in original.

[43]Ibid., 22.

[44]Ibid., vol. 13, no. 4:22.

[45]Archibald Thomas Robertson, *Word Pictures in the New Testament* (Grand Rapids, MI: Baker Book House, 1933) 6:148.

[46]*New Living Translation* (Wheaton, IL: Tyndale House Publishers, Inc., 1996).

[47]See Green, 62; Robertson, 148.

[48]Green, 62, emphasis in original.

[49]Ibid., 65.

[50]Hillyer, 161.

[51]Ibid., 91.

[52]See John's use of *logos* ("word") in John 1:1-14 and I John 1:1-4 and Paul's use of *sophia* ("wisdom") in I Corinthians 1:21.

[53]Green, 63, n. 1, and 65.

[54]Moo, 41.

[55]Green, 65.

[56]Ibid., 24-25.

[57]Ibid., 65.

[58]Keener, 726.

[59]Ibid., 724.

[60]See Bruce M. Metzger, *A Textual Commentary on the Greek New Testament* (Stuttgart, Germany: 1971, corrected edition, 1975), 699.

[61]Green, 63, n. 1.

[62]Hillyer, 162.

[63]See Exodus 16:7, 10; 24:16-17; 33:18, 22; 40:34-35; Leviticus 9:6, 23; Numbers 14:10, 21-22; 16:19, 42; 20:6; Deuteronomy 5:24; Romans 9:4.

[64]See Moo, 42.

[65]Ibid., 43.

[66]See Romans 8:1-2; 12:5; 16:7; I Corinthians 1:2, 30; 3:1; 15:18; II Corinthians 5:17; Galatians 3:27; Ephesians 2:10; 3:6.

[67]Green, 66.

[68]See Moo, 50-54. For such lists, see Galatians 5:22-23; I Timothy 4:12; 6:11; II Timothy 2:22; Romans 5:3-4; Colossians 3:12-14.

[69]Green, 66.

[70]Hillyer, 164.

[71]Ibid.

[72]Blum, 269.

[73]Ibid.
[74]Hillyer, 164.
[75]Ibid.
[76]Green, 67.
[77]BAGD, 106.
[78]Green, 67.
[79]Hillyer, 165.
[80]BAGD, 216.
[81]Green, 68.
[82]Ibid., 69-70.

[83]See Acts 3:12; I Timothy 2:2; 3:16; 4:7-8; 6:3, 5-6, 11; II Timothy 3:5; Titus 1:1; II Peter 1:3; 3:11.

[84]BAGD, 858.
[85]Moo, 46.
[86]BAGD, 531.
[87]See Moo, 48.
[88]See Green, 73; Hillyer, 167.
[89]Green, 73.
[90]Hillyer, 167.

[91]B.C. Caffin, in H. D. M. Spence and Joseph S. Exell, eds., *The Pulpit Commentary, II Peter* (Grand Rapids, MI: William B. Eerdmans Publishing Company, reprinted 1977) 22:5.

[92]Blum, 270.
[93]Moo, 48.

[94]See comments on I Peter 3:21 in Segraves, *I Peter*.

[95]Both "remission" and "forgiveness" are translated from the Greek *aphesis*. The KJV translates the word as "remission" in Matthew 26:28; Mark 1:4; Luke 1:77; 3:3; 24:47; Acts 2:38; 10:43; Hebrews 9:22; 10:18 and as "forgiveness" in Mark 3:29; Acts 5:31; 13:38; 26:18; Ephesians 1:7; Colossians 1:14. In Luke 4:18, the word is

translated as both "deliverance" and "liberty." As far as the KJV is concerned, the differences in translation seem to be more for stylistic purposes than for any other reason.

[96] See Matthew 28:19; Acts 2:38, 41; 8:12-16, 36-38; 9:18; 10:47-48; 16:15, 33; 18:8; 19:5; 22:16; Romans 6:3-4; I Corinthians 1:13; Galatians 3:27; Ephesians 4:5; Colossians 2:12; Hebrews 6:2; I Peter 3:21.

[97] Speculations of this kind led to the so-called Lordship salvation debate, which revolves around the possibility of accepting Jesus as Savior without accepting Him as Lord. Some have gone so far as to suggest that not only is water baptism not necessary but neither is repentance. Conjectures such as these do not reflect the biblically holistic view of regeneration. In Scripture, faith, repentance, water baptism, and Spirit baptism are all essential and normative to the new birth. Perhaps an analogy would be natural birth, which is comprised of conception, gestation, delivery, and the severing of the umbilical cord.

[98] See Romans 11:29; I Corinthians 1:26; 7:20; Ephesians 1:18; 4:1, 4; Philippians 3:14; II Thessalonians 1:11; II Timothy 1:9; Hebrews 3:1.

[99] See Acts 9:15; Romans 9:11; 11:5, 7, 28; I Thessalonians 1:4.

[100] Green, 73.
[101] Ibid., 74.
[102] BAGD, 727.
[103] Green, 74.
[104] BAGD, 727.
[105] Moo, 49.
[106] Hillyer, 169.

[107]Blum, 271.

[108]See Luke 1:30-33; Revelation 19:11-21; 20:1-6; Psalm 2:6-8; 22:1-31; 24:1-10; Isaiah 1:2-3; 11:1, 10-13; 60:12; Jeremiah 23:5-8; 30:7-11; Ezekiel 20:33-40; 37:21-25; Zechariah 9:10; 14:16-19.

[109]See Blum, 272.

[110]See comments on I Peter 5:10 in Segraves, *I Peter*.

[111]Green, 79.

[112]See the excellent discussion of Paul's anthropology in Ben Witherington III, *The Paul Quest: The Renewed Search for the Jew of Tarsus* (Downers Grove, IL: InterVarsity Press, 1988), 204-18.

[113]Moo, 70.

[114]Earl D. Radmacher, gen. ed., *The Nelson Study Bible* (Nashville, TN: Thomas Nelson Publishers, 1997), 2058.

[115]Green, 82.

[116]Ibid., 80.

[117]Moo, 63.

[118]Blum, 273.

[119]Matthew 24:3, 27, 37, 39; I Corinthians 15:23; I Thessalonians 2:19; 3:13; 4:15; 5:23; II Thessalonians 2:1, 8; James 5:7-8; II Peter 1:16; 3:4, 12; I John 2:28.

[120]I Corinthians 16:17; II Corinthians 7:6-7; 10:10; Philippians 1:26; 2:12.

[121]See Moo, 71; Green, 82.

[122]Green, 84.

[123]In the view of classical trinitarianism, the Father, Son, and Holy Spirit compose the one God, but we are limiting our discussion here to the Father and Son because of the content of the Scriptures under consideration.

[124] John Sanders describes references to God as "father" as metaphorical language. See John Sanders, *The God Who Risks: A Theology of Providence* (Downers Grove, IL: InterVarsity Press, 1998), 85. It is commonly acknowledged that when Tertullian first used the Latin *persona* in reference to God, the word did not have the current meaning of "individual." In ancient usage, *persona* had to do with the various "personas," or characters, portrayed by a single actor. It would be a mistake, however, to think that God could function in only one *persona* at a time (as would be the case with a human actor). Contrary to the typical description of Sabellianism, God is simultaneously all that He is, including Father, Son, and Holy Spirit.

[125] Leland Ryken, James C. Wilhoit, and Tremper Longman III, gen. eds., *Dictionary of Biblical Imagery* (Downers Grove, IL: InterVarsity Press, 1998), 918-19.

[126] One might think that Hebrews 1:8 is an example of the Father speaking to the Son as God, but see Daniel L. Segraves, *Hebrews: Better Things* (Hazelwood, MO: Word Aflame Press, 1996) 1:54-58.

[127] Moo, 72.

[128] Some of those who heard the voice from heaven at the conclusion of one of Jesus' prayers thought it was thunder. See John 12:29.

[129] See Green, 86-87.

[130] For other imagery, see Ryken, et al., 91.

[131] Ibid., 568.

[132] Blum, 275.

[133] Green, 89.

[134] See Moo, 91-92.

[135] Green, 94.

Second Peter & Jude

[136]Alfred Marshall, *The Interlinear Greek-English New Testament* (Grand Rapids, MI: Zondervan Publishing House, 1958), 925.

[137]See Hillyer, 185.

[138]Ibid.

[139]See Moo, 93.

[140]See BAGD, 95.

[141]Green, 96.

[142]Hillyer, 185.

[143]For a discussion of Paul's use of the Septuagint translation of Isaiah 52:5 in Romans 2:24, see Daniel L. Segraves, *Living By Faith: A Verse-by-Verse Study of Romans* (Kearney, NE: Morris Publishing, 1998), 73-75.

[144]See Moo, 94.

[145]See Hillyer, 186.

[146]This is the only appearance in the New Testament of *tartarus*, which was viewed in ancient Greek tradition as the holding place of the wicked dead where they suffered the most severe torture conceivable. See Keener, 728.

[147]Moo, 103.

[148]For example, John used *logos* to represent the deity and preexistence of Jesus Christ, even though to the Greeks *logos* was reason as the impersonal controlling principle of the universe. See John 1:1-14; I John 1:1-3. Paul quoted a pagan poet but certainly invested new and true meaning into the poet's words. See Acts 17:28.

[149]We should consider Peter's other uses of the "darkness" and "light" motif in interpreting this verse. See I Peter 2:9; II Peter 1:19; 2:17.

[150]Moo, 102-3.

[151]Instead of "chains" (*seirais*), some manuscripts have "pits" (*sirois*). The parallel account in Jude 6 uses a

different word (*desmois*), but it also has to do with chains or bonds of some kind: "And the angels who did not keep their proper domain, but left their own abode, He has reserved in everlasting chains under darkness for the judgment of the great day" (NKJV).

[152] See Louis A. Barbieri, *First and Second Peter* (Chicago, IL: Moody Press, 1977), 110.

[153] Ibid.

[154] Ibid.

[155] See comments on *tartarus* above.

[156] See Blum, 278; Green, 98; Hillyer, 193; Moo, 101-2; Keener, 728.

[157] The pseudepigrapha ("false writings") consist of a collection of ancient Jewish writings, many of which are falsely attributed to well-known personages from the era of the Hebrew Scriptures (e.g., *The Additions to Daniel, The Rest of the Book of Esther, Baruch, The Epistle of Jeremiah, The Wisdom of Solomon, I Enoch, The Assumption of Moses, The Book of Adam and Eve, The "Martyrdom of Isaiah," The Testament of Job*, etc.).

[158] Compare Jude 14-15 with I Enoch 1:9.

[159] See Blum, 393.

[160] See the comments on I Peter 3:20-21 in Segraves, *I Peter*.

[161] See Green, 99.

[162] See ibid., 100.

[163] See Moo, 104.

[164] See Green, 100.

[165] C. I. Scofield, ed., *The New Scofield Study Bible*, New King James Version (Nashville, TN: Thomas Nelson Publishers, 1989), 31, n. 1.

[166] Hillyer, 194.

[167] See ibid.

[168] See Marshall, xviii. Here, "knows" is translated from *oida*, but the idea of ability, not just knowledge, is seen also in *ginosko*. See Matthew 16:3; 27:65; Luke 12:56; Acts 21:37; I Thessalonians 4:4; I Timothy 3:5; James 4:17.

[169] Green, 102.

[170] See Matthew 19:23-24; Luke 1:53; 6:24; 12:16-34; 16:19-31; I Timothy 6:3-11, 17-19; James 1:9-11; 2:5-7; 4:3, 13-16; 5:1-5; II Corinthians 6:4-5; 11:23-28; I Timothy 5:23; II Timothy 4:20.

[171] See Hillyer, 195.

[172] Depending upon the context, "flesh" (*sarx*) can mean "human nature" (e.g., I Timothy 3:16), "human beings" (e.g., Acts 2:17), "human resolve" (e.g., Matthew 26:41), "skin" (e.g., Luke 24:39), "human perspective" (e.g., John 8:15), "human body" (e.g., Acts 2:26, 31), "human life under law" (e.g., Romans 7:5), the "sin principle" (e.g., Romans 8:1), the "way of thinking that is opposed to God" (e.g., Romans 8:7, where *sarx* is translated "carnal"), the "physical bodies of various creatures in contrast with the physical human body" (e.g., I Corinthians 15:39), and "human heritage" (e.g., Philippians 3:4).

[173] See Green, 103.

[174] Moo, 107.

[175] Ibid.

[176] See Moo, 107-8.

[177] See Green, 105-7.

[178] Ibid., 106.

[179] See ibid., 109.

[180] See Keener, 755.

[181] See Green, 110.
[182] See Moo, 127.
[183] See Ryrie, 873.
[184] See Green, 114.
[185] John G. Stackhouse, Jr., *Can God Be Trusted? Faith and the Challenge of Evil* (New York: Oxford University Press, 1998), 122-23.
[186] C. S. Lewis, quoted by Stackhouse, 123.
[187] Hillyer, 207.
[188] Green, 117.
[189] See ibid., 116.
[190] See Moo, 144.
[191] For example, a study released in August 1999 by the American Psychological Association indicated that as many as six percent of those who use the Internet are addicted to the point that broken marriages, job loss, and law suits result. Dr. Kimberly S. Young, founder and CEO of the Center for Online Addiction said "Internet addiction" meets the American Psychiatric Association's definition of addiction, viewed as "an impulse-control disorder that does not involve an intoxicant," such as drugs or alcohol. She further reported studies which show that "the addictive use of the Internet directly leads to social isolation, increased depression, familial discord, divorce, academic failure, financial failure, and job loss." Dr. Young recommended further study to examine "how personality traits, family dynamics, or communication skills influence the way people utilize the Internet." See "Internet addiction affects lives, marriages," *New York*, Aug. 24 (Reuters Health), available at http://dailynews.yahoo.com/h/nm/19990824/hl/web3_1.html.)
[192] Moo, 158.
[193] Ibid., 144.

[194] Ibid.

[195] For a discussion of these verses in Romans, see Segraves, *Living by Faith*.

[196] For a full discussion of these passages in Hebrews, see Segraves, *Hebrews*.

[197] For a discussion of these verses in James, see Daniel L. Segraves, *James: Faith at Work* (Hazelwood, MO: Word Aflame Press, 1995).

[198] Douglas Moo offers a candid and extended discussion of this text from the perspective of someone who embraces the idea of "eternal security." (See Moo, 151-55.) He acknowledges that "Peter here uses language to describe the false teachers that he elsewhere uses to depict conversion to Christianity" (151). "A first 'reading' of these verses, then," Moo writes, "seems to teach that genuine Christians can permanently fall away from their faith if they persist in holding heretical ideas and/or in pursuing a sinful lifestyle" (151). Moo points out that in Romans 11 "Paul seems to tell genuine believers (they have been grafted into the people of God) that they are in danger of losing their status among the people of God, of forfeiting the salvation they once enjoyed" (153). Because of his understanding of the "theological context" of Scripture (i.e., his understanding that Scripture teaches elsewhere the impossibility of losing one's salvation), Moo is unsure how to understand Peter at this point. He suggests that "perhaps the warnings are only "hypothetical," or "perhaps the people are not really being warned about eschatological condemnation," or "perhaps the people being warned are not really Christians at all" (153-54). But Moo then acknowledges that "[a] hypothetical warning is not of much use . . .

Endnotes

[n]either is it satisfactory to think that these warning passages hold out only temporal penalties" (154). He is left, then, with his third option, "that the false teachers were never really Christians at all" (154). But, Moo confesses, "I find a problem here as well: Peter uses 'conversion' language ('knowing' Christ) to describe them" (154). He says the view that the false teachers were never really Christians "does not ultimately satisfy me at the exegetical level" (154). Although he "admit[s] that this is not the most natural reading of the text in its immediate context," Moo comes to the "hesitant conclusion" that "Peter is not talking about truly regenerate believers" (155). He writes, however, "I will honestly admit that I am not finally satisfied with this conclusion. . . . I certainly do not accord 'eternal security' . . . nonnegotiable status. . . . I am in process on this issue, still convinced that eternal security is a biblical doctrine, but less convinced of it than I used to be" (155).

[199] The translation "actually escaped" (*ontos apophugontas*) or "barely escaping" (*oligos apopheugontas*) depends on which Greek reading is followed. But regardless of the text, the escape is real.

[200] See Moo, 147, n. 21.

[201] On the concept of the Christian life as a "way," see comments on 2:2, 15.

[202] See the discussion of the parallels between chapters 1 and 3 in Moo, 160-61. This treatment is adapted from Moo.

[203] See Green, 123.

[204] See I Corinthians 5:9; II Corinthians 7:8; Colossians 4:16. In the last reference, it may be that the "epistle from Laodicea" is a reference to Ephesians as a circular letter.

[205] See Moo, 162-63.

[206] Moo, 162. See also Moo, 65-66.

[207] See, for example, Exodus 13:3; 20:8; 32:13; Numbers 15:39-40; Deuteronomy 5:15; 7:18; 8:2, 18; 9:7; 15:15; 16:3, 12; 24:9, 18, 22; 25:17; 32:7.

[208] See Moo, 162.

[209] Green, 123.

[210] Moo, 164.

[211] Ibid.

[212] See ibid.

[213] For example, the Greek *eikon* (image) is ordinarily used of something that represents some reality but is not the reality itself, like the image of Caesar on a coin. But in at least one context, it is used to represent the reality itself. See Hebrews 10:1.

[214] Moo, 165.

[215] The ancient Greek philosophers taught that "word" (*logos*) was "the principle and pattern that gave the world or cosmos its character and coherence." Paul J. Achtemeier, gen. ed., *Harper's Bible Dictionary* (San Francisco: Harper and Row, 1985), 572. Philo, a contemporary of Paul, "sought to reconcile Greek philosophical theories about the universe . . . with the biblical accounts of God's creating the world by his spoken word. God's *logos* became a clearly identifiable entity, mediating between God and the world, the mode of divine creativity and revelation." Ibid.

[216] See Keener, 264; Achtemeier, 572-73.

[217] All the references to creation by the word of God find their roots in Genesis 1. We must understand them in a way that harmonizes with the original account of creation, which occurred as "God said." Jesus validated the

necessity of returning to the essential root of biblical teaching and interpreting all subsequent references from the perspective of the first teaching. (See Matthew 19:4-5, 8.) In the first reference to creation in the Word of God, there is no hint that God's Word is merely a principle. Neither is there any indication that the Word of God is a divine being of some kind distinct from God. Neither is there any suggestion of either of these ideas in the subsequent references in the Old Testament. (See Psalm 33:6, 9; 148:5.) The personification of wisdom as a female present with God at creation is only a figure of speech that depicts the wisdom of God as displayed in His creative acts. (See Proverbs 8:1, 12, 29-30.)

It is the "apocryphal books [that] develop the motif [of the wisdom and word of God] with the imagery of Wisdom present at God's side, active in creation and taking up residence in Israel." Ryken, et al., 445. If we allow this apocryphal background to be the determining factor in Jesus' relationship with God, as "the word . . . with God" (John 1:1), New Testament Christology then becomes dependent on apocryphal Judaism. If, instead, the Hebrew Scriptures influence the motif of the "word with God," the relationship between Jesus and God mirrors the relationship of the word with God.

The New Testament identifies Jesus as "the Word of God" (John 1:1-3, 14; I John 1:1-2; Revelation 19:13). The connection of Jesus as the Word of God with creation demonstrates that the background of thought in John's mind was Genesis 1. The Hebrew word for "word" (*dabar*) includes in its range of meanings "word, thing, affair, matter." The general and specific contexts in which *dabar* is used in reference to creation indicates that the meaning is "word," as in what God actually spoke. *Dabar* does not have within its range of meaning any idea of a distinct visible form or person. The word in the Old Testament is not some kind of permanent, visible form of God. It is simply a reference to God expressing Himself by means of a spoken word. God's words are in a spectrum far above human words as to their efficacy. His words are dynamic and creative, as seen in Genesis 1, because He is God.

The Greek *logos* ("word") has to do with a thought or concept or the expression or utterance of that thought or concept. Since *logos* is apparently used as the Greek equivalent of the Hebrew *dabar*, its range of meaning in the context of creation must be "word" as the expression or utterance of a thought or concept.

The idea that the *logos* is distinct from God is a result of the syncretism widespread in the first century, in the Jewish wisdom literature, and in Philo. BAGD, 478. To interpret the Hebrew Scriptures in this way is anachronistic. Since the writers of the New Testament wrote, to a large degree, from the perspective of the Hebrew Scriptures, and since they saw Jesus as the fulfillment of the Messianic prophecies of the Old Testament, it is doubtful that they poured their theology through the speculations of Greek philosophy. Moreover, there is no evidence that they used the musings of later Hellenistic thought to shape their perspective.

In straightforward terms, to say that creation occurred by the Word of God means that God spoke the created realm into existence. To say that Jesus is the Word of God means that He is for these "last days" (Hebrews 1:2) what the spoken Word of God was for the

Endnotes

"time past" (Hebrews 1:1). He is God Himself made known to us. In "time past" (before the Incarnation), God made Himself known by speaking "in various ways" (Hebrews 1:1, NKJV). In the Incarnation, He makes Himself known in the person of Jesus Christ. (See John 1:18; I John 3:1-2.) God's spoken words at creation and throughout the history of Israel do not constitute a being with identity distinct from God. Nor is Jesus Christ a being distinct from God. He is God manifest in genuine and full human existence (I Timothy 3:16). Just as God was revealed or made known or shown through His Word, so He is revealed or made known or shown through Jesus Christ. (The Greek word *phaneroo*, translated "manifest" in I Timothy 3:16, can mean "reveal, make known, show." BAGD, 852.)

There can be no difference in meaning between John 1:14 ("the Word became flesh," NKJV) and I Timothy 3:16 ("God was manifested in the flesh," NKJV). John identified the Word as God Himself (John 1:1). That John did not intend his readers to understand by "Word" something other than "God" is seen in his assertion that it was the Father the world did not know and who will be revealed at the Second Coming (I John 3:1-2; compare with John 1:10-11). In I John 1, John identified Jesus as "the Word of life . . . that eternal life which was with the Father and was manifested to us" (I John 1:1-2, NKJV). John no more saw the Word as a person distinct from God in John 1:1 than he saw the "eternal life which was with the Father" as a person distinct from God. The remarkable parallels in these passages indicate that John equated the Word and the "life" with God Himself. God's Word and God's life could be personified just as wisdom

305

could be personified. (See Proverbs 8.) But personification does not bestow distinct personal identity. Jesus certainly does possess personal identity, but this does not mean He had some kind of identity distinct from God before the Incarnation. It means that He is the personal God revealed in human existence. Due to the reality and completeness of His human existence, He possesses all the personal characteristics of any human, with the "fullness of the Godhead" (Colossians 2:9) dwelling in, or manifested in, every aspect of His being.

We should not interpret words like "bodily" (Colossians 2:9) or "flesh" (John 1:14; I Timothy 3:16) to mean that Christ's humanity was only physical. As with "Word," we must understand these terms from the historic perspective of Hebrew thought as expressed in the Scriptures. From this frame of reference, human existence cannot be fragmented. Whatever is said about a human being, whether of the material or immaterial aspects of existence, takes into account the entirety of human existence. In this regard, Hebrew thought is much more holistic than Greek thought. Even the "voice" of God represents God Himself. (See Genesis 3:8; Psalm 29:3-8.)

[218]Hillyer, 215.

[219]In the Old Testament, the synonymous words and phrases include "that day" (Isaiah 24:21), "the days" (Jeremiah 9:25-26), and "latter days" (Hosea 3:5). In the New Testament, they include "day of judgment" (Matthew 10:15; 11:22, 24; 12:36; II Peter 2:9; 3:7; I John 4:17), "the judgment" (Matthew 12:41, 42; Luke 10:14), "that day" (Matthew 7:22; Luke 17:31; 21:34; I Thessalonians 5:4; II Timothy 1:18; 4:8), "those days" (Mark 13:17, 19,

24), "a day" (Acts 17:31), "the day" (Romans 2:16), "day of God" (II Peter 3:12), and "the great day" (Jude 6).

Terms like "day of our Lord Jesus Christ" or "the day of the Lord Jesus" (I Corinthians 1:8; 5:5; II Corinthians 1:14), "day of Jesus Christ" (Philippians 1:6), and "the day of Christ" (Philippians 1:10; 2:16) seem to refer to the rapture of the church, after which the Day of the Lord begins. See the article "judgment, day of" in Achtemeier, 516-517. *The New Scofield Study Bible*, in its comments on I Corinthians 1:8, points out that the "expression 'the day of our Lord Jesus Christ,' identified with His coming [I Corinthians 1:7], is the period of blessing for the Church beginning with the rapture. This coming day is referred to as 'the day of the Lord Jesus' (1 Cor. 5:5; 2 Cor 1:14), 'the day of Jesus Christ' (Phil. 1:6), and 'the day of Christ' (Phil. 1:10; 2:16). 'The day of Christ' in all six references in the NT is described as relating to the reward and blessing of the Church at the rapture in contrast with the expression 'the day of the LORD' (cp. Isa. 2:12 . . . Joel 1:15), which is related to judgment on unbelieving Jews and Gentiles, and blessing on millennial saints (Zeph. 3:8-20)." Scofield, 1391.

The rare "day of God" (II Peter 3:12; Revelation 16:14) seems to refer specifically to the cataclysmic events clustered at the end of the Day of the Lord, which introduces eternity. See the discussion in John F. Walvoord and Roy B. Zuck, gen. eds., *The Bible Knowledge Commentary, New Testament Edition* (Wheaton, IL: Victor Books, 1983), 876-77.

[220]The "delay" is only apparent. God has always known precisely when He will come. When that time comes, He will not delay. (See Hebrews 10:37.) God is not continu-

ally reassessing the situation to find the right time to fulfill His promise to judge those who have rebelled against Him.

[221] Moo, 188.

[222] Ibid.

[223] Quoted in ibid.

[224] Ibid.

[225] A textual variant reads "toward you" rather than "toward us." Either word could refer to the believers to whom Peter wrote.

[226] Green, 136.

[227] Ibid., 138.

[228] See ibid.

[229] For a brief discussion of the textual problem by Daniel B. Wallace, see www.bible.org/docs/soapbox/2pet310.htm.

[230] See Romans 13:11-14; I Corinthians 15:58; Ephesians 5:11-16; Philippians 4:5; I Thessalonians 5:1-11; I Timothy 6:11-19; II Timothy 4:1-5; I Peter 1:13; 4:7-17.

[231] See Green, 139-40.

[232] Quoted in ibid., 139.

[233] Hillyer, 220.

[234] Green, 69-70.

[235] Following his discussion of the rapture of the church (I Thessalonians 4:13-18), Paul wrote, "For you yourselves know perfectly that the day of the Lord so comes as a thief in the night" (I Thessalonians 5:2, NKJV). That Paul did not expect the Day of the Lord to be a concern for the church (which is caught up to meet the Lord before the start of the Day of the Lord) is seen in his words, "But you, brethren, are not in darkness, so that this Day should overtake you as a thief" (I Thessalonians

5:4, NKJV). The "thief" motif focuses on the surprise element of the Day of the Lord. Since no one but God knows when it will be (see Mark 13:32), the Day of the Lord will be a surprise to all who experience it. It will not be a surprise to the church, for it does not have to do with the church, which is already with Jesus when the Day of the Lord begins. The Day of the Lord is connected to the judgment of God upon those who have rejected Him, and this does not include the church. Thus, Paul wrote, "For God did not appoint us to wrath, but to obtain salvation [i.e., deliverance] through our Lord Jesus Christ" (I Thessalonians 5:9, NKJV).

[236] See Moo, 198.

[237] And perhaps we can take some comfort in our attempt to understand these things from Peter's statement that Paul, writing in his letters about "these things" (i.e., eschatological events), wrote "some things hard to understand" (II Peter 3:16, NKJV).

[238] Green, 141.

[239] Some have made a distinction between the inhabitants of the new heavens and the new earth, suggesting that the new earth will be inhabited by those who are righteous and that the new heavens—specifically the New Jerusalem (Revelation 21:2, 10)—will be inhabited by those who are holy. They appeal to Revelation 22:11: "He who is righteous, let him be righteous still; he who is holy, let him be holy still." It would be difficult to defend this view by an appeal to II Peter 3:13, for the relative pronoun "which" in the phrase "in which righteousness dwells" is plural, referring both to the new heavens and the new earth. Righteousness dwells not only in the new earth, but also in the new heavens. It is also doubtful if

the intent in Revelation 22:11 is to distinguish between the righteous and holy or that the earlier part of the verse distinguishes between the unjust and the filthy. It seems, rather, that two categories of people are in view: In one category are those who are unjust and filthy; in the other category are those who are righteous and holy.

[240] The view discussed in the previous note tends to identify the new earth as the permanent abode of the righteous, who are barred from access to the New Jerusalem. It seems, however, that all who inhabit the new earth also have access to the New Jerusalem. (See Revelation 21:24-26; 22:14.) Those who are barred from the New Jerusalem are those who have already been cast into the lake of fire. (See Revelation 21:27; 22:15.)

[241] See Moo, 206.

[242] See Hillyer, 223; Green, 145-46.

[243] This does not include Hebrews. See the discussion of the author of Hebrews in Segraves, *Hebrews* 1:14-15.

[244] In I Timothy 5:18, Paul placed Deuteronomy 25:4 and Luke 10:7 side by side and identified both as Scripture.

[245] See I Corinthians 1:7; 15:23; I Thessalonians 2:19; 3:13; 4:15; 5:23; II Thessalonians 2:1, 8; I Timothy 6:14; II Timothy 4:1, 8; Titus 2:13.

[246] Green, 145-46.

[247] Hillyer, 224.

[248] See ibid., 226.

[249] See Green, 150.

[250] See ibid., 150-51; Moo, 214.

[251] Blum, 289.

[252] See Romans 11:36; 16:27; Galatians 1:5; Philippians 4:20; I Timothy 1:17; II Timothy 4:18;

Endnotes

Hebrews 13:21; I Peter 5:11; Jude 25; Revelation 1:5-6.

[253] See Green, 151.

[254] See discussion under Introduction in comments on II Peter.

[255] See Blum, 383.

[256] Ibid.

[257] See Segraves, *James*, 20-21.

[258] Green, 43-44.

[259] Moo, 27.

[260] For a discussion of the dating of Jude, see Green, 46-48.

[261] Keener, 753.

[262] Ibid.

[263] The chart is adapted from Hillyer, 19, and Edward C. Pentecost in Walvoord and Zuck, 917.

[264] See Green, 43-44.

[265] See the discussion under "Author" above.

[266] This includes Abraham (Genesis 26:24), Job (Job 1:8), Caleb (Numbers 14:24), Moses (Joshua 14:7; II Kings 18:12; I Chronicles 6:49; Nehemiah 10:29; Daniel 9:11; Revelation 15:3), David (II Samuel 3:18; 7:5; Ezekiel 34:23), Isaiah (Isaiah 20:3), Zerubbabel (Haggai 2:23), and the nation of Israel (Isaiah 41:8).

[267] Moo, 225.

[268] Ibid., 225-26.

[269] In His encounter with Satan, Jesus endorsed the Septuagint rendering of Deuteronomy 6:13 ("Him only shalt thou serve"). The word "only" does not appear in the Hebrew text, but it does in the Greek of the Septuagint. A common Hebraism implies "only" in certain contexts.

[270] For a fuller discussion of the way the claim to be a "servant" of Jesus Christ implies His deity, see the com-

ments on II Peter 1:1 and Segraves, *James*, 29-30.

[271] Moo, 225.

[272] Ibid.

[273] Metzger, 723.

[274] This discussion of sanctification follows Segraves, *First Peter*, 34.

[275] See comments on I Peter 1:5 in ibid., 47-48.

[276] BAGD, 436.

[277] For a discussion of election, see Segraves, *First Peter*, 30-34.

[278] See Moo, 225.

[279] F. W. Beare, *The Gospel according to Matthew* (San Francisco: Harper & Row, 1981), 545.

[280] Moo, 225.

[281] See Romans 1:7; I Corinthians 1:3; II Corinthians 1:2; Galatians 1:3; Ephesians 1:2; Philippians 1:2; Colossians 1:2; I Thessalonians 1:1; II Thessalonians 1:2; Philemon 3; II Peter 1:2.

[282] Moo, 224.

[283] Ibid. See Romans 5:5, 8; 8:39; II Corinthians 13:11, 14; Ephesians 2:4; Titus 3:4; I John 3:1, 16; 4:8-11, 16, 19.

[284] Green, 157.

[285] Paul's commendations usually focus on his readers' faith, hope, and love. For a discussion of Paul's commendations, see Daniel L. Segraves, *Themes from a Letter to Rome* (Hazelwood, MO: Word Aflame Press, 1995), 134-36.

[286] See Moo, 229.

[287] See discussion in Moo, 228, especially n. 3.

[288] See Galatians 1:23; 3:23; Ephesians 4:13; Philippians 1:27; Colossians 1:23; 2:7; I Timothy 4:1; 5:8; 6:10; II Timothy 3:8; Titus 1:13.

[289] Moo, 229.

Endnotes

[290] See the chart under "Style and Structure" in the section on II Peter.

[291] Green, 160-61.

[292] See the discussion under "Date of Composition."

[293] Moo, 230.

[294] Ibid.

[295] For a discussion of the relationship between faith and works, see Segraves, *James*.

[296] See Robertson 6:147-48, 187.

[297] See I Corinthians 4:17; 15:1; Galatians 1:8-9; II Thessalonians 2:5; II Timothy 1:6; 2:14; Titus 3:1; Hebrews 2:1; II Peter 1:12-13, 15; 3:1-2; Jude 17.

[298] See Exodus 12:14, 42; 13:3-16; 17:14; Deuteronomy 5:15; 7:18; 16:13; Joshua 4:7; Psalm 77:11; 105:5; 143:5.

[299] Green, 164.

[300] Moo, 110.

[301] Richard Laurence, trans., *The Book of Enoch the Prophet* (Chicago, IL: Lushena Books, n.d.), 5-6.

[302] A cubit is 17.5 inches.

[303] Charles Cutler Torrey, *The Apocryphal Literature: A Brief Introduction* (New Haven: Yale University Press, 1945), 114.

[304] Ibid., 111.

[305] A literal translation of the Hebrew text of Daniel 3:25 would read, "The form of the fourth is like a son of the gods." Nebuchadnezzar was a pagan with no accurate insight into the spirit realm. He simply described what he saw in a way consistent with his worldview.

[306] Chapter and verse divisions are not, of course, original.

[307] See Moo, 243.

[308] See Deuteronomy 29:23; 32:32; Isaiah 1:9; 13:19; Jeremiah 23:14; 49:18; 50:40; Lamentations 4:6; Ezekiel 16:48-50; Amos 4:11; Zephaniah 2:9; Matthew 10:15; 11:23-24; Mark 6:11; Luke 10:12; 17:29; II Peter 2:6. For the Apocrypha, see *Wisdom of Solomon* 10:6-9; *Ecclesiasticus* 16:8; *III Maccabees* 2:5.

[309] See Exodus 22:21; Leviticus 25:14, 17; Deuteronomy 24:14; Psalm 10:18; 12:5; 62:10; 73:8; 107:39; Proverbs 22:22; Isaiah 5:7; 30:12; 59:13; Jeremiah 7:6; 22:17; Ezekiel 22:7; 22:29; Micah 2:2; Zechariah 7:10; Malachi 3:5; James 2:6.

[310] See Green, 166, n. 4.

[311] Author's translation.

[312] See Hillyer, 247.

[313] See the discussion of Hebrews 13:4 in Segraves, *Hebrews* 2:223-24.

[314] Moo, 245.

[315] See ibid.

[316] Hillyer, 248.

[317] See Torrey, 114-16; Green, 169-70.

[318] Hillyer, 249.

[319] See Moo, 250.

[320] Quoted in Hillyer, 249.

[321] See Job 19:26; Daniel 12:2, 13; Matthew 22:31; 27:53; John 5:28-29; 6:40, 44, 54; 11:24; Acts 23:6; 24:15; I Corinthians 6:14; 15:12; II Corinthians 4:14; Hebrews 6:2; Revelation 20:5-6.

[322] See Green, 171.

[323] Blum, 392.

[324] Ibid.

[325] Moo, 257.

[326] Quoted in ibid.

[327] Ibid.
[328] Quoted in ibid.
[329] Hillyer, 251.
[330] Scofield, 1511, n. 1.
[331] Ibid., 1524, n. 2.
[332] Ibid., 1529, n. 2.
[333] Hillyer, 253.
[334] See Moo, 258.
[335] Quoted by Green, 172.
[336] Blum, 392.
[337] Bauckham, quoted by Moo, 258.
[338] Moo, 258, n. 6.
[339] See discussion in Green, 174. *Spilades* is rendered "rocks" or "sunken rocks" by Alford, Weymouth, NASB and Kelly; it is translated "spots" by the KJV, NKJV, RSV, NEB, NIV, TEV. See Blum, 392.
[340] Green, 175.
[341] Ibid., 176.
[342] Moo, 260.
[343] See the comments on James 1:6-8 in Segraves, *James*.
[344] Blum, 392.
[345] Green, 176.
[346] See Moo, 261.
[347] These examples follow Green, 49.
[348] See Blum, 393.
[349] See Torrey, 110; Moo, 269-70, n. 4.
[350] Laurence, 2.
[351] See Hillyer, 257; Green, 177
[352] See Moo, 270; Green, 177; Hillyer, 257.
[353] For a discussion of the four eschatological judgments, see Segraves, *First Peter*, 342-44, n. 314.

[354] See Green, 178.
[355] Blum, 393.
[356] See Moo, 271.
[357] Hillyer, 259.
[358] See Moo, 271.
[359] Hillyer, 207.
[360] Moo, 280, n. 1.
[361] Hillyer, 261.
[362] Green, 180.

[363] For a discussion of the importance of remembrance in avoiding error and the transformation of one's life, see the comments on II Peter 3:1.

[364] See the discussion on II Peter 3:1-3.

[365] For a discussion of the significance of the eschatological term "last time" or "last days," see the comments on II Peter 3:3.

[366] See Green, 181.

[367] There is no variant here between the critical text and the Textus Receptus. The Greek text of the phrase is *houtoi* ("these") *eisin* ("are") *hoi* ("the [ones]") *apodiorizontes* ("making divisions").

[368] Moo, 282.
[369] See Green, 182.
[370] Quoted in ibid., 184, n. 1.
[371] Ibid., 184.
[372] Moo, 284-85.
[373] Ibid., 285.
[374] Hillyer, 264.

[375] Pentecostals believe in speaking with tongues. Many understand that there is a difference between the initial sign of speaking with tongues, which occurs when a person is baptized with the Holy Ghost, and the gift of

Endnotes

"divers [different] kinds of tongues," which some, but not all, receive (I Corinthians 12:10, 28, 30). There is, however, some confusion over the continued role of speaking with tongues on the part of the person who has been baptized with the Holy Ghost, but who may not have received the gift of divers kinds of tongues.

There are two extremes of thought on this issue. Some claim that a person must speak with tongues every day in order to maintain his salvation. There is no biblical warrant for this position. On the other hand, some have so de-emphasized speaking with tongues that they see no further purpose for it after the initial Spirit baptism, unless a person has the gift of divers kinds of tongues for the purpose of communicating a message from God to the church, accompanied by an interpretation (I Corinthians 14:5). The latter position leads to the problem of people receiving the Holy Ghost and never speaking with tongues again.

The biblical evidence supports the view that all those who are baptized with the Holy Spirit can, and should, continue to speak with tongues. This is true whether or not one has the gift of divers kinds of tongues. Indeed, this latter gift involves different *kinds* of tongues (languages). The simplest explanation is that a person with this gift is able to speak in more than one language unknown to him. The gift may also involve various *purposes* for the tongues, as they are related to the gift of interpretation. That is, one message in tongues may be for the purpose of edification, another for exhortation, and another for comfort (I Corinthians 14:3-6). A person without this gift, but who has been baptized with the Holy Spirit, has the ability on a continuing basis to speak in at least one language unknown to him.

The question under consideration here is whether the Bible teaches that a person without the gift of divers kinds of tongues does indeed have the continuing ability to speak with tongues, whether the individual should regularly exercise that ability, and to what purpose.

Jesus said, "And these signs shall follow them that believe; In my name shall they cast out devils; they shall speak with new tongues; they shall take up serpents; and if they drink any deadly thing, it shall not hurt them; they shall lay hands on the sick, and they shall recover" (Mark 16:17-18).

The "new tongues" here are new or different languages. This is not a reference to a new believer "cleaning up his language." It is a miraculous sign, as are all the others, involving a new *language* [tongue=language]. This prediction of Jesus began to be fulfilled on the Day of Pentecost and continued to be fulfilled in the lives of the early believers throughout the New Testament era. (See Acts 2:4; 10:44-46; 19:6; I Corinthians 14:18-39.)

The language of Jesus' promise in Mark 16 suggests that these signs would continue in the lives of the believers. There is no indication that any of them would occur only once in a believer's experience. The word translated "shall follow" (*parakolouthesei*) in Mark 16:17 is in the future tense, active voice, and indicative mood. This can mean that in the future, these signs shall *continue to follow* believers. Whenever the opportunity and need arises, a person who is a believer can minister to the sick through the laying on of hands. He will do this even daily, if need be.

The same is true of the prediction by Jesus that

believers will "speak with new tongues." Speaking with tongues is one of the things that will characterize believers. They will not speak with tongues just once and then cease. Speaking with tongues will be a way of life for them. Whenever the opportunity and need present themselves for them to speak with tongues, they will do so, even if it is daily.

If a believer were expected to speak with tongues only once, it would seem strange that Jesus would use the phrase, "And these signs shall *follow* them that believe. . . ." This phrase indicates continual evidence, something that follows believers throughout their lives.

Believers first spoke with tongues on the Day of Pentecost as they were filled with the Holy Ghost and as "the Spirit gave them utterance" (Acts 2:4). While the mind gives utterance to speech in one's own language, the Holy Spirit gives utterance to speaking with tongues.

And this is not gibberish. The amazed multitude said, "We do hear them speak in our tongues the wonderful works of God" (Acts 2:11). It is worthy of note that on the first occasion when people spoke with tongues, they described in languages unknown to them the wonderful things God had done. This account indicates that one of the uses of tongues, even by those who do not have the gift of divers kinds of tongues, is to glorify God for His mighty acts. (See Psalm 150:2.)

When the Holy Spirit was poured out at the house of Cornelius, the amazed Jewish believers "heard them speak with tongues, and magnify God" (Acts 10:46). While one could speculate that the Gentiles here first spoke with tongues, then later magnified God in their own language, that does not fit the model of Acts 2, nor does

Second Peter & Jude

it explain fully the amazement of the Jewish onlookers. The visitors were amazed because they heard the Gentiles, in languages unknown to themselves, magnify God.

When Paul confronted the disciples of John the Baptist and declared to them that Jesus is the Messiah, they were baptized in the name of the Lord Jesus. Then Paul laid his hands upon them, and "the Holy Ghost came on them; and they spake with tongues, and prophesied" (Acts 19:6). It is possible that the spiritual gift of prophecy was at work here (I Corinthians 12:10; 14:3-4). It is also possible, however, that they prophesied *in tongues*, i.e., in languages unknown to them. This is possible since interpreted tongues equal prophecy (I Corinthians 14:5). For an interpretation of tongues to be prophecy, the tongue itself would have to be prophecy in another language. Some would understand I Corinthians 14:6 to support this view: "Now, brethren, if I come unto you speaking with tongues, what shall I profit you, except I shall speak to you either by revelation, or by knowledge, or by prophesying, or by doctrine?" Under this view, Paul referred to tongues, which, uninterpreted, do not profit or edify the church, but when interpreted, result in revelation, a word of knowledge, a prophecy, or teaching. Whether or not the prophecies of the newly Spirit-baptized believers in Acts 19 were related to their speaking with tongues, it remains that on the Day of Pentecost believers declared the wonderful works of God in tongues and, at Cornelius' house, magnified God in tongues.

The only other place in the New Testament that explicitly mentions tongues, in addition to Mark and Acts, is I Corinthians 12-14, in the discussion of the gifts of the

Spirit. I Corinthians 12 lists nine gifts of the Spirit and compares their function to that of the various members of the human body working together for the common good. The discussion assumes that not everyone has each gift but that all have at least one gift. The gift of divers kinds of tongues is one of the nine gifts mentioned.

I Corinthians 13 points out the emptiness of spiritual gifts when not motivated by love. It alludes to the possibility of speaking with human or angelic tongues (I Corinthians 13:1).

A great deal of I Corinthians 14 is devoted to the proper use of the spiritual gifts, including the purpose of speaking with tongues. While it clearly indicates the pointlessness of tongues without interpretation with regard to the edification of the church, it does recognize that uninterpreted tongues have value to the individual who is speaking with tongues.

For the moment, let us focus our attention only on the advantages of uninterpreted tongues:

- "For he that speaketh in an unknown tongue speaketh not unto men, but unto God . . . in the spirit he speaketh mysteries" (I Corinthians 14:2).
- "He that speaketh in an unknown tongue edifieth himself" (I Corinthians 14:4).
- "For if I pray in an unknown tongue, my spirit prayeth" (I Corinthians 14:14).
- "When thou shalt bless with the spirit . . . thou verily givest thanks well" (I Corinthians 14:16-17).

To sum up the value of uninterpreted tongues from Acts and I Corinthians, we note the following points:

- While speaking with tongues, a person may declare the wonderful works of God.

- While speaking with tongues, a person may magnify God.
- One who speaks with tongues speaks not to people but to God.
- One who speaks with tongues speaks mysteries in the spirit.
- One who speaks with tongues edifies himself.
- When a person prays in tongues, his spirit is praying.
- One who speaks with tongues can give thanks well.

All of these are noble activities and illustrate the value of continuing to speak with tongues following the initial baptism of the Holy Spirit.

Paul defined praying in tongues as praying "with the spirit" (I Corinthians 14:14-15). While uninterpreted tongues do not help the natural mind, whether in prayer or otherwise, the spirit is edified. Rather than rejecting prayer in tongues, Paul said, "I will pray with the spirit, and I will pray with the understanding also: I will sing with the spirit, and I will sing with the understanding also" (I Corinthians 14:15). This statement introduces another possible function of tongues: not only can a person *pray* with tongues; he can *sing* with tongues.

When a person is moved to speak with tongues, but there is no interpreter in the congregation to render the message in the language of the people, the person with the tongue is to keep silence in the church, i.e., he is not to speak aloud in the public assembly. But rather than forbidding him to speak altogether, I Corinthians 14:28 instructs this person to "speak to himself, and to God." In other words, even if speaking in tongues in this case would have no value to the congregation at large, it could still have value to the individual speaking in tongues because he would be speaking to God and at least he himself would be edified.

Even though Paul gave clear instructions on the proper use of tongues, emphasizing the importance of interpretation for the edification of the body, we can in no way interpret him as denigrating tongues. He said, "I thank my God, I speak with tongues more than ye all," and "forbid not to speak with tongues" (I Corinthians 14:18, 39).

For our purposes here, it is important to note that Paul equated praying in tongues with praying in the spirit (I Corinthians 14:14-15). This gives insight into other passages of Scripture that discuss the role of the Spirit in prayer.

"Likewise the Spirit also helpeth our infirmities: for we know not what we should pray for as we ought: but the Spirit itself maketh intercession for us with groanings which cannot be uttered" (Romans 8:26). Some disagree that this is a reference to praying with tongues. They point out that the Spirit's work here results in "groanings which cannot be uttered" rather than words which can be articulated, albeit in a language unknown to the speaker. Perhaps this is true, although the possibility remains that these could be groanings which cannot be uttered with the aid of the natural mind, but which can be uttered by the direction of the Spirit. The Holy Spirit did, on the Day of Pentecost, give utterance to words that would otherwise have remained unspoken.

But whether or not this is a reference to praying with tongues, this verse does point out important features of praying in or with the Spirit:

- Our natural understanding is insufficient to give us direction in prayer.
- The Spirit compensates for this human weakness by giving us direction in prayer, even leading us to pray with "groanings" (possibly deep sighs).

Paul concluded his discussion of the armor of God with these words: "Praying always with all prayer and supplication *in the Spirit*" (Ephesians 6:18, emphasis added). He apparently referred to prayer that goes beyond what springs from human understanding alone.

Another reference to prayer in this spiritual dimension is found in Jude 20: "But ye, beloved, building up yourselves on your most holy faith, praying in the Holy Ghost." While praying in the Spirit no doubt also includes praying in a language understood by the speaker with words impressed upon him by the Holy Spirit, prayer in tongues is always—by definition—prayer in the Spirit.

Once a person's human spirit is reborn (John 3:6), he possesses the ability to speak with tongues on a continuing basis. This is inherent in Jesus' prediction that speaking with new tongues is a sign that will *follow* believers and in that the very first evidence of the indwelling Holy Spirit is the ability of believers to speak with tongues by the utterance of the Spirit.

If we see the new birth as comparable to the birth of a child, it would be unreasonable to expect any of the abilities inherent in the new birth to cease as one matures. Instead, we would expect the abilities—including the ability to speak—to increase in proficiency and effectiveness.

By praying or singing with tongues, the believer can:
- give evidence that he is a believer

- declare the wonderful works of God
- magnify God
- speak to God in a way that surpasses human understanding
- speak mysteries
- edify himself
- allow his spirit to pray
- give thanks well.

A sincere believer in Jesus Christ who loves the Lord does not need to worry about the origin of the tongues he speaks. Jesus said, "If ye then, being evil, know how to give good gifts unto your children: how much more shall your heavenly Father give the Holy Spirit to them that ask him?" (Luke 11:13).

No loving human father would allow an evil person to slip his children poison when they ask for food. How much more will our heavenly Father not allow Satan to deceive His beloved children by giving them a false gift! The fact that some witch doctors or practicing Satanists may have spoken with counterfeit "tongues" has nothing at all to do with sincere believers in Jesus Christ who come to God on the basis of the promises of Scripture to receive a good gift from God. (See James 1:17.)

During the last years of his life, Andrew D. Urshan devoted his ministry almost exclusively to stressing the importance of believers continuing to speak with tongues on a frequent basis after their initial Spirit baptism. He told Phillip Dugas that if a person would speak with tongues every day, he would always be able to live in victory. (Phillip Dugas, a stepson of Andrew D. Urshan, confirmed this to me.) That is good counsel for our day, a day when some are de-emphasizing tongues, but a day when the need for praying in the Spirit is greater than ever before.

[376]Blum, 395.

[377]Green, 186.

[378]For a discussion of faith, hope, and love as the virtues connected with spiritual maturity, see Segraves, *Themes*, 134-36.

[379]See Metzger, 725-27; Moo, 286-89; Green, 186-89.

[380]Green, 186.

[381]See comments under "Author" and "Style and Structure."

[382]Moo, 287.

[383]Scofield, 1092, n. 3.

[384]Moo, 289.

[385]Ibid.

[386]See Romans 16:25-27; Ephesians 3:20; Philippians 4:20; I Timothy 6:15-16; I Peter 4:11; 5:11; II Peter 3:18.

[387]Moo, 302.

[388]Ibid.

[389]Green, 190.

[390]See the discussion of the textual evidence in Metzger, 727-28.

[391]Moo, 303.

[392]This series of questions reflects the theory of textual criticism championed by Westcott and Hort in their work on the Revised Version of 1881-85.

[393]Green, 192.

[394]Several doxologies ascribe divine attributes to God through Jesus Christ forever, i.e., from the point of the Incarnation onward, but not "before all ages." See Romans 16:27; Hebrews 13:21; I Peter 4:11.

[395]See Luke 2:11; John 4:42; Acts 5:31; 13:23;

Ephesians 5:23; Philippians 3:20; II Timothy 1:10; Titus 1:4; 2:13; 3:6; II Peter 1:1, 11; 2:20; 3:2, 18; I John 4:14.
[396] Moo, 301.
[397] Ibid.
[398] Ibid.
[399] Ibid.